The Wisdom of History
Part II

J. Rufus Fears, Ph.D.

THE TEACHING COMPANY ®

PUBLISHED BY:

THE TEACHING COMPANY
4151 Lafayette Center Drive, Suite 100
Chantilly, Virginia 20151-1232
1-800-TEACH-12
Fax—703-378-3819
www.teach12.com

ISBN 978-1-59803-355-7

J. Rufus Fears, Ph.D.
David Ross Boyd Professor of Classics, University of Oklahoma

J. Rufus Fears is David Ross Boyd Professor of Classics at the University of Oklahoma, where he holds the G.T. and Libby Blankenship Chair in the History of Liberty. He also serves as the David and Ann Brown Distinguished Fellow of the Oklahoma Council of Public Affairs. He rose from Assistant Professor to Professor of History at Indiana University and was chosen as Indiana University's first Distinguished Faculty Research Lecturer. From 1986 to 1990, he was Professor of Classical Studies and Chairman of the Department of Classical Studies at Boston University. He is currently the David and Ann Brown Distinguished Fellow of the Oklahoma Council of Public Affairs.

Professor Fears received his Ph.D. from Harvard University and is an internationally distinguished scholar and author of numerous studies in Greek and Roman history, the history of freedom, and the lessons of history for our own day. His books and monographs include *Princeps A Diis Electus: The Divine Election of the Emperor as a Political Concept at Rome*; *The Cult of Virtues and Roman Imperial Ideology*; *The Theology of Victory at Rome*; and *The Cult of Jupiter and Roman Imperial Ideology*. He has edited a three-volume edition of *Selected Writings of Lord Acton*.

Professor Fears has been a Danforth Fellow, a Woodrow Wilson Fellow, and a Harvard Prize Fellow. He has been a Fellow of the American Academy in Rome, a Guggenheim Fellow, and twice a Fellow of the Alexander von Humboldt Foundation in Germany. His research has been supported by grants from the American Council of Learned Societies, the American Philosophical Society, the National Endowment for the Humanities, the Zarrow Foundation, and the Kerr Foundation. He is listed in *Who's Who in America* and *Who's Who in the World*.

On 24 occasions, Professor Fears has been recognized for outstanding teaching excellence. In 1996, 1999, and again in 2000, students chose him as University of Oklahoma Professor of the Year. In 2003, he received the University Continuing Education Association (UCEA) Great Plains Region Award for Excellence in Teaching. UCEA is the national association for colleges and universities with continuing education programs. In 2005, Professor Fears received the National Award for Teaching Excellence from UCEA, which cited his "outstanding teaching and contribution to continuing higher education."

In 2005, Professor Fears was the recipient of the Excellence in Teaching Award from the Classical Association of the Middle West and South. In 2005, students at the University of Oklahoma named him "Most Inspiring Professor." In 2006, the state-wide Oklahoma Foundation for Excellence awarded him its medal for Excellence in College and University Teaching.

Professor Fears is very active in speaking to broader audiences. His comments on the lessons of history for today have appeared on television and in newspapers across the United States. He is a regular guest on national talk radio programs. Each year, he leads study trips to historical sites in Europe and the United States.

The *Wisdom of History* is the sixth course Professor Fears has produced with The Teaching Company. His other courses include *A History of Freedom*, *Famous Greeks*, *Famous Romans*, *Churchill*, and *Books That Have Made History: Books That Can Change Your Life*.

Table of Contents
The Wisdom of History
Part II

©2007 The Teaching Company.

The Wisdom of History

Scope:

The Wisdom of History is defined as the ability to use the lessons of history to make decisions in the present and to plan for the future. The Founders of the United States used the lessons of history to do just that. The success of our Constitution is enduring testimony to their ability to think historically and, thus, to apply the wisdom of history to the great task of building a new republic in a new world. This course examines the lessons that history might hold for the contemporary United States, particularly in a post–9/11 world. To apply the wisdom of history, we focus on six questions of profound importance for America today:

1. Is there meaning to history? Do we learn from history? And are there consequences to our failure to learn from history?
2. Is freedom a universal value? If so, then why is world history largely a story of tyranny, misery, and war?
3. Why has the history of the world seen the rise and fall of superpowers and empires? Why has the Middle East been, throughout history, the crucible of conflict and the graveyard of empires?
4. What do the lessons of history teach America about the destiny of a nation that is both a democracy and a superpower?
5. How do we distinguish between a politician and a statesman, and what makes a great leader in a time of crisis?
6. What will the wisdom of history teach later generations about America and its place in history?

The Wisdom of History builds upon five earlier courses from The Teaching Company: *A History of Freedom, Famous Greeks, Famous Romans, Winston Churchill*, and *Books That Have Made History: Books That Can Change Your Life*. Produced in the fall of 2000, *A History of Freedom* traced the idea of freedom in Europe and the United States. *Famous Greeks* and *Famous Romans* were courses in Classical history emphasizing the outstanding individuals who made that history. *Winston Churchill* was a detailed examination of an individual statesman who changed the history of the world. *Books That Have Made History: Books That Can Change Your Life* was a search for universal moral and religious values through a study of seminal works of literature that still speak to each of us.

The Wisdom of History distills the narrative of these courses into broad thematic lessons. Far more, however, *The Wisdom of History* reflects my own intellectual growth and the transformation of our country in the wake of September 11, 2001. This terrorist attack upon our country is a watershed in American history and presents the United States with a challenge as profound as the American Revolution, the Civil War, and World War II. *The Wisdom of History* was conceived in my conviction that if America and its leaders are to meet that challenge, then we must learn and apply the lessons of history.

September 11 and the ensuing American involvement in the Middle East forces Americans to consider anew their naïve belief that we are immune to the laws of history that have marked the destiny of every empire and democracy before us. The Middle East barely appeared in our consideration of *A History of Freedom* and only tangentially in *Famous Greeks* and *Famous Romans*. Our foreign policy since 9/11 places the Middle East at center stage in our reflections on the lessons of history.

Current foreign policy is a continuation of our belief at least since World War I that America must make the world safe for democracy. However, the simple empirical lesson of history is that freedom is not a universal value. Throughout history, nations, like many individuals, have chosen the perceived security of autocratic rule over the awesome responsibilities of self-government. This has been the historic choice of the ancient and modern Middle East, China, Russia, and Latin America. Having chosen autocracy over freedom, these areas of the world received little attention in *A History of Freedom*. They now play a major role as we ask why world history is primarily a story of tyranny, oppression, and war.

The repetition of such a tale of woe suggests that the ancient Greeks and Romans and the Founders of the United States were correct in their assessment that history is cyclical. Because human nature never changes, similar circumstances will always produce similar events. Because human nature prevents our learning from history, we are doomed to repeat it. Thus we consider, as did the Founders, the portentous lessons to be learned from the rise and fall of the democracies and empires of the past. However, the Founders also believed that these cycles of rise and fall could be delayed, even broken, by leaders and citizens wise enough to guide themselves by the lessons of history.

In the American Revolution, the Civil War, and World War II and the Cold War, democracy proved its superiority to dictatorships in producing leaders worthy of the challenge. However, such leaders were but a reflection of the robust love of freedom held by their fellow citizens. We conclude our course by asking if we can find in the lessons of history the wisdom to choose such leaders today and what the lessons of history teach us as private individuals, as well as citizens.

To find these answers, we begin our course in Lecture One by defining what we mean by the *wisdom of history* and by stating in bold terms the 10 primary lessons of history that we shall learn in this course.

Lectures Two through Four ponder the history of the 20th century and our own brief new millennium as evidence of the first lesson of history, that is, that we do not learn from history.

Throughout the 20th century and still today, we Americans continue to believe that freedom is a universal value. All men and women in all places and times want freedom. However, this belief flies in the face of the lessons of history. In Lecture Five, we define what we mean by *freedom* and explore the unique character of freedom in the United States.

The lessons of history teach us that freedom is not a universal value. Power and empire are, in fact, the universal values of human history. The core of our course, Lectures Six through Twenty-Six, discusses the lessons of the superpowers of the past for America today.

In Lectures Seven through Nine, we ask why the Middle East has been the crucible of conflict and the graveyard of empires throughout history.

The United States is both a democracy and a superpower. In Lectures Ten through Twelve, we follow the Founders of our country in reflecting on the lessons of the ancient Athenian democracy for a modern nation intent on bringing the values of democracy to the entire world. To these same Founders, Rome, as well as Athens, was a model for our new republic. Lectures Thirteen through Sixteen consider the lessons that the rise and fall of the Roman Empire hold for the contemporary United States.

The fall of the Roman Empire took place amidst the rise of Christianity and Islam. Lectures Seventeen and Eighteen examine religion as a primary force for historical transformation and the rise and fall of empires.

The United States has inherited the consequences of the imperial powers of the last five centuries in Europe, the Middle East, the Far East, and Latin America. Lectures Nineteen through Twenty-Five discuss the lessons of these great empires and their enduring impact on contemporary politics throughout the world.

The lessons of history might make us pessimists. Our Founders knew the lessons of history but remained optimists. For them, as for us, history should be a guide, not a straightjacket. In Lectures Twenty-Six through Thirty-Four, we have as our theme America and the unique course the United States has charted in world history. Here, we find our models for what distinguishes a true statesman and leader from the politicians, tyrants, and tin-pot dictators who strut across the stage of history. We ask whether by combining the legacy of the past with the power of modern technology, the United States can chart a new course in history.

The Founders believed that history has profound lessons for the individual as well as the nation. We conclude our course in Lectures Thirty-Five and Thirty-Six by addressing the lessons of history for you and me as citizens and as private individuals.

Lecture Thirteen
The Roman Republic as Superpower

Scope:

America is an empire founded to spread freedom across a continent and the world. This idea would not have surprised our Founders. But the Founders would have worried about what history teaches concerning the consequences of empire for a free republic. Republican Rome was their model, but they feared that one day America would come to resemble Rome of the Caesars. History teaches that it is difficult to be a superpower with a constitution designed for a small city-state, such as Rome, or for 13 struggling republics along the eastern seaboard of North America. Rome was ultimately forced to choose whether to remain a republic or become a superpower. Its choice determined the future of Europe and the Middle East down to our own day.

Outline

I. The next four lectures focus on the lessons of the Roman Empire for America today.

   A. Alexander the Great left no heir when he died. His generals carved up his empire, including Ptolemy in Egypt and Seleucus in Syria.

   B. The Romans inherited Alexander's vision to build and run the most successful empire in history. The Roman Republic was the model for the Founders of our country, both of vices to be avoided and virtues to be emulated.

   C. The historians Polybius and Edward Gibbon studied the Roman Empire as a model for the present and the future. They looked for examples to be followed by future statesmen and individuals.

   1. Writing in the 2nd century B.C., Polybius attributed the Roman Empire's early success to a balanced constitution and the fact that every Roman citizen was inculcated with civic virtue.

2. Writing in the 1770s and 1780s, Gibbon traced the decline of the Roman Empire, in part as a lesson to the British Empire of his day, which seemed intent on following the course of Rome.

II. Rome began as a small city by the Tiber River. In 509 B.C., the Romans drove out the last of their kings and swore never again to have a monarch. From then on, Rome was a republic, a representative government in which the people are sovereign.

    A. The *balanced constitution* of Rome mixed three fundamental elements: broad popular support (the democratic element), leadership by a small group of wise advisors (the aristocratic element), and strong executive leadership (the monarchical element).

    B. The Roman constitution rested power in two elected *consuls*, executives whose primary function was to serve as commanders-in-chief. One consul's "no" vote could override the other's "yes" vote. When they had an army in the field, their power was absolute—except over the purse strings, which were controlled by the Senate.

    C. The Senate was indirectly elected, as our Senate was originally. In Rome, a man who reached a certain step on the ladder of offices could be brought into the Senate by its members, where he served for life unless removed by the Senate. About 300 senators controlled the purse strings and guided foreign policy.

    D. The senators could not make law, but traditionally, no law was presented to the people without the recommendation of the Senate. The Roman people were the ultimate sovereigns. They elected magistrates, decided questions of war and peace, and passed all laws.

III. In Rome, every citizen was taught to be a patriot. Fathers taught their children to read and write and about Roman history and traditions. The Roman army was a citizen militia of males 18 and older. The Romans believed that a professional standing army had no purpose except to oppress the liberties of a free people.

    A. Our Founding Fathers believed that Rome had risen to greatness because of the moral fiber of its people. The

Romans were pious people who believed that the gods had chosen them to rule an empire. They were faithful and honest. Allies were protected; enemies were destroyed.

B. The Romans did not believe in preemptive or undeclared wars, but they were warriors first and foremost, always defending their liberty. The proudest claim a Roman could make was to have fought for his country.

C. In its long history, ancient Rome was officially at peace only twice. Through war and diplomacy, Rome united small tribes into the Latin League. Step by step, Rome expanded until, by the year 270 B.C., it was the master of Italy up to the Po River.

D. The Romans established a coalition of all Italian city-states, including the Greeks of the south, tying each of them to Rome by individual alliances.

IV. Soon after Italy was unified, Rome went to war with Carthage (264–241 B.C.); the conflict was justified, in the Roman view, because the Carthaginians had attacked Roman allies. This was a naval war, but Rome was not a naval power and lost many battles.

A. But the Romans did not give up. After failing to build efficient ships of their own, they captured a Carthaginian ship, put it on a beach, and taught themselves to row. Finally, they defeated the Carthaginians. As a result, Rome gained its first overseas territory, Sicily.

B. Carthage, a great commercial city, and Rome, an agrarian democracy, struggled for dominance in the western Mediterranean. They fought again in an all-out war from 218 to 201 B.C. Again, Rome saw itself as the victim of Carthaginian aggression.

　1. Hannibal, Carthage's military genius, invaded the lands of Rome. In three great battles, he killed one in four Italians of military age and threatened Rome itself.

　2. Rome conquered Carthage, then turned to the kingdoms of the Hellenistic east. By 167 B.C., Rome was master of the Mediterranean world.

C. Rome became a superpower, dominant militarily, politically, and economically. Its statesmen learned Greek, the language of diplomacy and culture, and Greek ideas were adapted to fit a Roman mold. The favored philosophy of Rome was the Stoic view of a world ruled by those worthy to be its masters.

V. Rome, the empire and the republic, offers fascinating history lessons. The Founders of the United States regarded it with both awe and trepidation.

A. The Founders believed that a nation with a balanced constitution vitalized by citizens' civic virtue would expand, as Rome had done. They also believed, along with Polybius and Gibbon, that empire brings with it dangerous consequences. Among them, the ancients believed, were wealth and contact with foreigners, which corrode civic virtue and destroy the constitution.

B. The Spartans recognized this danger, which is why they were reluctant to build an empire after defeating the Persians. They did not want to destroy their civic virtue.

C. The Founders asked, as the Romans did, whether a republic can rule as a superpower. By the 1st century B.C., Rome was trying to rule an empire with a constitution made for a small city-state by the Tiber.

D. Similarly, the United States is a superpower with a constitution made for 13 struggling republics along the eastern seaboard. Our constitution is based on the Roman constitution, both made for small city-states.

VI. By 70 B.C., the weaknesses in Rome's government were clear. The empire's wealth had completely corrupted the powerful Senate. In fact, wealth corroded every aspect of Roman political life.

A. Ordinary Romans were better off than ever, but the gulf between wealthy businessmen and senators and ordinary citizens was huge. Money eroded the political process. The only way to get elected in 70 B.C. was to spend lavishly.

B. To get citizens' votes, politicians sponsored gladiatorial games. Wealthy businessmen traded campaign contributions for political favors. Newly elected provincial governors recouped their campaign expenses by plundering the provinces.

C. The Senate and the governors reflected the corruption of the ordinary Roman. The small farmer was almost gone in Italy by the 1st century B.C. Rome replaced its citizen militia with a professional army. The Founders traced the demise of Roman liberty to the decision to give up the citizen militia.

D. Rome had always resolved its differences peacefully and for the good of the country. Now, there were two major political parties, the Optimates and the Populares.

    1. The Optimates stood for old moral values. They supported political reforms from within the Senate.

    2. The Populares—which literally means "democrats"—believed that Rome needed more democracy, not less. It needed leaders responsive to the popular will.

VII. Rome had a serious problem in 70 B.C. with pirates who terrorized the Mediterranean and took hostages, including senators' wives held for ransom. One hostage, a young student named Julius Caesar, later caught the perpetrators and had them crucified.

A. When the Senate failed to stop this network of terrorists, the citizens gave absolute power to Cnaeus Pompey, a military commander. In six months, he destroyed the terrorist network.

B. The people, again overriding the Senate, made Pompey commander-in-chief, with absolute authority in the Middle East. To handle the rogue regime of Mithradates, Pompey used ruthless force, annexing some areas and turning others into client states dominated by Rome.

C. The Romans had lost confidence in their republican government. They stood at a crossroads and asked: Do we wish to be a superpower or a free republic? Do we want a dictator who will give us good government, the wealth and prestige of empire, and personal freedom, or do we want the awesome, toilsome responsibility of self-government?

Essential Reading:

Polybius, *The Rise of the Roman Empire*, Book VI.

Reinhold, *Classica Americana*, pp. 94–115.

Supplementary Reading:

Fears, *Famous Romans*, Lectures One through Fourteen.

Starr, *The Emergence of Rome*.

Questions to Consider:

1. What other parallels between the Roman Republic and the United States occur to you?

2. Based on what they learned from Roman history, the Founders of our country believed that a large professional army was a danger to the liberty of a republic. Do you agree?

Lecture Thirteen—Transcript
The Roman Republic as Superpower

We turn now, in Lecture 13, to a series of four lectures on the lessons of the Roman Empire for America today. The Romans were the true heirs of Alexander the Great. He had been the most successful conqueror of the Middle East, and he was the statesman with a vision of how to bring peace, order and stability to the Middle East over a long period of time. Indeed, he dreamed of a brotherhood of the human race, all under the rule of Alexander the Great, but that was never to be. He died shortly before his 33rd birthday, and he left no real heir. His son by Roxane became simply a pawn in the struggles among his generals, who carved up his empire—men like Ptolemy, who ruled Egypt, and Seleucus, who ruled over Syria. The little boy, Alexander, like his mother, died in a cold castle in Macedonia by assassination.

It was to be the Romans who would inherit his vision of bringing order to the whole world. The Romans were remarkable as the most successful imperial nation in history and as a nation that grew morally into its role as the superpower of its day. The founders of our country believed that the most significant lessons were to be found in Rome. They learned from Greece, but Rome was their great model, both of vices to be avoided and of virtues to be emulated. In following the lessons of the Roman Empire for America today, we walk in the footsteps of two of the most thoughtful historians of all time, Polybius and Edward Gibbon. Both were truly philosophical historians; that is, they studied history to draw lessons for the present and to look into the future. Both believed in laws of history. You have to have your facts straight—that's crucial—and both were very serious in their research. But both believed that history was without any real point unless it gave models to be followed by both statesmen and individuals.

Polybius, writing in the 2nd century B.C., traced the rise of Rome's Empire and found the reason for the success of the Romans in their balanced constitution, and in the fact that every Roman citizen was inculcated with civic virtue, with a willingness to subordinate his own interests to the good of Rome as a whole. Gibbon traced the *Decline and Fall of the Roman Empire*—he was writing as a Member of Parliament—the first volume of his *Decline and Fall* came out in 1775, and the last volume in 1787. In other words, it exactly spanned the period from the Battle of Lexington down to the Constitution. He believed that in tracing the fall of the Roman Empire, he was giving lessons to the British Empire of his own day, which seemed intent on following the course of Rome.

The Romans were the most successful imperial people in history. They began, as tradition had it, in 753 as a small city by the Tiber, founded by Romulus and Remus, and we have no reason to doubt that tradition. In 509 B.C. they drove out the last of their seven kings and swore never again to have a monarch, and that the words "king" or "tyrant" would be the most hateful words in Roman ears. They gave themselves a free constitution. From that moment onward, they were a republic that came to be the greatest superpower of its day. Their constitution had much that our founders admired. It was a *balanced constitution*, and in the ancient view that meant it was a proper mix of the three fundamental elements that every government must have. It must have a broad base of popular support; that is the democratic element. It also must have leadership by a small group of wise advisors, which is the aristocratic element, *aristos* meaning "the best." Finally, it must, in times of crisis, have strong executive leadership; this is the monarchical element.

The Roman constitution, developed first in 509 B.C. and then evolved by a number of trials and errors, rested supreme power in two *consuls*. They were the executives, and their chief function was to be commanders in chief. That's where our idea of a strong president came from. The consuls also had duties at home, convening the Senate. They could convene an assembly of the Roman people, but they were chiefly the generals, and they were elected every year. The Romans believed strictly in terms of office, in term limits. Secondly, there were always two. The "no" vote of a consul overrode the "yes" vote. When they had the army in the field, their power was absolute, except over the purse strings; that resided with the Senate.

The Senate was indirectly elected, very much the way our Senate was in the original Constitution. In our original Constitution, the state legislature, which the people elected, then appointed the United States senators. So, too, in Rome; the people elected you to one of a series of offices. If you reached a certain step on the ladder of offices—if you, for example, became a *quaestor*, who was in charge of financial affairs, well below the Consul, but a responsible office—

then the senators could co-opt you, bring you into the Senate, if they thought your record and your moral character deserved it. Then you served for life unless you were removed by the Senate. The number varies, but there were roughly 300 of them, and they provided complete control over the purse strings, and they guided foreign policy.

The senators could not make a law, but no law traditionally went before the Roman people unless the Senate had made a recommendation about it, so their power was enormous. Polybius said if you saw the consuls in the field in their regal robes, leading an army, you would think Rome was a monarchy. But if you saw the grandeur of the Senate, and foreign ambassadors coming before the Senate making supplication for Rome's intervention, then you would think it was an aristocracy. When you saw the Roman people assembled in their majesty, the *fasciae*—the symbol of office of the Roman Consul, a bundle of rods with an ax in it, symbolic of his power on campaign to beat or execute a Roman citizen—lowered before the might of the people, then you would think it was a democracy. The Roman people were the ultimate sovereigns. They elected their magistrates, decided all questions of war and peace and passed all laws. This was the mixture.

Polybius went on to say that what made Rome so very special was the fact that every citizen was taught from their earliest days to be a patriot. Most Romans were taught to read and write by their fathers, who were the source of their knowledge of Roman history and Roman traditions. A Roman senator brought his son with him into the Senate house for the deliberations. The Roman citizen, from the age of 18 through the rest of his life, just as in Athens, was subject to military duty. They could serve every year, and the Roman army was a total citizen militia. This, too, our founders admired greatly. Like our founders, the Romans believed that a professional standing army had no purpose except to oppress the liberties of a free people. That army was a school for citizenship and for patriotism. They were highly disciplined and highly effective.

Polybius said—this is Polybius speaking, not me—that you could take a dozen Greeks, and take a chest full of gold, and wrap all kinds of chains and locks around it, and send it on a ship with all 12 of them as witnesses. When that chest arrived, there would not be a single gold piece left in it, and no one would know what had happened. You could take one Roman, put that same chest there without a lock, and every gold piece would arrive. That was, he said, the character of the Romans. The founders of our country believed, with the Romans, that Rome had risen to greatness because of the moral fiber of its people, their values. At the top was religion; they believed they were the most pious of people. They believed that the gods—above all, the god Jupiter—had chosen them for world empire. They were faithful and honest; they kept their word. If you were an ally, they protected you. If you were an enemy and crossed them, they would destroy you.

They always fought just wars. They did not believe in preemptive wars or undeclared wars. There had to be a just cause. They would bring it before the gods. They had a special class of priests called the *fetiales*, who brought it before the gods and asked them to give a sign through the heavens that this was truly a just war. Then they declared war upon the enemy by hurling a spear into the enemy's territory. They were honest, pious, true to their word, and warlike—*virtus*, which gives us our root word virtue—but thought nothing about turning the other cheek. It meant what made you a *vir*, a man. The Romans were warriors first and foremost. The proudest claim a Roman could have was to have fought for his country in battle, and to have won the highest of medals, like our Medal of Honor. It was generally awarded for saving the life of a citizen at extreme peril to you in time of combat. That was Rome.

Rome was a republic, a *res publica*; it gave us our very word, republic; it was the thing of the people, the commonwealth, our thing, the *res publica*. They had a strong democratic base, and they did not make for good neighbors. Nothing bothers me more than when people say democracies make for good neighbors; it's just historically dead wrong. The Romans were very bad neighbors in the same way that the Native Americans might have said, of our 19th-century republic, that we were very bad neighbors. The Mexicans and the Canadians might also have made that claim. After all, we invaded them first at the time of the American Revolution, and then in the 1812 war, each time convinced that they really wanted to become part of the United States when they did not.

Rome was an aggressive, warlike republic. They believed in their liberty. They always believed that they were defending their liberty, but somehow someone was always trying to take their liberty away from them. In fact, in the long history of Rome, down until the year 27 B.C., Rome was officially at peace only two times. Every year they had to go to war. They began with the small tribes around them, tribes that even spoke the same Latin language. Through war and diplomacy, they first united them into a league, the Latin League. That was the first step, this coalition, in spreading Rome all across the peninsula of Italy. Step by step, Rome expanded until, by the year 270 B.C.—a long expansion—they were absolute masters of Italy up to the Po River.

They established a coalition of all the Italian city-states, including the Greeks of the south, tying each of them to Rome by individual alliances. No sooner had they unified Italy than their liberty, they felt, was threatened by Carthage, just a day's sail away from Sicily, which had always been a Carthaginian sphere of influence. In 264, Rome went to war with Carthage. It was a just war in Roman view— the Carthaginians had attacked Roman allies—and it was a naval war. The Romans were not a naval power; they were an infantry power. They really didn't know much about ships, and they lost again and again to the Carthaginians in those mighty naval battles.

Another aspect of Rome was "never give up." They are the example of staying the course and doing it successfully. They lost many battles, but they never lost a war; that was their motto. They'd try these ships, and they'd fail. They'd have Greek cities build ships for them, and they'd still fail. Finally, they took a captured Carthaginian ship, in Roman tradition and put it up on a beach, and on land taught themselves to row then went out and promptly lost again. But they came back and finally defeated the Carthaginians. The great difference between Carthage and Rome was that Carthage lost this one battle—this is 264 to 241, a long war of attrition—and immediately surrendered. Rome gained its first overseas territory, Sicily. We never lose a war—that was the Roman motto.

Then it was a struggle for dominance in the western Mediterranean. Again, if you think having two republics sharing the sphere of influence is a model for peace, you are dead wrong. The American Civil War teaches us this as well. After all, the North and South were republics, democracies. Their constitutions were almost identical, and yet they could not stay at peace for more than a couple of weeks; so with Rome and Carthage, both republics, both having mixed constitutions. In fact, Aristotle admired the constitution of Carthage, that great commercial city. The founders pointed out that being a commercial city did not make you peaceful. They said Carthage was one of the most warlike nations of the ancient world. They said Britain was a commercial nation, and the most aggressive imperialistic nation the world had ever seen.

We had Rome, which was an agrarian democracy, and Carthage, which was a commercial republic, and they both went to war a second time around. This was a knock-down-drag-out war. It was parallel to our Second World War in terms of its impact upon the Roman mind. From 218 to 201, Rome was in a death struggle with Carthage. It saw itself as the victim of Carthaginian aggression. Hannibal, the military genius, had invaded the land of Rome. In three great battles, he destroyed one in four Italians of military age, and he threatened Rome itself. Rome decided as a result of this war never to be in danger of national extinction again. When they conquered Hannibal in 201 and won the final peace, they then turned to the eastern Mediterranean. They found reason after reason to bring war with the kingdoms of the Hellenistic east, the legacy of Alexander the Great—the kingdom of Macedonia, then the kingdom of the Seleucids in Syria, dominating Egypt and destroying the commercial power of roads until, by 167 B.C., Rome was absolute master of the Mediterranean world.

From that day on, Rome would be the absolute superpower—dominant militarily, politically and economically. They had reared the generation of the second war with Carthage, the generation that produced leaders like Scipio and Cato. They had produced a generation of statesmen to rule a world empire. They had learned Greek, the language of diplomacy and culture. They had become fully imbued with Greek ideas, at the same time pushing them into a Roman mold. It was no coincidence that their favorite philosophy from Greece was the Stoic view of a universal world state ruled by those worthy to be the masters.

The Empire of Rome, the republic, offers some of the most fascinating lessons for us today. The founders looked at it with both awe and trepidation. The founders believed that if you had a balanced constitution, motivated and vitalized by the civic virtue of its citizens, it would expand, as Rome had done. They also believed, along with Polybius and Edward Gibbon that empire brings with it dangerous, perhaps fatal, consequences. The ancients believed that there was an invariable iron law of empire. That is to say a republic would rise to greatness and gain an empire, which would bring with it wealth and contact with foreigners. Wealth and contact with foreigners would corrode civic virtue and ultimately destroy that constitution.

The Spartans already recognized this. That was why Sparta was so reluctant to take up an empire after the defeat of the Persians. They did not have wealth in Sparta—in fact, they didn't even have gold and silver—nor did they have contact with foreigners because they believed it would destroy their civic virtue. This, the founders believed, had happened in Rome, the republic that tried to be a superpower and an empire. The founders asked the question, as the Romans did, can a republic rule as a superpower for long, or must it change? Rome, in the last part of the 2nd century B.C., and then by the 1st century B.C.—let's take 70 B.C. as our date—was trying to be a superpower and rule an empire with a constitution made for a small city-state by the Tiber.

In that same way, we are now a superpower attempting to play a major role in the world, at the least, with a constitution made for 13 struggling republics along the eastern seaboard; the Roman republican constitution, upon which our own constitution was modeled; the wise Senate in charge of foreign policy, the commander in chief who is the consul. We now have a constitution that is based on the Roman constitution, both made for small city-states. The Roman constitution cracked. By 70 B.C., these cracks were clear. Rome was a republic, and everything seemed the same, but it was not. First, the wealth of empire completely corrupted the Senate. It had been the wise advice of the Senate that had guided Rome on its path to empire. The people had given enormous authority to the Senate to guide it through these difficult paths of becoming a world empire. But wealth was just too much for the civic virtue of senators. It corroded every aspect of the Roman political life.

Ordinary Romans were better off than they'd ever been before. Most of them had ceased to be farmers, and they were in various service industries. They were fairly well off, but the gulf between wealthy businessmen and senators and the ordinary Roman was huge. In the old days of the free republic, men like Cato had sat down alongside their workers and eaten a dinner of turnips. Not now; Romans like Cicero owned numerous huge villas with hundreds of rooms and vast numbers of servants. Huge amounts of money were spent on delicacies bought from all over the world for the table. But more than that, money eroded the political process. The only way you were elected in 70 B.C. to any office—starting at the lowest level, such as an *edile*, who was in charge of the street sweeping and prices in the market—was by huge spending, vast advertising and, particularly, by paying for gladiatorial games.

The Romans had a cult of violence very much like our own cult of video games today. They had these gladiatorial games, and if you wanted to run for office and gain the vote of the ordinary Roman citizen—because their vote still was what made the process possible—you put on these games for them. In fact, you even bought their vote openly. To do this, you didn't want to spend your own money, so you took campaign contributions, and the biggest campaign contributors were businessmen. The Empire had created an enormous number of wealthy businessmen with huge government contracts to supply the army and collect taxes in the provinces of the Roman Empire.

Their profits depended on good laws being passed in their favor, measures going through. Thus, they paid the campaign contribution and promised not to ask for any favors in return. No sooner were you elected than there they were saying you have to put this measure through the Roman Assembly. You took all this money, and you had to come through in order to have the next campaign contribution. All through your career, you looked forward to first being a consul and then governor of a province. As soon as you were governor of a province, then you could begin to recoup your money by plundering the provincials.

The provinces groaned under Roman rule in this 1st century B.C., but it was not only political corruption. The Senate and the governors that were sent out by the Senate were but a reflection of the corruption of the ordinary Roman, the sturdy men who had fought at Connae and lived on a diet of oatmeal. They were small farmers and patriots. The small farmer was almost gone in Italy by the 1st century B.C., and the Romans had given up their citizen militia. By 100 B.C., you simply could not find Romans who were willing to be drafted. They evaded the draft in every way possible, and a very good reason was give—why do we want to fight some small colonial war in Asia Minor, Syria or Spain?

What we need is a professional army of Roman citizens, but they'll serve for 20 years, starting off with a five-year term, and they will have professional generals. They are the ones to handle these colonial wars and deal with insurgencies. That's what the Romans had. The founders traced, in their view, the demise of Roman liberty to that decision to give up a citizen militia. Rome had a professional army by the year 70 B.C. It had a corrupt political process in which the ordinary Roman had lost complete faith, and it had a number of problems that were small in themselves, but which, collectively, the Senate refused to solve. The Senate, like Rome itself, was torn by bitter partisan political struggles.

Rome, like any free republic, had always had political differences. It had had political differences of a major sort during the war with Hannibal—how to fight Hannibal—but they had always been resolved peacefully and for the good of the country. Then there were two major political parties, the Optimates and the Populares. The Optimates believed they were the best people—that was what it stood for—and they were for strong old, Roman moral values, and for having the Senate rule Rome in the old-fashioned way. They believed that yes, Rome needed some reforms, but it would come from within the Senate itself in the political process. The Populares—which literally means the democrats, the party of the people—believed that Rome had just changed, that Rome needed more democracy, not less democracy. It needed leaders and a Senate very responsive to the popular will, and it tended to be championed by generals, who gained great authority from commanding armies. They were the darlings of the Roman people, and those powerful generals turned statesmen had things done.

Rome had a serious problem with terrorism in 70 B.C. In fact, pirates, most of them coming from the Middle East and in league with Middle Eastern rulers, would terrorize the whole Mediterranean and carry away hostages. They even snatched the wives of senators from their villas on the coast of Italy and held them for ransom. They made the mistake of holding as hostage a young student, on his way to a junior year abroad in Greece, named Julius Caesar, who caught them and crucified them later. The Senate just couldn't deal with these terrorists, couldn't find this network of terrorists. The people, overriding the Senate, gave absolute power to Cnaeus Pompeius, who had won a reputation as a military commander in Italy and

Spain. In six months, he utterly destroyed the terrorist network. He simply divided the Mediterranean into five districts, sent his fleet up and down, crucified a good many of the terrorists, and let the rest become farmers, peacefully transported away. The terrorism just disappeared.

Then the people, again overriding the will of the Senate, made Pompey commander in chief with absolute authority in the Middle East. Among the foreign policy issues the Senate simply could not find a way to settle was a rogue regime in the Middle East, the regime of Mithradates. He had been a problem since 88 B.C. His coin portraits bear a striking resemblance to Saddam Hussein. In 88 B.C., he had carried out the greatest single mass act of terrorism in history. He had 80,000 Roman citizens throughout the Middle East killed in one day. The Senate had fought a little war with him, but then had left him in place. Then finally in 63 B.C., Pompey the general showed it wasn't hard to rid them of him. He went in and used absolutely ruthless force. Pompey settled the Middle East, annexing some areas, making others into client states dominated by Rome, bringing back huge amounts of money and giving enormous rebates to Roman citizens.

The way was clear to the Romans. They had lost confidence in a republican government, and they stood at a crossroads, as another nation might one day. Do we wish to be a superpower, or do we wish to be a free republic governing ourselves under laws that we give ourselves? Do we want a dictator, like a Pompey or a Julius Caesar, who will give us good government, the wealth and prestige of empire, and personal freedom to live as we choose, but relieve us of the awesome, toilsome responsibility of self-government?

Lecture Fourteen
Rome of the Caesars as Superpower

Scope:

The Roman Empire was, in the terms of its day, a global empire, marked by a global economy, a global culture, and a global political world. The Roman Empire conjures up visions of oppression, because we tend to see a dichotomy between the ideals of empire and those of freedom. In fact, the Roman Empire did far more than the Roman Republic to advance the cause of individual freedom. The Roman Empire offers a model of how to achieve peace and prosperity over a large geographical area, while securing individual rights, ethnic autonomy, and local political freedom. The Romans grew to the challenge of empire and provide an enduring model that an empire can be a great force for the public good and world peace and prosperity. The model of the Roman Empire teaches the lesson that we must judge an empire by the values for which it stands.

The Roman Empire was an age of creativity with few parallels in history. It was, in its own way, as creative as our own age of technology and science. As America today builds upon the intellectual heritage of Europe, so Rome built upon its legacy from Greece. In art, literature, and architecture, the Roman Empire laid the cultural foundations for the next 1,000 years of European history. Roman science and medicine shaped the history of both the medieval Christian and Muslim worlds. In law and religion, the legacy was even greater and remains with us today on a daily basis.

Outline

I. By the 1st century B.C., the Roman Empire, the superpower of its day, began to crack under the weight of its wealth, political scandals, and other problems. A gridlocked Senate could not resolve pressing social, economic, or foreign policy issues.

    A. As a result, ordinary citizens lost faith in republican freedom. They wanted a leader who would solve Rome's political problems and give them prosperity and individual freedom.

B. Julius Caesar and his adopted son, Augustus Caesar, solved these problems and introduced two centuries of unparalleled peace and prosperity throughout the empire. Julius Caesar was a great general and a visionary politician. Augustus Caesar was probably the most successful statesman in history.

C. Julius Caesar believed that Rome could no longer stand as a republic. It needed a strong leader. By 44 B.C., he had risen to supreme power as dictator for life.

D. After Caesar's assassination, Augustus came to power, knowing that the Roman citizens still wanted to think of themselves as free. He left in place the façade of the old republican constitution but held all real power himself.

E. The Roman Empire of the 1st and 2nd centuries B.C. provides a uniquely instructive lesson in history. The Roman people gave up political freedom in return for individual freedom and to remain a superpower. Rome became a military dictatorship of the Caesars—Augustus, Nero, Trajan, and Marcus Aurelius.

II. The vast Roman Empire of the 1st and 2nd centuries B.C. stretched from Britain to Iraq, from the forests of Germany to the sands of the Sahara. It included what is today western and central Europe, parts of the Middle East, and northern Africa.

A. One language, Latin, was spoken throughout the empire. One coinage united commerce. One law protected all inhabitants. Roman citizens' individual rights were more clearly defined under the empire than they had been under the Roman Republic.

B. High-quality roads and bridges crossed the empire—some are still used today. A free-market economy brought the goods of the world to citizens. It was an age of social mobility, in which men were born slaves, bought their freedom, and became multimillionaires.

C. The seas were kept clear of pirates and terrorism, thanks to a professional army of 360,000 soldiers. The Roman troops were drawn evenly between citizens and noncitizens. By serving in the army for 25 years, the latter became Roman citizens. By 212 A.D., every freeborn inhabitant of the

Roman Empire became a citizen. Thus, a city had grown into the entire world.

D. Rome was a tolerant empire. The emperors built temples to the gods of Gaul and Egypt and were regarded as pharaohs in Egypt. This tolerance spawned tremendous creativity.

    1. The basis of science was established during the empire for the next 1,000 years of European civilization. Galen's medical textbooks were used in Europe in the 15th century A.D. Ptolemy's map of the world was still the standard in Europe in 1492.

    2. The architectural foundations for the next 1,000 years were laid. The Pantheon, designed by the emperor Hadrian (117–138 A.D.), spawned the intellectual framework and construction techniques for Gothic cathedrals.

    3. In art, the Column of Trajan portrayed military campaigns in narrative reliefs. The use of such visual forms to convey the message of imperial victory became the basis of Christian mosaics in churches of the 4th and 5th centuries A.D. in Rome.

E. Christianity spread over this vast empire. The early church fathers believed that it had been God's will to send a Messiah to the world in the age of Augustus to ensure peace and spread the Gospel.

F. In the 1st and 2nd centuries A.D., the foundations of Roman law were laid, and this law became the basis of the legal codes of France, Germany, Italy, and Latin America.

III. The Roman imperial system produced a set of able, dedicated leaders with few parallels in history. Augustus shaped the empire. Claudius conquered Britain and began administrative changes that would create one of the best civil service organizations of its time. There were no grand wars or struggles. Historian Edward Gibbon described this age, the 1st and 2nd centuries A.D., as the happiest in human history.

A. The civil service of the Roman Empire in the 1st and 2nd centuries A.D. was large but efficient. The bureaucrats saw their mission as bringing peace and order to the world.

B. The Roman Empire was multicultural and diverse. The Romans did not force inhabitants to learn Latin or Greek or prohibit the worship of native gods.

C. The empire was also expansionistic. Claudius conquered Britain, and Trajan carried out a long, successful war against the Dacians in what is now Romania.

D. The imperial age was one of philanthropy. Many Roman ruins seen today—aqueducts, baths, and gymnasiums—were the gifts of successful, civic-minded Roman citizens. Emperors sponsored professors and other learned commentators.

E. In this prosperous free-market economy, citizens paid taxes to support roads and other public benefits. The Roman emperors understood personal investment and its benefits for the general economy.

IV. The emperor and his advisors made all important decisions, but government otherwise was decentralized. Local political life was extremely active. However, foreign policy problems remained difficult to resolve, particularly on the frontiers of the empire.

A. Augustus was a shrewd judge of the limits of expansion. He tested the waters first in the Near East, where he came to an understanding with Iran.

B. In 9 A.D., the Romans decided to expand into German lands, then ruled by tribes. Three legions marched into Germany and were destroyed. The Roman army stopped at the Rhine River. Augustus saw no purpose in expanding deep into Germany.

C. Augustus also set limits in the Middle East, along the northern border (central Europe), and to the south (northern Africa).

V. Augustus Caesar inherited the throne of the Roman emperor at age 19 after the assassination of Julius Caesar. He returned to Rome from Greece, raised an army, and punished the assassins. By 31 B.C., he had risen to supreme power over the Roman world.

A. The world he inherited was in the midst of chaos and economic disaster. The provinces wanted to break away. The

Roman people were disenchanted. Augustus Caesar revived the empire, step by step.

B. In 27 B.C., Augustus announced his retirement from political life, leaving his successors to determine how to govern the provinces and maintain prosperity. In a carefully orchestrated demonstration, the Senate begged him to stay. Thus, Augustus held onto a few of his powers, and those powers would grow over the years. His new name, Imperator Caesar Divi Filius Augustus, meant the "Conquering General Caesar, the Son of God, Augustus, the Messiah."

  1. *Imperator* expressed his absolute domination of the army. As *Caesar*, he continued the vision of the Roman Empire under an absolute ruler, bringing peace and prosperity to all. *Divi Filius* was not blasphemy but literally meant that Augustus was the son of the deified Caesar, who had risen to the stars. The best rendition of *Augustus* is "the Messiah."

  2. Across the empire, he was hailed as the "prince of peace," the savior of the human race. Through his wisdom, prudence, and patriotism, Augustus created a model empire.

Essential Reading:

Fears, "Natural Law."

Gibbon, *The Decline and Fall of the Roman Empire*, chapters I–III.

Supplementary Reading:

Kelly, *The Roman Empire*.

Questions to Consider:

1. Do you believe that a global economy ensures peace?

2. The Romans saw national freedom of the many ethnic groups in the empire as disruptive forces. Does that have lessons for today?

Lecture Fourteen—Transcript
Rome of the Caesars as Superpower

In our last lecture we saw how Rome, by the 1st century B.C., had become the absolute superpower of its day—dominant militarily, politically, economically and even culturally. Rome was the heir of Greek civilization, and this Greco-Roman culture became the way of rising up in the social scale for people all over that vast empire. It was a superpower trying to rule that empire with a constitution made for a small republic, and it collapsed. When people ask me where I think America might stand on the scale of the Roman Empire, I say it has nothing to do at the moment with the Rome of the 1st or 2nd century A.D., the Rome of the Caesars. It is the Rome of the 1st century B.C., the Roman Senate, which had provided such superb guidance for Rome during the struggle with Hannibal and the rise to superpower status, and the Roman people, whose civic virtue and constitution, Polybius said, was the key factor in why Rome, in one generation, rose from being a small nation to being master of an empire.

Those began to crack under the weight of the wealth, affluence, political problems and complications brought about by empire. The Senate reached gridlock in the 1st century B.C. The partisan politics were so savage that neither party, the Populares nor the Optimates, could allow its compatriots, its rivals, to gain the political victory. Thus, those problems just went unsolved—pressing problems of social and economic needs, and above all, foreign policy issues. Moreover, at every critical moment, when clear thinking was required, the Senate always found itself in some scandal—sex and religion scandals bubbling up from time to time, having to set up committees to investigate each other. That was their way out of these serious questions.

The result was that the ordinary Roman citizen lost faith in republican freedom. They had already given up the desire to serve in their army and fight in these far-off wars. They wanted a leader who would give them prosperity and individual freedom, and solve those political issues, but it would not be Pompey, whom we discussed in our last lecture. It would be Gaius Julius Caesar and his adopted son, known to history as Augustus. They would be the rulers who would solve Rome's problems and introduce two centuries of unparalleled peace and prosperity throughout the Mediterranean world, a good part of Western Europe and the Middle East. They were two of the most visionary statesmen in history. Julius Caesar was one of the greatest generals in history, and a visionary politician. Augustus was probably the most successful single statesman in all of history.

Julius Caesar had a vision, but Pompey wanted to be the first man in Rome. He would be at home today in politics. He wanted to be in office; he wanted admiration. Caesar wanted to change things. He believed that Rome could no longer be a republic. The Roman people were not worthy of freedom, and they needed one man who could solve their problems and the problems of the Empire. Therefore, with foresight, vigor, and a desire and a goal to be king over that vast empire, Caesar, by 44 B.C., had risen to supreme power in Rome, dictator for life. He wanted one thing more; he wanted the title of king. Caesar pushed too far too fast, and he was assassinated. But his adopted son Augustus, who would be known to his contemporaries as Gaius Julius Caesar, would know that people would not give up the shadow of freedom. The Roman people still wanted to think of themselves as free.

In his long life—he died in bed peacefully at the age of 77 in 14 A.D. as absolute master of the world—Augustus kept coming up with little compromises, which left the façade of the old republican constitution, but gathered all real power into his hands. He was the true founder of the empire of the Caesars. The founders of our country hoped that the Rome of the republic would be our model, but they feared that one day the Rome of the Caesars would indeed become our model. That Roman Empire of the 1st and 2nd century B.C.—that age of the *Pax Romana* and the immense majesty of the Roman Empire—is one of the most instructive lessons in history. Yes, the Roman people made a deal. They gave up the political freedom they had enjoyed in order to have individual freedom and to remain a superpower. They could not be a superpower with a republican government, so they gave up their republic and became an empire, a military dictatorship, of the Caesars.

The Romans would have told you they made a good bargain. We now have the freedom to live as we choose, to raise our families, and to rise far on the social scale without all the silly political nonsense that goes on. That's why we have an emperor. That was the Roman Empire of Augustus, Nero, Trajan and Marcus Aurelius. The Roman Empire of the 1st and 2nd century B.C. stretched from Britain and the

North Sea, all the way out to the Tigris and Euphrates River Valley. It stretched all the way from Germany, the forests of that distant land, to the sands of the Sahara.

If you were going to go through the Roman Empire today, you would start off in Britain, come down to France, to Belgium and Holland, down through western Germany, on into Switzerland and Austria and pass through France, of course. You would go through Hungary, Romania, Bulgaria—which we now call Croatia and Slovenia and Serbia—all at peace with one another, on down into Greece, through Turkey, through Syria, Lebanon, Israel and Jordan. You would pass into Egypt, through Libya, through Tunisia, Algeria, Morocco and up into Spain. In other words, you would need a dozen languages to do this on your own. You'd need a series of visas. You would need to change your money time and time again, losing a little bit of money every step of the way. There would be places you would not want to go. Is that not true?

But in the Roman Empire of the 1st and 2nd century A.D., there was one language, Latin. If you had Greek, so much the better, but one language, Latin, would carry you anywhere in this empire. One coinage, the coinage of Rome, would carry you anywhere. One law, the law of Rome, protected you all over this vast empire. As a Roman citizen, you had not lost your individual rights; you had gained them. The Roman citizen had a more clearly defined nexus of individual rights, including the freedom to speak, than he had had under the Roman republic. The best display of this Roman freedom is St. Paul in the book of Acts, very historical. Paul has been taken prisoner by a tribune for causing a riot, and the tribune was about to give him a beating. Paul said, you can't beat me without charges. The tribune asked, why? Paul said, I'm a Roman citizen. The tribune was astounded. He asked that Paul show his papers, and then he was terrified that Paul would bring him up on charges of violating his civil rights.

That was the Empire. It was crossed by a series of roads of the highest quality. We still travel over Roman roads today. Where I used to do archaeological studies, south of Rome, every day I went to work over a Roman road. There are bridges in Rome that still carry traffic today, which were built in 63 B.C. There was a superb network of roads, and a sea that was kept clear of pirates and terrorism. That frontier, that vast world, was guarded by a professional army of 360,000 soldiers, the best-equipped professional army the world had ever seen—for all of this, a free market economy that brought the goods of the whole world to you.

Towns like Pompeii or Roman London—towns that would become Vienna in Austria, or towns like Leptis Magna in what is now a desert in Libya—which were like a mosaic composing the Roman Empire, had in their markets a display of goods like a modern super market, like a Wal-Mart today. You could buy in Leptis Magna oysters brought from Britain, cloaks made in Gaul, pottery made in the north of Italy, or silverware formed in Greece. Your wife, or husband, could drag you to an interior decorator's store and demand to redo your whole house in marble. That marble could be cut all over the Empire, depending on your fancy, and be shipped to you, be in your house in a few weeks. This was an economic unity that would not exist again until our own day.

It was an age of social mobility in which men were born slaves, bought their freedom, and rose to become multimillionaires. Their sons could go on to lives in the Roman civil service, and their grandsons could even become senators. The army provided a means for social mobility. The Roman army was divided in half; 180,000 of its troops were Roman citizens, and the other 180,000 were drawn from various people of the Empire who did not yet have Roman citizenship. By serving in the army for 25 years, they then became Roman citizens, and their children became Roman citizens. The language of Rome, and the benefits of Roman civilization, spread throughout this Empire to such a degree that by the year 212 A.D., every free-born inhabitant of the Roman Empire became a citizen. It truly was, as one of its admirers said, a city that had become an entire world, bringing everybody its benefits.

It was also a tolerant empire. Roman emperors built temples to the gods of Gaul and to the Egyptian gods. In fact, many of the temples you see as you go up the Nile today were erected or restored by Roman emperors. Roman emperors were regarded as pharaohs over Egypt. It was an age of religiosity, an age of spiritual seeking, all over that vast empire; as it was indeed an age of creativity. Yes, democracy and political freedom can spawn creativity. We live in one of the most creative ages in history, I believe, because more people are free today, and have political freedom, than any other time in history.

But the Roman Empire of the Caesars was a tremendously creative age. It was the age in which, in science, the foundations of the next 1,000 years of European civilization were laid. It was the age in which Galen wrote his textbooks, which would still be the medical textbooks of Europe in the 15th century A.D. It was also the age of Ptolemy. In 2nd century A.D. in Egypt, Ptolemy laid out latitudes and longitudes and drew a map of the world. You may ask what Ptolemy has to do with me, living here in the 21st century? That map was still the standard map in Europe in 1492. Studying that map, Christopher Columbus was taken in by one of the actual mistakes of Ptolemy. Ptolemy had shown that China was much closer to Europe than it really was. Columbus, believing in that map, thought if he could sail westward, he would come to China. Instead, he found a whole new world.

It was an age in which, in architecture, the foundations for the next 1,000 years were laid. The Pantheon, designed by the emperor Hadrian, was erected around 119 and 138 A.D. This Pantheon laid the intellectual, as well as constructional, techniques of the Gothic cathedral. It was meant to be a spiritual experience. You went inside the Pantheon, and your soul was swept up into eternal union with God. In art, the Column of Trajan, which he had designed to celebrate his victories of the Dacians, portrayed campaign after campaign in a spiral of narrative reliefs. Those narrative reliefs, the use of these visual forms to convey the message of imperial victory, then became the basis of the Christian mosaics that would decorate the churches of 4th and 5th century Rome, and then of Byzantium itself.

It was in this very age that Christianity would spread all over this vast Empire. Paul, as a Roman citizen, would travel through this Empire in safety because of the peace that had been brought. In fact, the early church fathers believed that it had been the will of God to send a Messiah to the world in the age of Augustus so that there would be the peace to spread the Gospel all over the world. It was also an age of law. In the 1st and 2nd century A.D., going on down into the 3rd century A.D., the foundations of Roman law were laid by the great jurists of the age, like Ulpian. That law would then go on to be the legal basis for more than half the world still today. Roman law was the basis of the law codes of France, Germany, Italy and Latin

America. It even played a role in shaping the law codes of Japan, this magnificent achievement.

The Romans were also a people who grew into their imperial destiny. The poet Virgil, writing under Augustus, created his *Aeneid* to proclaim that the gods themselves had chosen Rome. In it, he portrayed the mission of the Romans. Other people will make better sculpture than you; other people will give better orations than you Romans. You Romans have as your duty to wear down the haughty and to raise up the weak; to conquer the arrogant, and to raise up the weak. You Romans will bring law and peace to the world. That is your mission. That is how the Romans came to see themselves.

The Roman imperial system brought forth a set of leaders of ability and dedication with few parallels in history, including Augustus, who shaped this empire. It has been truly said of Augustus that only two times in history has a very serious problem been solved as well as it possibly could be. Once was with the founders of our country, and the other was with Augustus. Claudius seemed a little strange to some of his fellow Romans—he was a scholar who learned Etruscan—but he conquered Britain. He began a series of administrative changes that would create one of the best civil services of its day.

The civil service of the Roman Empire in the 1st and 2nd century A.D. reached a marvelous equilibrium, large enough to carry out the duties of governing the Empire, but efficient, filled with civil servants who saw their mission was to bring peace and order to the world, and governing the Empire with such regularity that strange emperors, like a Nero or Domitian, were nothing more than a blip upon the stage of history. Peace, order and tolerance—it was a multicultural diverse empire. The Romans did not force you to learn Latin or Greek. You could plead your case in court in Gaul in Celtic, in Carthage in the ancient Punic language, or in Syria in the Syriac language that Jesus spoke. It was multicultural and diverse, allowing people to worship whatever gods they worshipped; however, as long as they were Roman citizens, they also had to worship the gods of Rome. Other than that, you were free to worship as you chose.

The Roman Empire of the 1st and 2nd century A.D. was also expansionistic. Roman emperors like Claudius conquered Britain, and the emperor Trajan carried out a long and successful war to reduce the Dacians in what is now Romania, bringing back massive amounts of money to spur the economy of Rome. It was also an age of philanthropy. Many of the monuments you see throughout the Roman world, today in ruins, were given by civically minded Roman citizens who had been successful in the Empire, made a lot of money, and then wanted to build an aqueduct or baths for their city, to build a gymnasium where people could be healthy or to build schools. It was an age of professors and commentators on the great classics of the past, chairs that were sponsored by the emperors themselves.

It was an age of philanthropy and of free market economy—to have a free market economy in which you could go down to your local bank and earn 6% on a CD. If you were more of a speculator, you could join a joint stock operation, make a merchant venture, and maybe come back with 12 times what you had invested. You might lose everything, but you might come back with 12 times what you had made. For all of these benefits—the peace and prosperity of the Roman Empire, this network of roads—you worked two days a year to pay your taxes. The Roman emperors understood that if you leave money with people, they will invest it, and the economy will continue to grow. It was an age in which all important decisions were made at the very top by the emperor and his advisors.

But politics were much decentralized, and when we study inscriptions from cities like Pompeii, we see that the local political life was extremely active. People were very interested in what happened in their own little city, and in what their taxes would be in their own local city—whether a new bath structure or new fitness facility was erected. So it was decentralized—very avid politics at the local level, but major decisions made at the imperial level. So great was the peace and prosperity of the Empire that the Roman historian Tacitus, writing in the 2nd century A.D., complained that, unlike those who wrote about the history of the republic, he had nothing but boring things to tell you. There were no grand wars and grand events. That was the happiest kind of age for ordinary people.

Edward Gibbon would describe this age as the happiest in human history, this age of the 1st and 2nd century A.D., when this vast empire was ruled by firm and efficient emperors, where individual liberty flourished, and where creativity in art and literature set standards for Gibbon's own age. The Romans would have told you that they had made a good bargain when they had given up their political liberty in order to raise their nation to new heights and to achieve a new level of individual freedom.

There were still foreign policy problems that remained difficult for the Roman emperors to resolve. There was the Near East, the Middle East and to that we will devote an entire lecture. There were the frontiers of the Roman Empire. Above all, there was the vast land across the Rhine and Danube Rivers, inhabited by fiercely independent tribes, the Germans—once the Dacians and Sarmatians—divided, but always capable of coming together in unified action. The emperor Augustus had been a very careful and shrewd judge of how far the empire could expand. He had tested the waters first in the Near East, where he had come to an understanding with the empire of Iran. He had tested the waters in Germany as well. In 9 A.D., it seemed as though the whole of the German tribes could be conquered, and the Romans would expand, and even annex, Germania.

So confident was Augustus that the civilian officer, Varus, was put in charge of three legions to march into Germany and complete the reorder and pacification of the Germanic tribes. There he encountered the German war chief, Arminius—Hermann the German. In the Battle of the Teutoburg Forest, all three legions were destroyed, and the Roman army would stop at the Rhine River. "Give me back my legions," Augustus would say as he walked the halls an old man. "Varus, Varus, give me back my legions."

But he learned from that warning, and the Romans came to understand that there was no purpose in expanding deep into Germany, to an endless land of forests, and then steps that went all the way out to Russia, and even to central Asia. They learned the limits of expansion and the wisdom of moderation. In the south, in Africa, there were forays into the Sahara. Was there any need to press deep into what we call the Sudan today? Once again, this wisest of statesmen, Augustus, decided no, there had to be a limit there, what the Romans called the *limes*, the frontiers. He set limits in the Middle East, along the northern border—what we call central Europe—and in the Sahara and in the south, moderation in terms of imperial expansion.

Augustus Caesar had been born Gaius Octavius, the great-nephew of Julius Caesar. Caesar knew him very little, but he had impressed the great general. Young Gaius Octavius was going out to be with his uncle in Spain. His boat had been shipwrecked, and he made his way there on his own. To his amazement, when Caesar was assassinated, this young Octavius had been designated as the heir of Julius Caesar. It was at the age of 19, on a junior year abroad studying in Greece, that he made his way back. Using the name of Caesar and his adopted form of Gaius Julius Caesar, he would raise an army on his own accord. He would punish and see to the death of those who had assassinated Caesar. He would make alliances and then break them with Marc Antony. By the year 31 B.C., he had risen to supreme power over the Roman world, but it was a world in chaos, in economic disaster, a world in which the provincials wanted to break away from the Roman Empire. It was a world in which the Roman people themselves had become utterly disenchanted.

He set about to create the system that we have been describing, step by step. In 27 B.C. he went before the Roman Senate and announced simply, I have had enough. I am retiring from political life. I have restored the republic. You now have your constitutional system back. Do with it what you can. You have peace. Come up with a means to govern the provinces well and have economic prosperity, but leave me out of it. Of course, the Senate had been very carefully organized to demonstrate against this, to beg him to stay on, so he kept a few powers, and over the years they grew ever larger. He was, in fact, absolute master of the army. The new name he took was Imperator Caesar Divi Filius Augustus, the "Conquering General Caesar, the Son of God, Augustus, the Messiah."

The first word, *Imperator*, expressed his absolute domination of the army. As *Caesar*, he continued the vision of Caesar; of the Roman Empire under an absolute ruler, bringing peace and prosperity to all. *Divi Filius* was not blasphemy to the Romans at all, but literally the son of the deified Caesar, who had risen to the stars. *Augustus* was carefully chosen, and the best rendition of it is indeed "the Messiah." All over the Empire, he was hailed as the "Prince of Peace," the savior of the human race. This one statesman, Augustus, through his wisdom, his prudence in domestic and foreign policy—but above all, his patriotism, for he was a genuine patriot who believed that the best interest of Rome could only be served by this military dictatorship—

sugared coated the pill so well that the Roman people gulped it down. That one statesman created this model empire, this model superpower.

Lecture Fifteen
Rome and the Middle East

Scope:

The Middle East offers a key to understanding the history of Rome. Rome first became involved in the Middle East out of self-interest and treaty obligations. It began with military intervention against a rogue regime. The Romans were then forced into nation building, then occupation, and finally, annexation. Terrorism was linked to the Middle East throughout the Roman Empire. The problems of the Middle East were fundamental to the failure of Rome's republican constitution and, later, to the fall of its empire. The attempt of the Romans to bring stability, peace, and Roman political values to Judea illustrates why the Romans found the problems of the Middle East so intractable.

Outline

I.   Of all the areas ruled by the Roman Empire, the Middle East was the most problematic. The Romans never fully solved the region's problems, and this failure ultimately led to the fall of the empire. The area of Judea, now Israel, was particularly troubling.

    A. In 6 A.D., Augustus Caesar received a delegation from Judea, seeking Roman annexation of the region. Judea had long been under Roman domination but not direct control. Augustus wanted to leave Judea, with its many feuding ethnic groups, as a client state of the Roman Empire.

    B. On the other hand, Judea was strategically vital to Rome because it was next to Egypt, an important source of grain. Much of Egypt's grain was brought to Italy, where it kept bread prices low and the people happy.

    C. Across the Roman border was the empire of Persia (Iran), which had made a peace agreement with Augustus in 19 B.C. Julius Caesar had dreamed of conquering Persia, but Augustus knew his limits. If he stirred up the Iranians, they might invade with their formidable army.

D. With much concern, Augustus decided to annex Judea. The Romans sought to build a Judea that was technically independent but under Roman control, with basic Roman forms of government and a king who functioned as a client king of Rome. The Judeans didn't want a king, however; they wanted to be part of the Roman Empire.

II. The annexation treaty set down the rights and privileges of the Jewish people in Judea, who had largely supported the Caesars.

    A. For example, Augustus agreed that the Romans' regional capital would be in Caesarea, not Jerusalem. In addition, Roman coins that circulated inside Judea would not have the image of the emperor on them, in keeping with the Second Commandment's ban on graven images.

    B. Also in Judea were a number of other ethnic groups, including the Samaritans and Greeks, both native Greeks and those who had adopted Greek customs and language.

    C. The Gospels and the book of Acts offer insight into the problems the Romans faced in the Middle East and why the region proved so troublesome. In the Gospel of Luke, for example, we read that the first task of the annexation was to carry out a census so that everyone could be taxed. Many Jewish people opposed the census and the tax. Judeans already harbored much resentment over foreign influence.

    D. For a group called the zealots—who were terrorists in Roman eyes—any foreign occupation broke God's commandment that he alone was king of Israel. From the beginning of Roman annexation, they stalked the streets of Jerusalem and other cities, killing Roman soldiers. They saw themselves as fighting for the freedom if Israel.

        1. By these acts of terrorism, the zealots hoped to provoke a Roman military response that would unite the Jewish people and foment a rebellion against Roman rule.

        2. They and others sought to establish a new kingdom of Israel, which would regain its status as a mighty power.

III. One incident recounted in the Gospels reveals why the Middle East proved so intractable.

A. A teacher, Jesus, aroused hostility among influential Jews in Judea, including the Pharisees, who were also teachers, and the Sadducees, important citizens whose worship was connected with the temple.

B. The Pharisees and Sadducees began to prepare a dossier on Jesus and brought his activities to the attention of the Roman governor, Pontius Pilate.

   1. Pilate, a typical Roman civil servant, wanted to resolve the situation without making waves or calling attention to himself in Rome.

   2. Pilate also knew that Augustus's successor, Tiberius, was a suspicious, paranoid old man, not unlike Joseph Stalin. Tiberius put to death any governor he thought was weak on treason.

C. Passover was a sacred Jewish holiday and the most difficult time of year in Judea. The Roman governor had permission to call up more troops to prevent riots. As in other parts of the empire, the governor also relied on a local council to handle community matters. Judea's council, the Sanhedrin, consisted of 71 leading Jewish citizens, including Pharisees and Sadducees.

D. The Sanhedrin had found Jesus guilty of blasphemy and brought him to Pilate, who reminded them that blasphemy was not a crime under Roman law. Even Jesus, who was not a Roman citizen, had basic guarantees of individual freedom.

   1. The Sanhedrin insisted that Jesus be put to death, charged him with treason, and threatened to contact Tiberius if Pilate did not find him guilty.

   2. Pilate tried to pardon Jesus but ultimately caved in to the crowd. Deemed a traitor by the Romans, Jesus was executed by crucifixion.

IV. With the spread of Christianity, more problems arose in Judea. All the Roman governors were worried about ethnic violence, and in Judea, a Roman citizen, Paul, was spreading the Gospel and inciting riots.

A. In traveling about the empire, Paul was protected by his status as a Roman citizen. By 64 A.D., however, the Roman government turned against this new religious group in Judea, and Paul and Peter perished in the first of many persecutions.

B. This persecution shows the character of Roman rule in the Middle East. The Jews were protected and were not required to worship the Roman emperor as a god. But the Christians were not protected and were put to death for refusing to worship the emperor, as required of all Roman citizens.

C. The situation in Judea worsened. The Romans tried to let each ethnic group rule itself, but time and again, violence broke out. In 66 A.D., this violence became a full-scale insurgency. The Romans regarded the instigators as terrorists, but the Jews saw themselves as freedom fighters.

   1. In 70 A.D., under a new emperor [Vespasian], Jerusalem was captured and the Jewish temple was destroyed. A small group of Jews held out in the fortress of Masada, but a Roman army slowly battered it into submission. The Jewish patriots killed themselves and their families rather than surrender.

   2. Even today, Israeli army recruits take their oath of allegiance at Masada, where their ancestors fought so bravely. Judea, known to us from the New Testament, is the most important example of Rome's intractable problems in the Middle East.

Essential Reading:

Gospel of John and Book of Acts.

Josephus, *The Jewish War*.

Supplementary Reading:

Millar, *The Roman Near East, 31 B.C.–A.D. 337.*

Questions to Consider:

1. Augustus believed that Iran was the key to stability in the Middle East. Do you agree?

2. The decision of Augustus about Iran in 19 B.C. was based on a prudent assessment of Rome's resources. Should America make that same assessment in terms of its policy in the Middle East?

Lecture Fifteen—Transcript
Rome and the Middle East

In our last two lectures, we explored the lessons of the Roman Empire for America today. In Lecture Thirteen we asked the question that the Romans had to ask themselves. Can a republic rule an empire? The Romans of the 1st century B.C., as we saw, faced the momentous decision—do we want to be a free republic, or do we want to be a superpower? The problems involved in being a superpower were too serious, too difficult and too complicated to be answered and handled well by a republic under a constitution meant for a small city-state. The Romans chose to become a superpower under a military dictator—Julius Caesar then Augustus. We saw in the next lecture that they made a pretty good decision by their lot. They gave up political liberty, it's true, but their individual freedom and their prosperity were enhanced. The Empire had peace, and the whole world, for two centuries, enjoyed an unparalleled golden age, called by Edward Gibbon "the happiest in human history."

Julius Caesar and Augustus, like Alexander the Great, whom they took as a model, are true world historical figures. These are men who moved history to an entirely new level. They were not bound by the ordinary morality of mortals. Caesar overthrew the freedom of his country to lead it into a new age of peace and prosperity. Augustus sacrificed everything for self-aggrandizement and personal power. In the process, he saved and regenerated the Roman nation, which then grew in its mission and destiny and saw itself chosen by God to war down the haughty and to raise up the weak. The legacy of the Roman Empire is with us still. In fact, it is with you right now as you look at your watch to see what date it is. The very calendar by which airplanes fly from Tokyo to New York was created by Julius Caesar and handed down to us. The languages of France, Spain, Italy, and even little Romania, are all legacies of the Latin language, but it is most interesting that these Latin-based languages are not spoken today as the languages of the Middle East.

We turn now to the Middle East and ask why, of all the areas the Romans ruled, the Middle East was most intractable, the most difficult. The Romans never fully solved the problem of the Middle East. We shall see how that failure ultimately led to the fall of its majestic empire. To understand Rome and the Middle East, let's take the year 6 A.D. We could be in Rome, and we could be in the home of Caesar Augustus. It was a modest home. He did not believe in flashy homes and in showing off his wealth. He was much richer than the Roman treasury, but he lived in a modest house. There he received a deputation from Judea, and they posed the question to him—would Rome be willing to formally annex the area of Judea, roughly what is modern Israel today? Augustus pondered this.

We saw in our last lecture that he believed in definite limits to the Empire. In fact, in his last will and testament, he told his successor, Tiberius, do not extend the Empire any further. It is already big enough for us to handle. Judea was a difficult proposition. It had long been under Roman domination. Syria had been annexed by the Romans in 63 B.C. as part of the political settlement of the Middle East made by Pompey, but Judea had stayed outside it. In fact, for quite a period early in Augustus's reign, it had been ruled by his good friend Herod. Augustus basically wanted to leave Judea as a client state of the Roman Empire, under Roman control, but not with all the formal problems of annexation. Judea and its large number of ethnic groups, quite different and hating one another, was a very ticklish problem.

On the other hand, strategically Judea was vital to Rome. Judea was the strategic key to Egypt, and the grain of Egypt was just as important to Rome then as the oil of the Middle East is to us today. Rome operated not on the basis of petroleum, but on human power, and you needed grain to feed people. Egypt produced three crops of grain a year. It was extremely well organized economically, and much of that grain was brought to Italy where it served to keep the prices of bread very low in Rome. What the Roman people had was a highly subsidized grain supply. As long as they could have all the bread they wanted, they were happy—in the same way that, as long as we can get all the gasoline we want, we're basically happy, and we'd rather not pay too much for it. They did not want long lines at the bread stores.

Right across the border in Iraq was the vast empire of Iran—the Parthians, as they were called, but they were Iranian people. Their empire had made a peace agreement with Augustus in 19 B.C. Augustus left the Iranians alone. That vast desert might be something Alexander could conquer. Julius Caesar had dreamed of conquering it before he was assassinated in 44 B.C. Again, Augustus was a leader who knew his limits. He knew he wasn't a general like Caesar or Alexander the Great, so he made a peace treaty by which Iran had its sphere of influence, and the Romans had theirs. Iraq was a buffer between them. If he had stirred up the Iranians, they might very well have invaded, striking up into Syria and Asia Minor, and down into Egypt. The Iranians were a formidable army. Their mounted archers and their heavy-mailed cavalry were things the Romans, with their infantry-based army, found difficult to deal with. He did not want to outrage the Iranians, but he wanted to maintain that strategic position of Judea.

With much concern, he decided to annex Judea. Rome and Judea, as well as other parts of the Middle East, had gone first from military intervention—which they had done in 63 B.C.—to nation building. The Romans had truly sought to build a Judea that was technically independent, but under Roman control and with basic Roman forms of government, a king who basically functioned as a client king of Rome, with a council to advise him, and with recognized forms of government that the Greeks and Romans understood. That had failed. The people of Judea had been outraged by their king, and they went and said, "Take us over. We want to be part of the Roman Empire and have all the benefits that other annexed areas, actual provinces, have." This had been done.

But Augustus then set about learning more about Judea. There were the Jewish people; he began to have that under control. In fact, he had great admiration for the Jewish people, as did Julius Caesar. The Jewish people had supported Caesar and Augustus very loyally. Part of the annexation treaty with Judea set down the rights and privileges of the Jewish people as an ethnic group. For example, Augustus agreed that there would not be a capital at Jerusalem for the Romans. They would have their administrative center at Caesarea, which is a heavily Greek city on the coast of Judea named after Caesar and Augustus by Herod. They would have the administrative structure at Caesarea, and they would keep only a tiny garrison in Jerusalem, lest the Roman soldiers outrage Jewish law by their behavior.

Moreover, Augustus agreed that the coinage of Rome that circulated inside Judea would not have the image of the emperor on it. Remember the Second Commandment—have no graven image. This would not have the image of Caesar on it. He also agreed that the battle standards carried by the Roman soldiers in Judea would not have a portrait of the emperor on them. Everything possible was done to satisfy Jewish public opinion. Augustus said, I'll tell you what—as a province, now you have to pay taxes. You understand that?—Yes, there's this two-day tax we have to work to pay, and we understand that it goes into a treasury in Rome that is dedicated to Augustus Caesar as a god. Augustus said, Yes, I know. That would make it seem as though you were worshipping me. We won't have that. Yours can go into a treasury at your temple, and I'll only ask that you pray to your God for my well being. Everything possible was done.

But the Jews weren't the only people in Judea. In fact, there was another whole group called the Samaritans. Aren't they Jewish? No, they're not quite Jewish. They think they're Jewish, but the other Jews think they're not, so they're a little different. Do they cooperate with each other? No, they hate each other. Then there were lots of Greeks of various kinds. There were real, ethnic Greeks, but most people there who were called Greeks in fact were of various ethnic groups who have taken over Greek customs and the Greek language. Greek culture was, for Judea—as it was for the whole Middle East under Roman rule—very much equivalent to American culture today. That is to say it was the cultural medium for everyone. You might speak a Semitic language at home, like Aramaic, but out in the world you would speak Greek. You saw to it that your children not only learned Greek, but if you could, that they were educated in a Greek school in order to take on the customs of Greeks. They dressed like Greeks and knew how to eat like Greeks. Culturally, they were Greek.

It is the same way today. Our American culture has spread all over the world. You can see a terrorist today holding someone hostage. They'll be speaking English, dressed in a Mickey Mouse T-shirt, wearing sneakers and dreaming of a McDonald's when this is all over. In fact, it is our fast foods and our music that the world takes over, not our democratic values, but all the lower aspects of our culture. I often believe that there is no cuisine so noble in the world that the Americans cannot turn it into fast food. This is what spread throughout the world. So, too, Greek culture was the common medium of exchange. There were lots of Greeks, and there were Syrophoenician people—these would be Lebanese—who were Greek by language; they were all there. Did they like the Jewish people? No, and the Jewish people hated them and regarded them as unclean.

Augustus said the first governor we sent out has the job of keeping those people in agreement. The Gospels and the book of Acts offer very good insight into the problems that the Romans faced in the Middle East and why it proved so intractable to the Romans, who throughout the rest of their empire, related fairly well, and on the whole had a lot of local loyalty. That was annexation and an actual mandate. The first task of a Roman annexation was to carry out a census so that everyone could be taxed. That, of course, begins the Gospel of Luke, "In those days, there went out a decree from Caesar Augustus that the entire world was to be taxed, and this was the first taxation when Quirinius was governor of Syria."

That's real history. Publius Quirinius was a Roman civil servant that we know about from other sources. He was governor of Syria. Syria, as a long-standing part of the Roman Empire, supervised that first census in Judea. In point of fact, the governor of Syria always exercised a certain limited supervision over the governor who was stationed in Caesarea, the governor of Judea. The census was carried out, and from that very moment Roman rule became suspect to many Jewish people. They didn't like that census, and they didn't like that tax. Even if it was only for two days a year, and was to be paid into the temple in Jerusalem, many Jewish people did not like it.

Moreover, there was already in Judea a great deal of national resentment over foreign influence, over what we call Western or Greek values. At the heart of it was a group of terrorists, in Roman eyes. They were called the Zealots, and they took their name from the Bible, from those who had been zealous for the worship of God, and had killed those who had gone over to the worship of foreign divinities. For these zealots, any foreign occupation, including that of the Romans, represented a revocation, a breaking of God's commandment that he alone was king over Israel. These zealots, from the beginning of Roman annexation, would stalk the streets of Jerusalem and other cities, striking by night, killing one Roman soldier here another Roman soldier there.

They saw themselves as fighting for the freedom if Israel, but by these acts of terrorism, they hoped to force the Romans into a military response on such a large scale that all the Jewish people would unite, and rebellion would break out. They believed, along with a number of quite peaceful Jewish citizens, that ultimately the Romans would be driven out by God and by war, and that a new kingdom of Israel would be established—the kingdom of God—and that Israel, as it had been in the days of King David, would be a mighty power once again. There was much hostility to the Romans as they came. Then the Gospels show us how one small incident, in Roman eyes, was handled by the Roman administration in Judea, and again why the Middle East proved so intractable.

There was a teacher, Jesus, the son of Joseph. He was a trained rabbi. I believe he spoke Greek and Aramaic, and knew Hebrew well. Almost from the beginning of his mission, he aroused hostility in important elements of the Jewish community in Judea; among the Pharisees, who were essentially his peers as teachers and professors; and among the Sadducees. The Sadducees were influential Jewish citizens whose worship of God rested upon the temple and the ceremonies connected with the temple. It was always the wealthy influential citizens of a province that the Romans sought to conciliate. The Gospels make it quite clear that in his brief mission, Jesus aroused such hostility and such suspicion that the Pharisees and Sadducees began to cooperate, prepare a dossier on him, and bring his activities to the attention of the Roman governor, Pontius Pilate.

Pilate was a very typical example of a Roman civil servant. He was the governor of this province. It was, by his likes, one of the worst places he could have been stuck, but he was on his way up. The governorship of Judea was not one of the plums of the civil service. Really good provinces like Syria or Asia Minor were governed by senators. He was not a senator, he was on a lower rung, but he was the procurator, the governor. What he wanted to do was to be out of this very difficult situation without causing major waves. For the previous 30 years—because we're down to about the year 36 A.D.— Judea has been a real worry to the Romans. Pontius Pilate had other worries. The emperor was no longer Augustus, who had died in 14 A.D., but Augustus's adopted son, Tiberius, a very different kind of man.

Augustus was affable and shrewd, and he knew how to relate to people and build a consensus. Tiberius was a suspicious man. His closest parallel among modern leaders would be Joseph Stalin. He was paranoid. He was old, perhaps having some problems with senility. His pet concern was treason. He believed that everywhere in the Empire there were traitors looking for a chance to overthrow Roman rule. He came down very hard—that is to say he had them tried by the Senate and put to death—on any governor he thought was weak on treason. There came before him the most difficult time of the year in Judea, Passover. The Roman governors did their best to understand the customs of the Middle East. Pontius Pilate could give you a pretty good discussion on what the Jewish religion was about. He knew Passover was their sacred holiday when they celebrated the passing over of the children of Israel by God to slay the children of the Egyptians. On that day, from all over the Diaspora—because Jewish people were spread all over the Roman Empire—pious Jews came to Jerusalem and offered up sacrifices.

During that period of time, even the most Roman-loving Jew dreamed of liberation. In those days during Passover the Roman governor had permission to bring up a larger troop of soldiers just to keep any riots from breaking out. Pilate was almost through Passover when suddenly, early in the morning, his aid came running in and said we have the whole Jewish Sanhedrin. Again, let's look at this simply from the point of view of Roman political life. The Sanhedrin was a council of 71 leading Jewish citizens, on which Pharisees and Sadducees were represented. In fact, it attempted to be a broad cross section of the educated wealthy Jewish population. The Sanhedrin had its parallels all through the Roman Empire. The Romans liked to have local matters handled by local administrative units. The Romans controlled the frontiers to see to military peace and security, but they liked domestic issues to be handled by the local people.

The Sanhedrin had found the teacher guilty of blasphemy against their gods. They brought him to Pilate, who told the Sanhedrin that blasphemy was not a crime under Roman law. He may blaspheme your god. That teacher, Jesus, the son of Joseph, even though he was not a Roman citizen, had the basic guarantees of his individual freedom. He had the right to appear before the governor. He had the right to be faced with his accusers because the Sanhedrin was demanding the death penalty. Pilate again explained to them carefully that, from the Roman point of view, he had not broken Roman law and could not be put to death. If you keep it inside your council, you can beat him for blasphemy, but you can't put him to death. But they insisted that he be put to death, and they brought the charge that he was a traitor, that he was teaching about the kingdom of God, and that he claimed he was the King of the Jews. Pilate was trapped. They then said if you do not find him guilty of treason, we will write to the emperor, Tiberius.

Pilate, a typical civil servant, finally caved in. He did have a heart, and the Gospels are quite clear that he scouted around through his aids for some means of releasing that man. He was told he could pardon one person a year during Passover. Pilate tried to pardon Jesus, but the crowd wouldn't have it, and Jesus must be put to death. The very Gospels show the difficulties faced by the Romans in the Middle East, and the extreme lengths to which they went to preserve not only peace, but individual rights, even for those like Jesus who were not citizens. The death of that traitor, as the Romans saw him, by the most terrible form of punishment, crucifixion, marked the end of the life of Jesus. But Christianity was based on the belief that he arose from the dead.

Another set of problems began for the Romans in Judea with the spread of Christianity. That time, the chief bearer of the Gospel message was a Roman citizen, Paul, whose Jewish name was Saul, a rabbi. His father had certainly been a Roman citizen, so he was born a Roman citizen, and he had even more rights. As we follow the book of Acts, as he made his way around the Roman Empire, ultimately to Rome itself, time and time again he was protected by his status as a Roman citizen. Again, not only in Judea, but in the cities of Asia Minor like Ephesus—even as far away as Greece, the city of Corinth—the various ethnic groups caused trouble for the Romans. The Roman governor was constantly worried about ethnic violence breaking into riots, and then into insurgency. That was why the Roman governor, Felix, in Judea was so eager to have Paul off his hands. Everywhere Paul went, there is a riot, and these riots could spread like wildfire. They could quickly take on a very anti-Roman sentiment.

The governor first tried to pass the buck to the local client king, Agrippa, who was left over from the Roman period, in a small little principality. He wouldn't take the trouble, but he did tell the governor that the man has not done anything evil. But the governor said well, he has appealed to Caesar, and now he has set that legal machinery in place, and Paul must go off to Caesar. The Middle East continued to cause problems, even in Rome. In 64 A.D., urged on perhaps by disturbances already brewing in Judea, the Roman government turned upon the religious group that had come to it from Judea, the Christians. Both Paul and Peter perished in 64 A.D. in the first persecution.

Once again, the very putting to death of Christians in this first persecution shows the character of Roman rule in the Middle East. The Jews had protection; they did not have to worship the Roman emperor as a god. That was part of their annexation treaty. But these Christians were clear to say they were not Jewish, and ethnically, many of them were not Jewish. They were put to death for refusing to worship the emperor. The emperor didn't care if they worshiped Jesus; that was fine. But they also, if they were Roman citizens, must worship the emperor as a sign of loyalty. That is why they were put to death.

The trouble in Judea becomes ever more difficult, spurred on in 66 A.D. by rather ferocious Roman reaction to the constant trouble. For 60 years they had governed Judea, and nobody appreciated them. Riots continued to cause trouble. There continued to be various difficulties between the ethnic groups. The Romans tried to let each ethnic group rule itself, but time and time again violence broke out. In 66, it became a full-scale insurgency, one of the noblest struggles ever fought against the Romans by the Jewish people—the "First Year of the Freedom of Israel," their coins proclaimed. The Romans regarded the instigators of this revolt as terrorists, but to the Jewish people, they were heroes fighting for freedom. But even in that insurgency, there were bitter divisions among Jewish people. One of the original leaders of the insurgency, Josephus, went over to the Roman side and wrote a history of the war from the Roman point of view, *The War Against the Jews*.

For four long years, the Romans fought the war. It was a civil war as well—Greek against Jew, with atrocities on both sides. Once you crossed the Romans, they never forgot. In 70 A.D. under a new emperor and his son Titus, Jerusalem was finally captured. The temple, which the Romans viewed as the source of this insurrection, was destroyed, and the sacred implements of Judaism were brought back to Rome in triumph. One small group still held out in the fortress city of Masada, looking out over the Dead Sea, in an almost impregnable castle. Again, once you had crossed the Romans, they stayed the course. Another mighty Roman army under a capable Roman general arrived outside this huge plateau, this mesa stretching up into the sky, and battered it slowly into submission.

With only 900 of the original defenders left, the Jewish patriots, with their wives and children, the last holdouts, were faced with surrender or death. They chose to kill their wives and children and then kill themselves, the last falling on his own sword after he had cut the throats of his comrades. When the Roman soldiers finally broke into the fortress and saw this heroism, they snapped to attention, voluntarily, in honor of such warriors. Nothing ever changes in the Middle East. Still today, on the plains of Masada, recruits to the Israeli army take their oath of allegiance there, where their ancestors fought with such bravery. Judea, known to us so well from the New Testament, is the most important example we can have of why Rome found it so hard to solve the problem of the Middle East.

Lecture Sixteen
Why the Roman Empire Fell

Scope:

Since the time Rome was declining and falling, historians and moralists have tried to explain why. The Middle East provides a major key. Rome's involvement in the Middle East became a quagmire from which the Romans could not withdraw. It strained the military and financial resources of the empire. More than that, focus on the Middle East distracted the Roman emperors from other critical foreign policy issues, especially in central Europe among the Germanic and other tribes that the Romans considered barbarians. Despite Rome's efforts, Iran could not be drawn into the Roman orbit. Ultimately, Iran, revitalized by religious fundamentalism, and the Germanic tribes united to shatter the Roman order. The fall of the Roman Empire is one more illustration of the lesson that the Middle East is the graveyard of empire.

Outline

I. In this last lecture on the Roman Empire, we learn a crucial lesson from the study of history: The Roman Empire offers a model of how a superpower can bring peace and prosperity to a large part of the world over an extended period of time. The Romans achieved this feat in three ways.

   A. The empire used complete military dominance and ruthless force when necessary.

   B. It allowed ethnic groups to govern themselves internally and respected their customs and values.

   C. At the same time, it recognized that every nation, even a superpower, must have a common set of shared values.

   1. The Roman emperors fostered the cults of many different divinities, but all with the idea that to be moral, people need gods and that Classical Greek culture offered the right moral values for the empire.

   2. Under Roman rule, Greek civilization throughout the eastern Mediterranean underwent a renaissance. It was a new age of excellence in Greek art, literature, and philosophy. Roman emperors from Julius Caesar to Marcus Aurelius wrote and spoke in Greek.

3. Greek moral tradition embodied the ideals of Stoicism, a philosophy that taught that there is only one all-beneficent God. That God had planned everything to happen in accordance with his will and had willed the Roman Empire and everyone's place in it. The *Meditations* of Marcus Aurelius (r. 161–180 A.D.) reveal his belief that a common set of moral values should unite the empire.

II. Given that it fell, how can the Roman Empire be a model for us? Pericles told us that all things human will pass away. Who doubts that we, too, will pass away? Five hundred years from now, archaeologists may probe the ruins of American cities.

A. For more than 200 years, the Roman Empire was a superpower that brought peace and prosperity to the world. That accomplishment alone makes it an important model.

B. Some people assume that we are immune to any lessons from the Roman Empire because of our science, technology, and global economy. That theory is nonsense, as we saw in the lessons of World War I.

1. The Romans did not possess atomic weapons, but the Roman army itself was a formidable weapon of mass destruction. The wrath of the Romans often meant ethnic cleansing.

2. We have a global economy and an information superhighway, but the Roman economy was also global. Traders traveled across the empire, and there was economic unity all the way to China.

3. In modern times, our advanced technology does not prevent human suffering.

III. A fundamental lesson of history is that human nature never changes. Since the Roman Empire collapsed in the 4th and 5th centuries A.D., thinkers have tried to understand its decline and fall.

A. St. Augustine noted a collapse in morality of the Roman people, which he said brought on the wrath of God and the fall of the empire.

B. Edward Gibbon's *Decline and Fall of the Roman Empire* blamed the extinction of political liberty. Having given up their political freedom—the patriotism and civic virtue that sparked their imperial greatness—the Romans were an empty shell.

C. William Hooper, who signed the Declaration of Independence, wrote that Rome at its height was like the British Empire. The British were trying to extinguish political liberty in America as they had done at home—and as the Roman Caesars had done in their time.

D. The moral dimension of the fall of the Roman Empire is a valid argument, especially considering the empire's culture of violence.

    1. The defeated Judeans were brought back to amphitheaters, such as the Colosseum in Rome, where people fought to the death. Gladiators were the heroes of the day.

    2. Even after buying their way out of slavery, many gladiators stayed in the arena because they loved the accolades of the crowd. The Romans enjoyed this vicarious violence.

    3. The Roman poet and satirist Juvenal spoke of "bread and circuses," meaning that the Romans had given up their freedom for the enjoyment of food and entertainment.

IV. The Roman Empire held together numerous ethnic groups, not by patriotism—as the old republic had done—but by prosperity. These various ethnic groups enjoyed the benefits of Roman rule, but many of them never fully embraced Rome. Rome was emulated and praised at the same time that it was hated.

V. Rome is testimony to our lesson that empires rise and fall because of specific decisions by individual leaders. Given that human nature never changes, the same mistakes are made again and again throughout history. The Roman Empire ultimately fell because its leaders failed to solve critical foreign-policy issues in central Europe and the Middle East.

A. For the Romans, central Europe was the vast land across the Rhine and Danube Rivers, which today includes Germany,

Poland, Ukraine, and Belarus. This area was inhabited by fiercely independent German tribes.

B. Rome first intervened in the Middle East in the 2nd century B.C. The Caesars tried military intervention, nation building—reconstruction on the basis of Roman political values—and occupation, but nothing brought true peace.

    1. In Judea, under the emperor Hadrian, a new Jewish revolt broke out. It was put down with much brutality, amidst ethnic violence and civil war. The Romans destroyed the Jewish temple and turned Jerusalem into a Roman colony.

    2. The Iranian Empire was another major issue. This empire stretched through today's Afghanistan, Tajikistan, Uzbekistan, Turkmenistan, and Kazakhstan.

        a. The Iranians, whom the Romans called Parthians, were Persian but influenced by Greek culture. They believed in a free-market economy. They had a formidable army that had defeated the Romans repeatedly.

        b. Augustus made peace with Iran and brought it into his sphere of influence. In contrast, Julius Caesar, before his assassination, had planned to lead an expedition to conquer and annex Iran.

C. Like Julius Caesar, Trajan (r. 98–117 A.D.) solved Rome's foreign-policy problems by military conquest. He was a warrior by nature and a shrewd administrator.

    1. Trajan made conquests along the Danube and exterminated the Dacians of central Europe

    2. He then led his army east and began the conquest of Parthia, starting in Iraq. City after city fell to him, but insurgencies broke out in his wake. Trajan died in the midst of this fighting.

D. Looking back to Augustus, Trajan's successor, Hadrian, rejected total conquest and sought to limit the empire's expansion.

    1. Trajan had planned to conquer Germany and Scotland, but Roman rule extended only to the northern limits of England. Hadrian built that massive Roman wall in

England, still the supreme symbol of Rome north of the Alps.

    2. In Germany, he erected a similar ring of forts and a wall along the Danube. In the Middle East, he put up fortifications along the frontier with Parthia. He literally walled the Roman Empire in and tried to wall out its foreign-policy problems.

VI. In the 2nd century A.D., the empire still held together, although the problem of the Middle East remained. Marcus Aurelius sought to conquer Iran one more time, but his troops brought back a plague that devastated the empire, weakening its manpower for generations to come.

    A. In the 3rd century A.D., the Parthians were overthrown, and a new native Persian dynasty, the Sassanids, took power. They ravaged the Roman Empire in the east, while new coalitions of Germanic tribes swept into the empire in the north.

    B. Rome beat back these attacks on two fronts, but the empire that emerged was fundamentally changed. The army became bloated and inefficient. Taxes on the middle class were onerous. The bureaucracy became a huge, swollen force. Above all, the sense of loyalty to Rome disappeared. Many citizens stopped supporting the empire.

    C. In the 5th and 6th centuries A.D., German princes dwelled in the ruined palaces of the Caesars in Italy. In the east, under the banners of Islam in the 7th century, Syria, Egypt, and North Africa were swept away. The Roman Empire became a relic.

Essential Reading:

Fears, *The Lessons of the Roman Empire for America Today*.

Gibbon, *Decline and Fall of the Roman Empire*, chapter 38.

Supplementary Reading:

Ermatinger, *Decline and Fall of the Roman Empire*.

Heather, *Fall of the Roman Empire*.

Questions to Consider:

1. What lessons do you think the Roman Empire can teach us today about how a superpower might bring peace, prosperity, and stability to our world?

2. Why did the Roman emperors fail to follow the example of Alexander and conquer Iran?

Lecture Sixteen—Transcript
Why the Roman Empire Fell

We come now to the last of our lectures on the lessons of the Roman Empire for America today. I want to say quite clearly that I believe one of the most crucial lessons of the Roman Empire, and one of the most crucial lessons we can draw from the study of history, is that the Roman Empire offers a model of how a superpower can bring peace and prosperity to a large part of the world over an extended period of time. It did so, one, by exercising complete military dominance and acting when necessary with the ruthless use of force; two, by allowing individual ethnic groups to govern themselves internally being respectful of their customs and values; and three, by not imposing a universal system of values and language upon its empire, recognizing that every nation—even a superpower—must have its citizens bound together by a common set of shared moral values.

The Roman emperors believed this had to be based on a belief in God, and they fostered the cults of many different divinities, but all with the idea that people need God to be moral; and moreover, that the culture of classical Greece offered the right moral values for the Roman Empire. Greece, in fact, under Roman rule, and Greek civilization throughout the eastern Mediterranean, underwent a renaissance in the Roman Empire. It was a new age of excellence in Greek art. Greek literature flourished, and Greek thinkers and orators went all over the Roman Empire lecturing to appreciative audiences. It was a new age of professors, and Greek was the common language of their intellectual exchange. Roman emperors from Julius Caesar, whose last words were in Greek (*kai su teknon*), through Augustus, right on through Marcus Aurelius, wrote and spoke in Greek.

In fact, the common moral tradition of Greece embodied the ideals of Stoic philosophy that had begun in Athens, saw itself as the successor of Socrates, and taught that there was only one God who was all good and all beneficent, who had planned all things to happen in accordance with his will, who willed the Roman Empire and everyone's place in the Roman Empire, and who believed that all men were created equal and endowed by their creator with certain unalienable rights, among which are life, liberty and the pursuit of happiness. These noble ideals were enshrined in the person of

Marcus Aurelius, who ruled as emperor from 161 to 180, and left us his meditations, his reflections to himself. We see how noble emperors like Marcus Aurelius were. A common set of moral values would unite this empire.

People say to me, yes, but how can Rome be a model to us, for it fell? Yes, the Roman Empire did fall. Pericles tells us that all things human will pass away. I'll ask you to raise your hand if you believe that 500 years from now, there will be a professor telling a group of students about a nation called the Americans. In a classroom, someone may raise his hand at the end and say, the Americans didn't last for very long, and you only devoted one lecture to them. Are they going to be on the test? We wonder if there will not be archaeologists probing the ruins of American cities, finding these strange golden arches and wondering what matter of cult—because archaeologists always like to identify any unidentifiable remain as a religious shrine—occupied these sites. What strange rites did they carry out in these huge kitchens, and who was this god worshipped all over the world, called Ronald? Who doubts that we, too, will pass away?

The Roman Empire, for more than 200 years—almost as long as we've been a nation—was a superpower that brought peace and prosperity to the entire world. I think it is an important model. But there is a second reason why people don't want to use the Roman Empire as a model, and that is the arrogant assumption that we are immune to any lessons from the Roman Empire because of our science, technology, information super highway and global economy. When we looked at the lessons of World War I, we saw that that was nonsense, but let's repeat it again for the Roman Empire as well.

Yes, transportation was much slower in the Roman Empire. Caesar traveled the same way that George Washington did, by foot or by sail. Messages were sent in the same way, and we see in the Gospels and in the book of Acts how difficult travel could be. St. Paul had a very hard time, and it took him a long time to travel from Judea to Rome to appeal to Caesar. The Romans did not possess atomic weapons; that is certainly true. However, the Roman army was a weapon of mass destruction of formidable character. The Romans killed hundreds of thousands. In fact, we are told by Plutarch that

Caesar killed one million Gauls, enslaved one million Gauls, and left one million free to become good Roman citizens.

The Roman army marched into Dacia under Trajan in 105 and 106 and ended by exterminating the Dacian people. That Column of Trajan that we discussed, with its narrative relief portraying the campaign against these Dacians in great detail, ended at its very top with sheep grazing because that was all that was left in Dacia. Only a few little words have come down to us from the Dacian language. They spoke a Latin-based language because the land had been resettled by Trajan's veterans. Thousands who had fought with such bravery against the Romans in Judea were brought back to the amphitheater at Rome, to amphitheaters all over the empire. The Roman army was a weapon of mass destruction. To bring the wrath of the Romans down upon you was to invite ethnic cleansing. I do not say this is right; I simply say do not be too sure that a weapon of mass destruction did not exist in Rome.

More than that, there is our information super highway and our global economy. Do not forget the Roman economy was also global in its terms. Traders went all over the empire. We have inscriptions of their going from one city to another. Trade goods moved; there was a real economic unity that went all the way out to China. Silks brought across the Silk Road played an important part in Roman markets. It was a global economy. Our information super highway today, our global economy; none of these prevent terrible human suffering. The very fact that we can send an e-mail across the world, and the very fact that we sit down at our breakfast table and watch the news being broadcast to us directly from Africa, for example, does not in any way change the fact that people starve to death, that ethnic cleansing is carried out—it's carried out in the Balkans, and it's carried out in Africa. The only difference is that we sit down and eat a high-fiber cereal in the morning, because we're so fat, while we watch these terrible things unfold.

Let us go back to one of our most fundamental lessons—human nature never changes. We have the same human nature as the Romans did, and their empire is an important model for us, just as the founders of our country understood. The fall of the Roman Empire is a lesson that still reverberates with us today. Since that empire was collapsing in the 4th and 5th century A.D., thinkers have tried to understand it. Thinkers like St. Augustine and other writers of the time attributed it to a collapse in the morality of the Roman people, bringing down upon themselves the wrath of God in the fall of their empire.

The best of all the works on the Roman Empire is Edward Gibbon's *Decline and Fall of the Roman Empire*. It was one of those books I would have with me on a desert island if I could only choose three or four works to read for the rest of my life. Gibbon, writing as we saw at the time of the American Revolution, found the cause of the fall of the Roman Empire in the extinction of political liberty. That is to say yes, the Roman Empire of the 1st and 2nd century A.D., under the military dictatorship of the Caesars, was the happiest time in human history, but happy meant that people were fat and satisfied because they didn't have the responsibility of political freedom anymore. But there was, Gibbon said, a secret poison gnawing at the vitals of the Roman people. Having given up their political freedom, that patriotism and civic virtue that was the spark of their imperial greatness, they were but an empty shell.

Many of the founders of our own country believed that, including William Hooper, who signed the Declaration of Independence. He wrote a letter saying that Rome, at its very height, was like the British Empire of today. It looked flush, but that was just the flush of a fever. The British were trying to extinguish political liberty in America as they had extinguished it at home, the same way that the Roman Caesars had extinguished political liberty. The Roman Empire had fallen, and so the British Empire was ripe to fall. The Americans would purge the British Constitution of its evils and build a new empire. The founders saw great lessons in the fall of the Roman Empire.

It is certainly true that the moral view, the moral dimension, of the fall of the Roman Empire is still valid. This is not to say that the Roman Empire fell because they were all engaged in orgies or, as a tabloid said once, because they were drinking wine out of vessels that were lined with lead and poisoned themselves. No, in fact, the ordinary Roman citizen of the 1st and 2nd century A.D.—and we have very good touching examples of this—was just as moral and devoted to his or her family as the ordinary American is today. But the Roman Empire did foster a culture of violence in a most interesting way.

When the Judeans were defeated, they were brought back to amphitheaters like the Coliseum. The Coliseum stands, still today, as the most enduring monument of the Roman Empire. There, people fought to the death. Animals were slaughtered; human beings were slaughtered. In fact, the Roman Empire of the 1st and 2nd century A.D. along with our own world today are the only two societies in which spectator sports have been all important. The boys who fought at Gettysburg did not watch spectator sports, and the Romans who fought at Connae saw little need for gladiatorial combats, but the Roman Empire of the 1st and 2nd century was all about spectator sports. Chariot racing was also just as important.

These gladiators became the heroes of their day. You could walk down the streets of Roman cities, and somebody might not be able to tell you who the emperor was, but they could tell you who the best gladiators of the day were. These men started life as slaves, but they were allowed to keep a small part of their purse, and they would then buy their freedom. Many gladiators, even after they had bought their freedom, stayed in the arena because they so loved the accolades of the crowd. They would invest their money and become wealthy owners of real estate. Just as today we sponsor a culture of violence, with all the video games in which you can slaughter thousands of people in an afternoon, the Romans enjoyed this vicarious violence.

The Roman poet, satirist and moralist, Juvenal, of the 2nd century A.D. spoke of "bread and circuses." By this, he meant that the Roman people had been systematically corrected by their emperors to give up their love of freedom for the enjoyment of plenty to eat and entertainment. Edward Gibbon, who had a much more cynical view of Augustus than I do, said that Augustus quietly corrupted the Roman people by providing them with entertainment and plenty of food, thinking that, in the satisfaction of their senses, they would forget their old love of freedom. The Roman Empire held people together, these large numbers of ethnic groups, not by patriotism—the way the old republic had been held together—but by prosperity. We're well off, and we're a lot better off under Roman rule than we would be independently. There was no deeply moral base for patriotism to this empire.

The various ethnic groups, while enjoying the benefits of Roman rule, in many parts of the empire never fully embraced a love of Rome. This you must remember if you are a superpower and the

Romans would tell you this. You will be emulated; you will find people praising you. At the same time, you will be hated and despised, and they will be jealous of you. They will mimic your values while at the same time, deep inside, long to see you fall and collapse. A Roman himself, Tacitus described this view when he put into the mouth of a warrior, a Caledonian—what we call Scotland today—Calgacus, fighting against the Romans, the words, "The Romans make a desert, and they call it peace." In fact, when some of the pro-Roman elements in Judea were trying to convince the Jews not to rise up in revolt, they basically said yes, Rome is a tyrant, but it's the best tyrant we can have. What's wrong with being the slaves of Rome when all others are slaves of Rome? You can't beat them.

There was no sense that Rome was truly beneficent. Despite all the benefits it brought to the world, the Romans still found themselves hated and despised. That is the fate, I fear, of every superpower. But Rome is testimony further to our lesson that empires fall, as they rise, not because of unavoidable social, economic and climactic changes—for Rome did not fall because of any climactic changes—they fall because of specific decisions made by individual leaders. Again, since human nature never changes, these same mistakes will be made again and again throughout history. The Roman Empire ultimately fell because the Romans failed to solve critical foreign policy issues. They failed to solve, above all, the problems of central Europe and the Middle East.

Central Europe was what we call today, perhaps, the problem of Russia. For the Romans, it was the vast land across the Rhine and Danube, the lands that today would certainly include Germany, stretching out to Poland and into the Ukraine and Belarus, inhabited by fiercely independent German tribes, tribes that were, in cultural terms, related. The other was the problem of the Middle East. We have seen in our last lecture how Rome certainly went to the Middle East with mixed intentions, but it went to bring peace. It intervened first in the Middle East already in the 2nd century B.C. It intervened first in Asia Minor, out of a need to protect itself from the kingdoms of the Middle East.

But military success did not allow the Romans to withdraw from the Middle East. They tried as long as they could to avoid annexing parts of the Middle East. It would not be until 133 B.C. that, quite reluctantly, they accepted a small province in Asia Minor. They tried nation building, to reconstruct the Middle East on the basis of Roman political values. We saw that, in Judea, this failed—military intervention, nation building and ultimately, as in Judea, occupation—nothing brought true peace. In point of fact, even in Judea, the utter ruthlessness of the Roman conquest of the Jewish rebellion did not bring lasting peace. Despite the thousands that were killed and thousands brought to fill the arenas in Rome and elsewhere, in the 130s, under the emperor Hadrian, a new Jewish revolt broke out in Judea, led by the hero Bar Kochba.

Once again, the Romans acted with the greatest vigor. The revolt was put down with much brutality, amidst a great deal of ethnic violence. The various ethnic groups within Judea fought against one another, and there was civil war among the Jewish people themselves. This insurgency was finally put down. This time, not only had the Romans already destroyed the temple, but they rebuilt upon the site of the old Jewish temple—the great temple that had been built originally by Solomon and restored by Cyrus the Persian—a temple to Jupiter. Jerusalem was made into a Roman colony called the Colony of Hadrian. The Jews now had to pay their taxes to the cult of the emperor there at the temple of the Roman god. This was a forcible statement.

Judea was but a microcosm for the resistance the Romans encountered in the Middle East. They perhaps could have stayed on and ruled the Middle East, had it not been for another major foreign policy issue, Iran. The Iranian Empire perhaps bears most relationship today to China in our world. The Romans traded with Iran. They had a sphere of influence with Iran. The Iranian Empire stretched all the way to Afghanistan. It reached into what we call Tajikistan, Uzbekistan and Turkmenistan, even as far as Kazakhstan—the central Asian republics. Iraq was the border between the two, between the Roman Empire and the Iranian Empire. The Iranians who are the ancestors of the Iranians today, the Romans called the Parthians. The Parthians were a central Asian tribe that spoke an Arabian language, like Tajik today, and had established their rule over Iran.

They had become not only "Persianized"; they had become very much influenced by Greek culture. They believed in a free market economy. In fact, they loved a free market economy, trading throughout the Roman world. They were a formidable fighting force.

Their basic forms of warfare were mounted archers and heavy-mailed cavalry. These forces had defeated Romans again and again. Crassus, in 53 B.C., was killed, and his legions destroyed, and Marc Antony nearly met disaster. We saw that Augustus made peace with Iran and carved the two into a sphere of influence. Julius Caesar had understood that there was only one way to solve foreign policy problems. You could not negotiate; you must conquer. Before he was assassinated in 44 B.C., he had planned to solve this problem. He was going to lead an expedition into Iran, conquer and annex all of Iran, then swing back through the Caspian Sea area into the steppes of Russia, conquering all the way back to the Rhine and annexing all of the land of the Germans, all of Germania.

No other emperor had been bold enough until the emperor Trajan. Emperor from 98 to 117, he too understood that ultimately Rome would have to solve the problem of central Europe, of the Germans and of the Middle East by conquest and war. He had already begun the process by conquering along the Danube. Dacia was a salient sticking into the Roman Empire, and he conquered and exterminated the Dacians. As with everybody else, they were given one chance to accept Roman rule. When they refused, they were conquered and exterminated. Dacia became the model for how he intended to deal with foreign policy. He was a warrior by nature, and a shrewd administrator. He was a very, very good builder of consensus.

Already somewhat old, he then led his army to the east and began the conquest of Parthia. He started in Iraq. City after city fell to him. He finally reached the Persian Gulf and watched as boats sailed off into the distance. He said, if I were only younger, I could be like Alexander and go to India. Behind him, as the Roman armies marched ever farther into Iraq, insurgencies broke out all over the Middle East. He had to return, offering up sacrifices—in the very palace where Alexander had died in Babylon—to the great conqueror who had ruled the Middle East. On his way back to put down these insurgencies, he died. He would never carry out his plan in Germany.

His successor, Hadrian, was an extremely talented man. The most capable man of his day, he had been personally selected by Trajan, who had no children, to succeed him as emperor. He had been educated to be emperor. Hadrian had accompanied Trajan on these campaigns in the east, but Trajan weighed the cost of empire. He looked back to Augustus, and he said, there is no way we can conquer the world. We must have a limit to our expansion. This limit took a very concrete form. Trajan had planned not only to conquer Germany, but to conquer what we call Scotland today. Roman rule in Britannia, their province, extended only to the northern limits of England, as we call it.

Hadrian said what is to be gained by conquering the Moors of Caledonia. He built that massive Roman wall, still the supreme symbol of Rome north of the Alps, the Wall of Hadrian, 77 miles across the island. In Germany, he erected a similar ring of forts and a wall all along the frontiers, the *limes*, along the Danube, and in the Middle East, all along the frontier with Parthia, fortifications. He literally walled the Roman Empire in, and its foreign problems out. You cannot wall out foreign problems. What the Wall of Hadrian was in Caledonia, in the land of the Germans and in Iran was a sign that Rome was afraid, was weak. Once you give the sign that you are weak, you bring disaster upon yourself. Moreover, as a superpower, you scare people. You bring together ethnic groups—or in the case of Germany, tribes—that normally hate each other, but they hate you more, so they will come together in temporary alliances. If they sense weakness, they strike.

In the 2nd century, the empire still held together, but the problem of the Middle East remained. Marcus Aurelius sought to conquer Iran one more time. All that happened with the troops was that they brought back a plague, which devastated the empire, weakening its manpower for generations to come. Those are the imponderables of war. Finally, in the 3rd century A.D., Iran was revitalized. The Parthians were overthrown, and a new native Persian dynasty took power; we call them the Sassanids. They went back to the ancient empire of Xerxes. They worshiped the fiery god, Ahura Mazda, and the Sassanid rulers believed that God had pressed into their hand a fiery sword. Monotheistic, fundamentalist in their religion, they swept into the Roman Empire. All through the 3rd century, the Roman Empire in the east was ravaged again and again by the attacks of the Persians—frequently carried out in conjunction with new coalitions of tribes along the Danube and Rhine sweeping into the fairest provinces like Gaul.

Rome would beat back these attacks on two fronts, but the empire that emerged from it was fundamentally changed. The army became big and inefficient. The taxes that had been so light on the middle class now were onerous. The bureaucracy became a huge swollen force. But above all, that sense of loyalty to Rome—that association of their best interest with Rome that had motivated so many provincials and the middle class—disappeared, and they simply failed any longer to support that empire. In the 5th and 6th centuries A.D., German princes, half barbarian, would dwell in the ruined palaces of the Caesars in Italy. In the east, under the banners of Islam in the 7th century, Syria—ultimately even Asia Minor—Egypt and North Africa would be swept away, and the Roman Empire would be but a relic.

Lecture Seventeen
Christianity

Scope:

The rise and spread of Christianity occurred fully within the historical framework of the Roman Empire. The triumph of Christianity came with its adoption as the official religion of the empire by the emperor Constantine and his successors in the 4th century A.D. In an important fashion, the triumph of Christianity was a triumph of the religious values of the Middle East over the tradition of Greece and Rome. Emperors before Constantine believed Christianity to be a grave threat to the Roman order and persecuted the faith. Christianity, like Islam, is a universal religion, seeing itself as the only way to salvation. Under the aegis of the Christian emperors, the Church itself began to persecute in the name of orthodoxy. The rise of Christianity and Islam, within the context of the Roman Empire, illustrates the power of religion as a motivating force in history.

Outline

I.   As we saw in the last lectures, the Roman Empire fell from superpower status in the 3rd century A.D. because of its involvement in the Middle East. Although the empire continued, it was only one of a number of competing powers.

  A. The Middle East distracted the Romans from solving pressing economic issues. The Roman Empire of Trajan had enjoyed an economic boom, but 60 years later, Marcus Aurelius had to auction the imperial jewels to pay for a war in the Middle East.

  B. The Roman Empire fell, but its legacy shaped the history of Europe and the Middle East into the Middle Ages. It continues to shape history in Europe, Latin America, and the United States today.

II. The empire's legacy includes Christianity and Islam, two world religions that arose within its historical, cultural, and political framework. Both religions make universal claims and offer only one way to salvation.

A. Not coincidentally, Christianity and Islam arose in an empire that was also universal in its claims and absolutist in its demands. Christianity could spread because of the intellectual, economic, and cultural unity of the Roman Empire.

B. Christianity began with the death of the teacher Jesus of Nazareth and the belief that he had risen from the dead and ascended to heaven. It was a belief that his apostles gave their lives for.

C. Our next four lectures will illustrate the lesson that religion is one of the most important motivating forces in human history.

III. Christianity entails a set of beliefs in a single God, that Jesus is the son of God, and that he can bring salvation to individuals. Its ethics are simple: Do unto others as you would have them do unto you.

A. The old Roman (and Greek) religion was a communal religion. To be a Roman citizen was to worship the gods of Rome. In contrast, Christianity was a religion of personal salvation.

B. The emperorship of Augustus (31 B.C.–14 A.D.) saw a notable religious revival. Indeed, from Augustus through the 17th century, it was religion—not money, not political power—that was the chief motivator of most individuals. Even emperors feared for their souls. These centuries were dominated by two religions, Christianity and Islam.

C. Christianity grew from the idea in the 1st, 2nd, and 3rd centuries A.D. that there was only one god. Mars, Apollo, and other divinities were just emanations from a single, all-powerful god. This philosophy was fundamental to the Stoics, who believed in one all-powerful, beneficent god [Jupiter, also known as Zeus, Providence, or Nature] who willed all things to happen.

D. But many Romans also believed in a god who could bring salvation. This idea went back to the 6th century B.C. in Greece, with Dionysus, literally meaning the "son of Zeus."

Variations of these savior gods existed throughout the Roman Empire in the 2nd and 3rd centuries A.D.

IV. The Roman mind was prepared for Christianity, but the Roman government was not. The government persecuted Christians, beginning in 64 A.D. in Rome, when the apostles Paul and Peter met their deaths after an investigation ordered by the emperor Nero.

  A. The Roman government used Christianity as a scapegoat. In the case of Nero, it was rumored that he had sung an opera while fire burned a good portion of the city. Because he needed to divert public attention from himself, he pointed the finger of blame at the Christians.

  B. The savior cults believed that people could worship multiple divinities, but Christianity insisted on one God. The Christians would not worship the gods of Rome, a requirement of all citizens. As the Roman Empire became more absolutist, emperors demanded more loyalty from their citizens.

  C. Christians displayed freedom of conscience. They put God's law over the state's law and were a danger to society; thus, they were persecuted.

  D. As the Roman Empire began to collapse in the 3rd century A.D., it faced war on two fronts, economic chaos, and leadership changes. Many Romans blamed the Christians for their troubles. In their view, people who refused to worship the old gods of Rome incurred those gods' wrath. Across the empire, persecutions of Christians increased.

  E. Instead of breaking Christianity, these persecutions seemed to strengthen it. Non-Christians watched Christians stand up to the Roman bureaucracy and risk death.

V. Seeking religious uniformity in the name of stability, the emperor Diocletian sought to rid the empire of Christians once and for all. Yet within a decade, Christianity became the official religion of the Roman Empire as a result of Constantine's decree.

  A. Constantine, like other leaders we have seen, was driven by the desire for power. In 312 A.D., he marched on Rome, then controlled by Maxentius. With a smaller army, Constantine seemed unlikely to prevail.

B. As Constantine marched, he had a vision of a cross in the sky with the words, "In this sign, you will conquer." He later said that he had seen Christ, who told him that he had been chosen to make the world Christian. Constantine won a tremendous victory at the Milvian Bridge and rode into Rome.

C. Constantine still had an opponent in the eastern part of the empire, but the west belonged to him, and that's where he began to transform Christianity from an oppressed sect into the empire's official religion.

   1. State funds paid the salaries of bishops and priests and for the construction of new churches, including St. Peter's.

   2. In 324 A.D., Constantine united the Roman Empire by defeating his opponents in battle and bringing east and the west together. He became not only emperor but head of the Church.

D. Constantine saw himself an apostle, meant to spread Christianity throughout the world. He began to persecute non-Christians. By the end of the 4th century, worshiping the old gods of Rome was a treasonable offense.

E. Christianity in this era meant orthodoxy, with beliefs dictated by the state. Those who didn't accept the proper theology were persecuted.

VI. So taken was Constantine with his mission as the first Christian emperor that he overthrew a millennium of Roman history and built a new capital at Constantinople. For him, Rome was too tied to the old gods. He founded a completely Christian city, which he named after himself.

A. There were no pagan temples in Constantinople, only elaborate Christian churches. Dedicated by Constantine in 330 A.D., Constantinople became one of the most magnificent, influential cities in history.

B. Still, Constantine could not escape the problems of the Middle East. A revitalized Iran—itself motivated by a universal, monotheistic religion—remained the greatest organized enemy of the Roman Empire.

C. Constantine also had to fight the Germans, but he moved the capital to Constantinople to focus on the Middle East. The empire took up the mantle against Iran and the spread of Islam.

D. Spiritual reasons aside, one man's decision to convert to Christianity, backed by the power of the Roman Empire, made Christianity a major world religion.

Essential Reading:

Eusebius, *Life of Constantine.*

Fears, *Cult of Jupiter.*

Supplementary Reading:

Jones, *Constantine and the Conversion of Europe.*

Questions to Consider:

1. Do we live in an age of spiritual longing comparable to that of the Roman Empire?

2. Is the intolerance of the Christian Church in the Middle Ages an example that all power corrupts?

Lecture Seventeen—Transcript
Christianity

We continue with our search for wisdom in history, and by the wisdom of history I mean the ability to use the lessons of the past, to apply them to make decisions in the present, and to plan for the future. As I thought about this course, what I wanted to do is to give the lessons of history that I wish every American citizen, every voter, could have as they consider the issues of today. You'll remember that as we studied Thucydides. He gave us the answer that a democracy cannot belong to a superpower because the issues of foreign policy are too complicated for ordinary citizens to act responsibly about. I think that's nonsense, but I do think the lessons of history are a fundamental element in that education for freedom.

In our last four lectures, we examined the lessons of the Roman Empire for America today, and we argued that the Roman Empire fell because of its involvement in the Middle East. But the Roman Empire of the 1st and 2nd centuries A.D. was the absolute superpower of its day—dominant militarily, economically, politically, culturally—and it lost that position as the absolute superpower in the course of the 3rd century A.D. Although it would continue, it would be only one of a number of competing powers. It lost this position as the absolute superpower because of its involvement in the Middle East. It began with good intentions. It began out of self-defense. It then went to nation building, finally to annexation, and ultimately the Middle East became such a preoccupation for Rome in the 2nd century A.D. that it distracted the Romans from crucial situations in central Europe and from the need to solve pressing economic issues.

In fact, the Roman Empire of Trajan—that is to say in the period from 98 to 117 A.D.—was economically a boom; it just flourished. Sixty years later, the emperor Marcus Aurelius had to auction the imperial jewels in order to pay for a war in the Middle East, so it was this preoccupation—the Roman Empire would fall; all things human pass away. What matters is the legacy, and in these next four lectures, we want to discuss the legacy of the Roman Empire, which continues to shape our world today. It shaped the history of Europe in the Middle Ages, the Middle East in the Middle Ages; and in point of fact, it continues to shape history in Europe, Latin America, even in our own country—a legacy of the Roman Empire.

If you had asked the emperor Augustus what his legacy would be, he would have said well, Roman law. He would have pointed to the aqueducts. He would have pointed to the many temples that he had restored in Rome. He never would have imagined that the legacy of the Roman Empire would be the result of the birth, during his time as emperor in 6 A.D., of a teacher in a distant portion of the Roman Empire. It makes us wonder what is going on in our world today that will change history, that the media is not aware of, that the politicians are not aware of, and that all those who shape our destiny are totally ignorant of. In fact, both Christianity and Islam are the legacy of the Roman Empire. These two world religions both arose within the historical, cultural and political frame work of the Roman Empire.

We'll start with Christianity. Christianity, like Islam, is a universal religion. It is a religion that makes universal claims, and in fact it offers only one way to salvation; again, just like Islam. So both are universal in their claims and absolutist in their demands; and it is not a coincidence, I believe, that both arise within an empire that was universal in its claims and absolutist in its demands. In fact, there's a parallel between the growth of an idea of world empire and the growth of an idea of a world religion. Christianity spread because of the economic and cultural unity of the Roman Empire, and it spread because of the intellectual forces in the Roman Empire. Christianity began with the death of the teacher, Jesus of Nazareth, and with the belief that he had risen from the dead and ascended into heaven. In other words, it began with an idea.

Our next four lectures will illustrate our second law of history, that religion is one of the most important motivating forces in all of human history. In fact, the British historian of freedom that has had so much influence on me, Lord Acton, wrote that freedom and religion have been the source of the greatest deeds for good and for evil in all of history. Both are ideas, and ideas shape history just as much as individuals, great individuals, shape history. Christianity began with this idea, this belief that the teacher Jesus had not died, but had risen into heaven. It was a belief for which his apostles, men like Paul, were willing to go all over the Empire, suffer much danger and ultimately give their lives; so that was the power of this belief.

So what does Christianity entail? One, a belief in a single God—I am the Lord thy God; thou shalt have no other gods before me; two, that

Jesus is the Son of God, and that he has conquered death; and third, that he can bring salvation to you as an individual. Like Islam, Christianity is a religion of the individual. And four, its ethics are quite simple; do unto others as you would have them do unto you, easy to say, though more difficult to follow. Abraham Lincoln once said that he would join any church that had as its only creed the golden rule, do unto others as you would have them do unto you, and actually followed it. But that's very simple ethics. In point of fact, all of these ideas, these beliefs, were extremely important and extremely dynamic in the Roman Empire of the 1st and 2nd century A.D.

The old Roman religion, like the religions of Greece, was a communal religion; you were born into it. We've seen how to be a Roman citizen meant to worship the gods of Rome, to be an Athenian citizen was to worship the gods of Athens, but Christianity was an individual religion of salvation. In point of fact, the emperorship of Augustus, the period from 31 B.C. down to 14 A.D., saw a notable religious revival in the Roman Empire. In fact, Augustus took it as one of his chief tasks to revitalize Roman religion, to have the Romans believe again in their ancient gods and to have the morality that came from this belief in their gods. This religious revival will continue all the way through the centuries, and the next 1,400 years of European history are the age of religion.

It's most interesting to me that we live primarily today in an age of economics. Men and women are economically minded, and everything we do is based on economics. Now this doesn't mean that many Americans are not very religious, deeply religious, and it does not mean that many Americans are not very political, but economics guides everything that we do. Universities run on the basis not of the search for truth but of raising money. That's how they judge their success, in their endowments. Science is all about raising money to do the work. Success is judged by economic means, economic standards. That was not true in the age of our founding fathers. They liked money; they liked economics. Many of them were religious, but it was politics, the political belief in liberty, that motivated them. So, too, in the age from Augustus right on through the 17th century and the wars of religion, religion was what motivated most individuals. They were greedy for money, they were very interested in political power, but even the emperor feared for his soul. That is why these ages, these centuries, were dominated by the two religions of Islam and Christianity.

Christianity partook of basic ideas in the Roman Empire. That is to say to the 1st and 2nd and into the 3rd centuries A.D., more and more Romans came to believe that there was only one God. Mars, Apollo, those other divinities, were just emanations from a single all-powerful God. And in his Pantheon, the emperor Hadrian, from 117 to 138, gave an architectural expression of the idea that one God ruled the whole world. It was fundamental to the philosophy of the Stoics, that there was one God who was all-powerful, all good and who willed that all things came to pass, and happiness lay in making yourself part of his will, and understanding his will, and accepting his will, submitting to the will of God.

But many Romans also believed in a savior God, going right back to the 6th century in Greece, the idea of Dionysus. The very name means the son of God, Dionysus—the son of Zeus, the son of God—who was born of a mortal woman by a divine father, Zeus, who suffered terribly, who in the myth even died and was resurrected by the power of his divine father who could bring salvation to you if you believed it and believed in him. You even partook of a sacred meal and drank the blood of his body, which was the wine. That was fundamental to the thought of Athens in the 6th century B.C., and it spread to Rome. In fact, in the 2nd and 3rd century A.D. all over the Roman Empire, there were several of these savior gods. Mithra was one of the most important, who was again the son of God, who had suffered, risen into heaven, and could bring you salvation. Then third, at the very basis of the Stoic ethics was the central teaching, do to others what you would have them do to you.

So the mind of the Roman of the 1st, 2nd and 3rd century was prepared for Christianity, but the Roman government was not prepared for Christianity. In the 1st and 2nd centuries A.D., and with even more intensity in the 3rd century A.D., the Roman government persecuted Christianity. It did not persecute any of these other salvation cults; it was Christianity. It began, as we have seen, already in 64 A.D. in Rome when both Paul and Peter, those two apostles, met their deaths in an official Roman investigation of Christianity—that is what it was—ordered by the emperor Nero. Now there were various reasons at various times why the Roman government fell upon the Christians as a scapegoat. In the case of Nero, it was related to the fact that the city of Rome had caught fire. A good portion of it had burned down, and the rumors in Rome were that he, Nero, had sung an opera while the city was burning, an opera on the burning of Troy, and he needed to divert public attention from him, put a spin on it. It was said that the Christians had actually done this.

But there was a deeper issue. All of these other savior cults—Dionysus, Mithra—they all believed that you could worship as many divinities as you wanted to. There was no single road to salvation. Many gods hast thou fashioned; all of them lead to the light. But Christianity, like Judaism, insisted that there be only one God, and the Christian would not worship the gods of Rome, which as a citizen he was duty bound to worship, nor would the Christian offer up sacrifices to the emperor, the symbol of loyalty to the whole empire, the same way that our flag is the symbol of loyalty to our country. The Christian would not do this, but there was something even more dangerous. As the Roman Empire became ever more absolutist—and it did; the imperial system of Augustus was still free-flowing—each emperor, generally for very good reasons of efficiency, gathered ever more power into their hands, and the empire made ever greater demands upon the loyalty of its citizens.

Christians presented that most dangerous of individuals to an absolutist nation, and that is the freedom of conscience—the Christian who would say, I don't care what the state tells me to do; God tells me, and I will act in accordance with the will of God. That's a very dangerous idea, dangerous enough that the Athenian democracy put Socrates to death for his freedom of conscience. That is what the Christians represented. Time and time again well meaning emperors determined the uniformity of the empire, along with well meaning bureaucrats such one of the bureaucrats we know best, Pliny—Pliny the Younger, he is called—who was governor of Bithynia in the Black Sea area in the early 2nd century A.D., a very human man.

Nonetheless, under orders from Trajan, he persecuted Christians because they represented a danger to society. All the Romans said was just worship our Roman gods, and everything will be fine, but Christians refused. Marcus Aurelius, perhaps the noblest of all the emperors, and a Stoic, did not do unto the Christians as he would have them do unto you. He, too, ordered their persecution. So there was something about the Christians—not their numbers, but the very ideas that they represented, that was such a danger. Last hour we saw how, in the 3rd century A.D., this immense majesty of the Roman Empire began to collapse, faced with war on two fronts—against the Persians in the east and the Germanic tribes coming down from the north, even invading from the Black Sea. With economic chaos, with constant changes of emperors, the Roman Empire stood on the verge of extinction, and there had to be a reason.

Romans asked themselves why all this trouble was falling upon them. Why are we suddenly unable to beat the Persians? Why are we suddenly overwhelmed by the Germans? Why is our economy in ruins? There had to be an answer, and it was the Christians. There are so many people in our empire now who refuse to worship the old gods of Rome that they have brought down the wrath of the gods upon us. It was the gods who raised us up, and now when we allow this defiling of their worship by Christians, we have suffered all this trouble. So the persecutions intensified. The 3rd century saw, all over the empire, elaborate attempts to root out Christians—anonymous accusations used, a real terror instituted, in which the very suspicion of being a Christian was enough to bring you before a tribunal, and with the prospect of death.

But instead of breaking Christianity, it only seemed to strengthen it. Non-Christians watched these men and women—these girls, even, and boys—who were Christians stand up to the Roman bureaucracy and say no, I will not worship your gods; put me to death. There must be something in that idea, which gave it power. The last and most ferocious of these persecutions was unleashed by the emperor Diocletian, who in 284 A.D. began the process of destroying the Roman world, and he did. He created an elaborate bureaucracy, a very elaborate army, but he brought stability back to Rome, and his final step was to bring intellectual uniformity to Rome, religious uniformity. He unleashed what he saw as the final persecution to rid the Empire once and for all of Christians.

He stepped down from his imperial power and never would imagine that within a decade from being a persecuted religion, Christianity would become the official religion of the Roman Empire, and that it became the official religion of the Roman Empire and would thus spread all over Europe and to the New World, was due to one man because once again, it was a single individual armed with a powerful idea that changed the world. That individual was Constantine, the

Roman emperor Constantine. Now just as much as Augustus, just as much as any of the figures, like Xerxes, who have paraded across our stage, he was driven by power, the desire for self-aggrandizement, and he wanted to be absolute master of his world. He murdered his own relatives, he waged war and in 312 A.D., he marched upon Rome itself.

Rome in Italy was held by his enemy, a claimant to the imperial power, Maxentius. Constantine had a smaller army. Maxentius was inside the walls of Rome, and it seemed impossible for Constantine to win. But as he marched, there came to him a vision, and later he would tell this to the Christian bishops—and I saw in the sky a cross, and on it the words, "In this sign, you will conquer," and I saw Christ, and he told me that I had been chosen out of the whole world to bring this message of Christianity and to make the world Christian—and he conquered. Contrary to all expectations, his enemy Maxentius came outside of the protection of the walls at Rome, and at the Milvian Bridge in 312, Constantine won a tremendous victory and rode into Rome itself.

Now he still had an opponent in the eastern part of the Empire, but the west belonged to him, and there he began to transform Christianity from an oppressed sect into the official religion of the empire. Bishops were paid, priests were paid out of state funds. Churches were erected on the basis of state funds, and Constantine began the erection of a mighty church over the bones of the simple fisherman, Peter, who had been buried there in Rome. In 324, he succeeded in uniting the whole of the Roman Empire, defeated his opponent in battle, and brought the east and the west together. One of his first actions in this same year, 324, was to assemble a convention of bishops there outside of the city of Byzantium where he had won his great victory, and he became head of the Church.

Don't you see—an idea as powerful as Christianity must be under the emperor himself and Constantine saw himself as another apostle, meant to spread the word of Christianity throughout the world. He wanted not only the whole world Christian, but he also wanted it uniform in doctrine. Now when they were a persecuted group, the Christians had written to the emperors like Marcus Aurelius, like Hadrian, and said, all we want is freedom to worship as we choose, and that is what you ought to have throughout your Empire, everybody free to worship any god that they choose. All of us are loyal Romans; let us worship any god. But as soon as they became the religion inside the state, they began to persecute the pagans. By the end of the 4th century, to be a pagan, to worship the old gods of Rome, was a treasonable offense.

But it was not only persecution of the pagans; one had to have orthodoxy, and that meant to believe the right way. Along with other powerful ideas, such as Communism in the old Soviet Union, it's not enough just to be a believer. One has to be the right true believer, and the state alone would determine what Orthodox Christianity was. Constantine was already bothered, when he had won his great victory in 324, by various churchmen coming to him and saying there's this terrible controversy destroying the Church and our sanctity. Constantine said, what is it? Well, it's the following. There are some who say that since God is the beginning and the creator, Jesus must be a creature of the father. See, he's the son, and doesn't a father create a son? It's logic; and the Christians had made the mistake of trying to bring the logic of Aristotle into this quite simple belief. So logically, if the father is supreme, then the son must be lesser. But that's heresy; that is false belief because there never was a time when there was not a son.

Constantine said, this is all very, very complicated for me. Why can't you just agree to cooperate? No, people's souls are in danger of eternal damnation because they don't have the right logical view of who Christ is. You're emperor, yes. You're a Christian, yes, and when you are called upon on the day of judgement, God will ask you, why did you allow all of these people to be damned because you would not interfere and make everybody have the same belief? Well, what do we have to do? We have to call together a convention of bishops. We have to come up with a formula, and everybody in the empire then must accept it. Well, what if some people say we don't want to accept this formula of who Jesus is; we have our own little formula? Well, then we persecute them, and we put them to death.

And so it would go on, the enforcement of orthodoxy; a world religion demanding that all believe in it—and that there is only one way to salvation, which the state and the Church together decide upon. So taken was Constantine with his mission as the first Christian emperor, and the successor to the apostles, that he overthrew a millennium of Roman history, and he built a new capital at Constantinople, there where he had won his great victory. Rome for him, religiously, was tied too much to the old worship, the old gods. Many senators in Rome were still openly pagan. He wanted a totally Christian city, and he named it after himself, Constantinopolus, the city of Constantine. There were to be no pagan churches, no pagan temples or shrines, only Christian churches of the most elaborate kind. It would be an exact replica of Rome, right down to having its own circus for the chariot races. The palace of the emperor there in Constantinople would be identical with that in Rome.

That city, dedicated by Constantine in May of 330, would live on to be one of the most magnificent, influential cities in all of history, still spanning the Bosporus where Europe and Asia come together, not very far from where Xerxes built his bridge. The city of Constantinople, the city of Constantine, was not only a testimony to the emperor's deep religiosity—and believe me, he needed lots of testimonies. He remained to the end of his life very, very violent. He strangled his own son, and then had his own wife put to death by boiling her alive in a hot bath. He waited to be baptized until he knew he was dying on his deathbed, lest in the meantime he'd do something else violent and cause his soul [to be lost]. So he deeply believed and stood in fear before this judgement of God.

Constantinople was certainly a testimony to his belief in Christianity and his assumption of the title of the apostle, but it also takes us back to Rome and the Near East because the empire of Constantine, just as much as the empire of Augustus, was deeply involved in the Middle East. In fact, the Middle East, under a new vitalized Iranian power— itself motivated by a universalist religion of one God that was the only true God—Iran was still the greatest single organized enemy to the Roman Empire. Constantine had to fight on both fronts against Germans, but he moved his capital to Constantinople, chose that to be his new Christian city, so that he could focus entirely upon the Middle East.

He chose other lesser emperors to watch out for the western part of the Empire, and there he stayed in the Middle East to deal with Persia. So the complete engagement of Rome in the Middle East remained, and it would set the tone for the next 1,000 years of history. For that city that Constantine built would be the magnet and the center of Christianity in the east, and the Christian Roman

Empire would take up the mantle, first against the Iranians and then against the spread of Islam. Army after army—Arab armies, Turkish armies, Slavic armies—would crash and break against the great walls of Constantinople. It would be the very center of the effort to spread Christianity throughout the world, to the Slavic lands of Russia and even far to the east. And that was the achievement of Constantine. Take away any spiritual reasons—and they may be powerful—it was this one man who converted to Christianity, with all the power of the Empire behind him, that made it the world religion.

Lecture Eighteen
Islam

Scope:

Christianity and Islam have much in common. They are monotheistic religions. They are revealed religions, resting on a book—the Bible and the Koran. Both Christianity and Islam arose in the Middle East within the historical context of the Roman Empire. Both teach an ethical belief based on justice, mercy, and peace in the name of an all-powerful God. Yet from the beginning of Islam in the 7th century, these two universal religions have been locked in conflict. The growth of the Byzantine Empire and the Crusades were epoch-making events in this struggle, illustrating the lessons that power and religion are the great motivating forces of history and that—again—the Middle East is the graveyard of empires.

Outline

I. Religion is one of the most powerful motivating forces in human history, a lesson that we, as a secular society, find difficult to understand. Most Americans believe strongly in the separation of church and state, but much of the world has taken a different view. Even today in the Middle East, the separation of church and state is not a favored idea.

II. Constantine, a devout Christian who held absolute power as Roman emperor, transformed Christianity from a persecuted sect into the official religion of the Roman Empire. He founded Constantinople, a Christian city between Europe and Asia.

    A. The Christian Roman Empire—also called the Byzantine Empire, from the older name of Constantinople, Byzantium—continued the struggle between the values of Europe and the values of the Middle East.

    B. The most immediate threat to the empire in the 4th century came from Iran, a formidable military foe from about 226 A.D. to the early 7th century. Iran has always been one of the most important strategic locations in the world.

III. The Iranians are an ancient tribal people whose language and its offshoots are spoken today in Afghanistan, Pakistan, and other areas. In the 3rd through the 7th centuries, Iraq was the buffer zone between Rome and Iran as both empires dueled to dominate the Middle East.

    A. Under Xerxes, the Iranians were a union of the Persians and the Medes. After Alexander the Great defeated them, they were dominated by Greek successors.

    B. By the mid-3rd century, Iran was ruled by the Parthians, a nomadic people from the north. While Augustus had made peace with them, Trajan had marched against them, as did Septimius Severus, whose assault led to the Parthians' fall from power.

    C. A new dynasty, the Sassanids, revitalized Iran, including the ancient religion of the prophet Zarathustra, who had taught the doctrine of one God, Ahura Mazda, Lord of Truth.

        1. Under this doctrine, the world is divided into good and evil. Every individual must decide whether to accept the truth of Ahura Mazda and lead a righteous life or to follow the evil one's way of the lie.

        2. On the day of judgment, those who follow Ahura Mazda will cross a bridge into heaven and eternal bliss. Others will fall into a deep pit and burn forever.

    D. The Persian emperors in the 3rd century A.D. saw themselves as chosen by the Lord of Truth to exterminate those who taught any other religion. They persecuted Christians and waged war on Rome into the 7th century.

    E. Ultimately, the Persians made their capital at Ctesiphon, near modern Baghdad, claiming Iraq as their own. In 615, the last of the Persian kings, Chosroes, carried back from Jerusalem the Relic of the Holy Cross as a sign of victory over the Christians.

IV. By 645, the Persian Empire was swept away by a new force, the force of Islam, taught by the prophet Muhammad.

    A. Muhammad was born around 570 in the city of Mecca, which was formally outside the Roman Empire but part of its economy. Mecca was a caravan city through which many foreigners passed. In this environment, Jews and Christians openly discussed their faiths.

B. Muhammad's father died before he was born, and he was raised by his grandfather. From the beginning, he was solitary and meditative. He married an older widow and helped run her caravan service.

C. When he was about 40, Muhammad began to have revealed to him the Koran. For Muslims, the Koran is not the equivalent of the Christian Bible; it is literally the word of God as dictated to Muhammad. Its main message: There is no God but God, and Muhammad is his prophet.

D. Muhammad's teaching competed with established interests in Mecca, and he was forced to flee. In 622, Muhammad found refuge in the city of Medina, where he proved to be not only a prophet but also a diplomat and a general.

V. By the time he died in 632, Muhammad had united the quarreling tribes of the Arabian Peninsula into a community of believers that overrode national and ethnic boundaries. There was no separation between church and state.

A. Muhammad taught that there is no God but God, all-powerful and all-merciful, who has preordained all things. The powers that be are put in their place by God, and believers must submit to their will as they submit to God's will.

B. To a non-Muslim, it seems that Islam leaves no room for free will. But Muslims believe that each of us has a free choice to accept or reject the word of God.

C. A good Muslim performs other acts, such as giving alms to the poor, fasting during Ramadan, praying five times a day, and making a pilgrimage to Mecca.

VI. The power of Islam united the Arab tribes and led them to undertake an expansion with few precedents in history. They swept out of the Arabian Peninsula, bearing the word of God against both the Iranian and Roman Empires.

A. The split between Sunnis and Shiites can be traced back to the generation after Muhammad, with the question of his true successor. Was it his son-in-law and cousin Ali, who became the martyr of the Shiite faith, or was it a successor to Muhammad chosen by the community, which is what the Sunnis came to believe?

B. For the Muslims, there was no reason Christians could not accept Muhammad. Muhammad had respected Moses and Jesus, but he was also the last of the prophets and the fulfillment of their message. Why wouldn't Christians understand that his was the ultimate revelation of God?

C. Christians and Muslims found themselves locked in an ongoing struggle. By the 8th century, the Muslims attacked Constantinople, swept through Egypt, and entered northern Africa. By 711, Islamic armies entered Spain and asserted control.

D. These competing religions, both based on values of peace and justice, found themselves engaged in a titanic struggle.

    1. *Jihad* (holy war) was fundamental to the Islamic view. It was the duty of every Muslim to spread the faith by the sword. Those who died in conquering unbelievers went immediately into paradise.

    2. Christianity was also spread by the sword. Medieval Christian rulers, such as Charlemagne, killed, conquered, and even burned pagans in the name of Christ.

VII. The Byzantine Empire, based in Constantinople and extending into Greece and most of Asia Minor, was the Christian bulwark against the Islamic tide. Christians continued to make pilgrimages to Jerusalem, though the city had fallen to Islamic armies.

A. At first, the Muslims tolerated these pilgrimages. But in the 11th century, Turkish dynasties, converts to Islam, rose to power. They were more intolerant than the Arabs had been. The pilgrimages ceased, and heavy taxes were imposed on Christians in the Islamic world.

B. The Crusades began in 1096, when Christians began to march from France into the Holy Land. They continued until the 15th century. Motivated by territorial gain, love of warfare, and religious belief, men left home to wage war to the death against those who believed differently. Muslims did the same. When the first crusaders captured Jerusalem, the Muslims were massacred en masse.

C. In the most famous of the Crusades, Richard the Lionheart; Frederick, the Holy Roman Emperor; and Philip of France came to the Holy Land in 1189. They met Saladin, a Turk who was willing to establish peace and toleration in the Middle East so that both Christians and Muslims could visit Jerusalem.

D. After Saladin's death, the Crusades began again, dragging for centuries and exhausting the Byzantine Empire, the Middle East, and even Europe.

VIII. During the Crusades, Constantinople—then called Byzantium, today called Istanbul—remained the great magnet of Christianity in the east. Its emperors looked to the legacy of ancient Greece and Rome.

A. Augustus's law codes formed part of the foundation of Byzantium's legal system. The city's scholars and monks spoke Greek, and the heritage of Greek literature and history was handed down.

B. As with its Islamic competitors, there was no separation of church and state in this Christian Roman Empire. The emperor followed in the path of Constantine as both high priest and ruler, with absolute authority in all matters of doctrine.

   1. This form of religion, *caesaropapism*, in which the Caesar is pope, is fundamentally different from Latin Christianity, in which the pope as spiritual leader stands above the secular king or emperor.

   2. Constantinople would pass Eastern Orthodox Christianity and its ideals of government to Russia.

C. Ultimately, Constantinople fell. The Turks rose to power in the Middle East, first defeating the Byzantines in 1071. Piece by piece, the Ottomans, descendants of the Turkish warlord Osman, began to conquer what was left of the Byzantine Empire.

D. In 1453, the Ottoman armies broke through the gate of Constantinople. The last Roman emperor, Constantine XI, died with his sword in hand, and Constantinople became an

Islamic city. The Ottoman Empire became a superpower and a dominant force in European history until the 18th century.

Essential Reading:

Carrithers, et al., *Founders of Faith.*

Koran.

Supplementary Reading:

Esposito, *Oxford History of Islam.*

Norwich, *Byzantium.*

Runciman, *History of the Crusades.*

Questions to Consider:

1. Muhammad was warrior and a statesman as well as a prophet of peace. Do you believe that this has had lasting consequences for Islam?

2. Why does the word "crusade" today have a somewhat negative implication?

Lecture Eighteen—Transcript
Islam

We continue to explore the wisdom of history, and to document our seventh lesson from history, which is that religion is one of the most powerful motivating forces in all of human history. That is a lesson that we, as a very secular society, find difficult to understand. Not that many Americans aren't religious, it is simply that we believe strongly in the separation of church and state, as we put it, a wall between church and state. We believe that personal religious views should not influence the political decisions of our leaders. We have removed much of religion from our public schools to maintain this sense of separation of state and church. For much of the world's history, this has just been wrong. Still today in the Middle East, the separation of church and state is simply not an idea that most people wish to have. It's not that they don't understand it, they think it is bad.

We explored the legacy of the Roman Empire in our last lecture, and saw how the two great world religions of Islam and Christianity are both legacies of the Roman Empire. We saw that Constantine, by his deep belief in Christianity and his absolute power as a Roman emperor, transformed Christianity from a persecuted sect within the Empire into the official religion of the Roman Empire. He founded as his city, the city of Constantine, Constantinople, the Christian city that spans the Bosphorus between Europe and Asia.

Constantine and the Christian Empire, which lasted all the way down to 1453, were important enough that Edward Gibbon devoted a long series of chapters to the fall of this Christian Roman Empire. The Christian Roman Empire took up the challenge of the Middle East. In fact, the Christian Roman Empire—the Byzantine Empire, as we sometimes call it, from the older name of Constantinople, Byzantium—continued the struggle that we have seen going all the way back to Herodotus and his view that the Trojan War, and then the later invasion by Xerxes in Greece, were all part of one ongoing struggle between the values of Europe and the values of the Middle East.

The immediate threat to Constantine and the Christian Empire in the 4th century A.D. continued to come from Iran. Just like the Romans of the late republic, such as Caesar and Marc Antony—such as the emperor Augustus, Trajan, and the emperor Marcus Aurelius— Constantine was forced to wage war against Iran. But never since the time of Xerxes had Iran, or the Persian Empire, been such a formidable foe as it was in the period from about 226 A.D. to the early part of the 7th century A.D. It was a revitalized Iranian Empire that the Roman emperors of the Christian Empire faced. Let's think a little more about Iran. It is one of the most important strategic places in the world, and has been all through history.

The Iranians are a very noble and ancient people. The Iranian language and its various offshoots are spoken today in Afghanistan and Pakistan. These tribal societies are very much a part of the Middle East as a whole, and very much a part of Iran. For much of Iranian history, Afghanistan and Pakistan have been part of its empire. The Iranian language extends into the Central Asian republics, including the republic of Tajikistan, and it extends all the way across to Iraq. In the period of the 3rd through the 7th centuries, the struggles between Rome and Iran, Iraq was the buffer zone. Both sides dueled to dominate that area.

The Iranians, under Xerxes, were a union of the Persians and the Medes, both closely related people. When Alexander the Great brought their empire to an end, for a while they were dominated by the Greek successors. But already in the middle of the 3rd century, a new empire had arisen in Iran, and we saw it as the Parthian Empire. The Parthians were nomadic people from the northern part of the Iranian territory that established a ruling dynasty. They quickly became very much Persian, as well as being influenced by the Greeks. It was against them that Augustus made his peace treaty. It was against them that Trajan marched, and it was against them that one of the most formidable of later Roman emperors, Septimius Severus, in the early 3rd century, launched another expedition. Once again, Rome gained no permanent results from this, but it did shake the Parthians so much that they fell, and a new dynasty—we call them the Sassanids—rose to power.

These vigorous new kings saw themselves as the heirs of Cyrus the Great, of the great Persian Empire, and they revitalized Iran. They also revitalized the ancient religion of Iran, the religion of the prophet Zarathustra. He had perhaps lived in the 6th century B.C. and had taught a fiery doctrine—there is only one God, the God of Truth, Ahura Mazda, the Lord of Truth. The Lord of Truth is locked in an eternal struggle with the evil one. The world is divided into good and evil, and every individual is called upon to make a personal decision to accept the truth of Ahura Mazda and to follow a righteous life, or to follow the way of the lie of the evil one. On the day of judgement, there will be a great bridge across to the sacred heaven and paradise, but it is as narrow as a razor blade. If you have taken the truth of Ahura Mazda, you will cross it into eternal bliss. If you have followed the lie, you will fall into a deep pit and burn for all eternity.

Darius and the Persians of the time of Herodotus followed this to some degree. The Parthians were not interested in it, but it was revitalized as the reason for the existence of this new Persian Empire of the 3rd century A.D. The emperors of the Persian Empire saw themselves as chosen by the Lord of Truth to exterminate the lie of all those who taught any other religion. They persecuted Christians with fervor, and they waged war after war upon Rome. Emperor after emperor, all through the 3rd, 4th, 5th, and into the 6th and 7th centuries, had to fight against the Persians. Both sides swept back and forth across Iraq until finally the Persians made their capital at Ctesiphon, which is not far from modern Baghdad, claiming Iraq as their own. In 615, the last of the great Persian kings, Chosroes, swept as far as Jerusalem and carried back in triumph the Relic of the Holy Cross there in Jerusalem as a sign of ultimate victory over the evil followers of the lies, who were the Christians.

Neither Rome nor the Persians understood that all they tried to do in the Middle East—all their wars, all the treaties they made, all the constant negotiations they made trying to avoid war—amounted to nothing. By the year 645, the Persian Empire was swept away, and a whole new force dominated the Middle East—once again, the result of the power of an idea and one single great individual. That was the force of Islam and Muhammad, the prophet. Muhammad was born around 570 in Arabia, in the city of Mecca, which was on the fringe of the Roman Empire. A small northern part of Arabia had been annexed as a Roman province. This was outside the formal limits of the Empire, but very much a part of the economic unity of that Empire. In fact, in the latter part of the 6th century, that economic unity was as great as it ever had been.

Mecca was a city of caravans. It was a city that many foreigners passed through, and it was a city that bubbled with ideas. In that age of religiosity, of spirituality, you could find Jews who lived in Mecca talking about their faith. Judaism in this period was a proselytizing religion; it sought converts. You could hear Christians talking about their religion. Of course, they were very closely related. Muhammad's father died before he was born, and he was reared by his grandfather. From the very beginning, he seemed to be a man much taken to solitude, meditation who pondered the lessons of life. He married an older widow and helped run her services of caravans, but spent much of his time just thinking.

When he was about 42, he received his great mission in life. He began to have revealed to him the Koran, the revelation of God to Muhammad. It was a call to reform the religion of his fellow Arabs there in the peninsula, to bring them to the understanding of one true God. The Koran, for the Muslim, is the equivalent of Jesus for the Christian. It is not the Bible; it is the actual physical revelation of God, dictated by God to Muhammad in the Arab language. That's why it should not be translated, in the view of a stern Muslim. It is the word of God to Muhammad, and it tells that there is no God but God; it's just that simple. There is no God but God, and Muhammad is the prophet of God. Muhammad had been chosen out of the whole of the human race to bear this word.

He told first his family about his message, and he tried also to convert his fellow citizens in Mecca. The trouble was that the new teaching came up against, and was a competitor to, old established, vested interests—particularly the pagan gods who were sources of economic benefit to Mecca, with people coming there on a pilgrimage to worship the ancient Black Stone, as it was called. Muhammad was forced to flee from Mecca. That year of his flight, the year 622, became the beginning of the chronology for the Muslim world, just as the birth of Christ was for the Christian world. He found refuge in the city of Medina, and proved not only to be a prophet infused with the law and the will of God, but also a remarkable diplomat, even a general.

By the time he died in 632, Muhammad had brought the quarreling tribes of the Arabian Peninsula together into a community of believers. That was always what was so important to the Muslims, the community of believers—overriding any national, or even ethnic, boundaries. He taught his simple message, and the Koran, for the good Muslim, had all you need to know of truth. It was a comprehensive worldview. It answered questions of government, morality, and social and family life. There was no separation between the word of God and the state. The powers that be were put in their place by God, and you must submit to their will as you submitted to the will of God. That, after all, is what Islam means, submission to the will of God. There is no God but God, and that God is all powerful, all merciful and all compassionate. He has preordained all things that will come to pass. "It is written," a Muslim will say, which means that is your destiny.

To the non-Muslim, it is hard to see that Islam leaves any room for free will. But the Muslim believes that each of us does have that free choice to accept the word of God and find everlasting life or to reject it. On a day of judgement, just like the day of judgement in Christianity, all souls will be tried and weighed. Just to say one time with complete belief and conviction that there is no God but God, and Muhammad is the prophet of God, is enough to make you saved. But there are other aspects, the deeds that a good Muslim will carry out, such as paying alms. Still today in the Middle East, you will see people sitting outside a mosque and ordinary people with obviously very little money stopping to give them just a little bit of change. That is your duty to those who are less fortunate than you.

To fast during the month of Ramadan, to pay a pilgrimage, if possible, to Mecca, and to pray five times a day. There's no more powerful tribute to the unity of the Islamic world spiritually than to see all over the world, far up on the reaches of the Nile, blacks and whites and Egyptians all sitting down together and kneeling in prayer to their God those five times a day. There is no God but God. Muhammad is his prophet. Come to prayer. It's a powerful idea that united first the Arab tribes and led them to undertake an expansion with no other precedent or parallel in history, except perhaps, later, the expansion of the Mongols under Genghis Khan. The Arabs swept out of the Arabian Peninsula, bearing the word of God against both the Iranian Empire and the Roman Empire. They swept into Syria, crushing Roman armies and a Persian army, and on into Egypt, carrying this powerful message. They were a warrior race.

They overcame even splits within the belief community of Islam. The debate we hear so much today, about Sunnis and Shiites, goes back to the generation right after Muhammad, and the question of who was the true successor of Muhammad. Was it his son-in-law and cousin Ali, who would become the martyr of the Shiite faith, or was it a "caliph," a successor to Muhammad chosen by the community as a whole, which is what the Sunnis came to believe? There's no doubt that this has been a historically extremely important division. At the same time, Protestants and Catholics were historically very much divided and fought one another, yet still worshiped the same fundamental God.

It was interesting that, for the Muslims, there was no reason why Christians would not accept this idea of Muhammad. Muhammad was very respectful towards Moses and Jesus. These were all prophets; Abraham and Jesus were prophets. Muhammad was the last of the prophets, and he was the fulfillment of the message they had been given. Why would Christians not understand that this was the ultimate revelation of God? Instead, these two great forces found themselves locked in a struggle to the death. Already by the 8th century, the Muslims were beginning to attack Constantinople. The Byzantine Empire found itself waging war against Arabs, as well as invaders on all corners of their empire. The empire of the Arabs swept through Egypt, all the way across North Africa, so that by 711—that is to say less than 100 years after Muhammad had begun to proclaim his message—armies of the Islamic faith passed on into Spain, and very rapidly reduced almost all of Spain to Islamic control. This was the power of the idea.

In medieval Europe, as in the medieval Islamic world, these two competing religions, both based upon values of peace and justice, found themselves engaged in an eternal struggle. The *jihad* was fundamental to the Islamic view, and it was the holy war. It was the duty of every Muslim to spread the faith by the sword. One of the noblest titles in the entire Islamic world is to be a *ghazi*, a warrior for the faith. Those who spread it by the sword and die in the midst of bringing the word, conquering the unbelievers, go immediately into paradise. It was a religion that was to be spread by the sword, but Christianity, despite the teachings of peace of Jesus, was equally a religion that was spread by the sword. The Christian rulers of the Middle Ages, such as Charlemagne, had absolutely no hesitation to go out with a sword and kill, conquer and even burn pagan Saxons, for example. Both religions became religions of the sword.

The Byzantine Empire—centered in Constantinople and extending into Greece and over most of Asia Minor—was the great bulwark in the east against the Islamic tide. Christians continued, all during this period, to go to Jerusalem as a place of pilgrimage. It had fallen to the Islamic armies very early in the surge of Islam, but Christians still went. For a long period, there was a certain tolerance of this Christian pilgrimage. But in the 11th century, there was a new change of leadership in the Middle East, and the rise to power of Turkish dynasties—of Turks from the central part of Asia Minor who had come into the Islamic world, frequently as mercenaries and slaves now became the masters—who were converts to Islam. They were more intolerant than the Arabs had been.

Suddenly, the pilgrimages to Jerusalem began to cease. Strong taxes were laid upon Christians inside the Islamic world, around Jerusalem, and the Crusades were proclaimed. In 1096, the first of the Crusaders took up their banners and crosses and began to march from France into the Holy Land. From then on, really until the 15th century, these Crusades would continue—men coming certainly for game, territory and the sheer love of warfare, but also testifying to the power of those ideas, that men would leave their homes, take a dangerous route all across Europe, and wage war to the death against those who just believed differently. So, too, the Muslims waged war to the death. When the first Crusaders captured Jerusalem, the massacre of the Muslims was terrifying to behold.

The most famous of the Crusades was that in which Richard the Lionheart, Frederick the Holy Roman Emperor and Philip of France all took up the cross, and in 1189, came to the Holy Land, bickering among themselves and ultimately encountering one of the noblest of all the figures of the Middle Ages, Saladin. Saladin was a Turk, ruling from his headquarters in Egypt, a man who was willing to establish a kind of peace and toleration in the Middle East centered on the rights of both Christians and Muslims to use Jerusalem. With his death, the Crusades began again in all their fury, dragging on century after century and wearing out, again, the Byzantine Empire, the states of the Middle East, and even Europe itself.

Constantinople, all through this long period, would remain the great magnate of Christianity in the east. Constantinople—its very name still echoes. It's called Istanbul today, but that means only the Greek words *eis tin polin*—to the city—Istanbul, for it was the city. The Russians called it Tsargrad, the city of the emperors. Those emperors who sat upon the golden throne in Byzantium looked right back to Augustus as the founder of their empire. In fact, the official name for the Byzantines was *Romaioi*, the Romans. The law codes of Augustus still form part of the foundation of the legal system of Byzantium. Greek was the language, but we remember that Greek was one of the two languages of the Roman Empire. There among the scholars and monks of Constantinople, that enormous heritage of Greek literature was handed down to us. There they copied Thucydides so that we might learn his lessons of history. There they copied Herodotus.

Such was their love of the ancient Greek heritage, and the legacy that had been handed down from Greece and Rome, that they even copied the scurrilous comedies of Aristophanes, filled with sexual innuendo and risqué language. They patterned their orations upon Demosthenes. They patterned their histories of the coming, for example, of the Crusaders, on the writings of Thucydides. They developed an art, which in its subtlety and religious power has few equals in all of history—the icon—as the window into the soul of the faith. That was a Christian Roman Empire. Just as in its Islamic competitors, there was no separation of church and state.

The emperor in Constantinople followed in the path of Constantine. He was both the high priest and the emperor of this great empire. He was priest and king, with absolute authority in all matters of doctrine. He decided what the Christian faith was. This form of religion, *caesaropapism*, in which the Caesar is pope as well, is fundamentally different from that which arose in Latin Christianity, where the pope stands above as the head of the spiritual kingdom, and the king or emperor is the head of the secular kingdom. In Constantinople, there was no limit on the power of the emperor. Constantinople would pass its Eastern Christianity, its Orthodox Christianity, and its ideals of government—as well as its ideals of art—to Russia, and continue its legacy right down to our own day.

Ultimately, Constantinople would fall. A new power began to arise in the Middle East, first defeating the Byzantines in a mighty battle in 1071, the Turks. In the form of new vigorous rulers, the Ottoman Empire—the descendants of the Turkish warlord Othman—began to conquer what was left of the Byzantine Empire. It had been shaken by the Fourth Crusade and the actual capture and rule of Constantinople from 1204 to 1261 by the Latin Christians, but it regained its power and the emperor still sat upon his throne. But piece by piece, this empire was taken away—first in Asia Minor, then crossing into the Balkans and conquering the Orthodox states of Serbia and Bulgaria. Finally in 1453, that last little tiny remnant, still there by the Bosphorus, the legacy of Constantine, found itself surrounded by the Ottoman armies under the command of their brave, efficient, capable sultan, Muhammad. He would be known as Muhammad the Conqueror in the west, and as Muhammad the Law Giver in the Islamic world.

On May 29, 1453, with huge kettle drums pounding, with great canons drawn before the walls of Constantinople, and with the Janissaries—the professional army of the Ottoman sultans—leading the way, the Ottomans broke through the Romanus gate. The last emperor of Rome, Constantine XI, died with his sword in hand, worthy indeed to be the last emperor of Rome. The armies of the Ottomans would march through this last relic of the Roman Empire, and Constantinople would become an Islamic city. The Ottoman Empire would go on to be one of the superpowers and dominant forces in European history, right down to the 18th century. It, and the Spanish Empire, continued this Crusade of the Islamic world against the Christian world, and this clash of values that goes all the way back to the Trojan War.

Lecture Nineteen
The Ottoman Empire and Turkey

Scope:

The Crusades were the first of many failed attempts to impose European values on the lands of Islam. The Ottoman Empire represented the farthest extension of Islam into Europe and the fulfillment of the Muslim ideal of holy war. The Ottoman Empire is also a lesson that ethnic autonomy under a centralized autocracy could be the best way to peace in the Middle East. The transformation of Turkey in the 20th century by Kemal Ataturk is a most instructive example of how to create a secular nation-state in the Middle East, based on European political and cultural values.

Outline

I. Despite their similarities, Islam and Christianity have battled since Islam arose in the early 7th century. Starting with the Crusades in the 11th century, holy warriors fought in the Middle East until 1453, when Turkish Muslims captured the Christian city of Constantinople.

   A. The fall of the Roman Empire is often dated to 476 A.D., when the empire in the west fell. The Roman Empire in the east did not fall until 1453, when the Ottomans became the successors to the Christian-Islamic struggle in the Middle East.

   B. The Ottoman Empire illustrates two lessons of history. One is that empires rise and fall because of individual leader's decisions. The other is that religion is a powerful motivating force.

   C. The Ottoman Empire was the most successful of the Islamic empires devoted to *jihad*. From the capture of Constantinople in 1453 to the Ottoman armies' retreat from Vienna in 1683, it dominated much of the political history of Europe.

   D. The Middle East was shaped by the long centuries of Ottoman rule. Indeed, the nation of Turkey in the 20th century is a remarkable illustration of successful nation-building.

II. The Ottomans were a Turkic people from central Asia with a nomadic heritage and close linguistic ties to the Mongols. They appeared in Europe early on; the Huns, who swept into the Roman Empire in the 5th century, were a Turkic people.

A. In the 11th century, the Turks became a major factor in Asia Minor. One group that fought the Roman Empire were followers of the war chief Osman, which gives us the name Ottomans.

B. Under the early sultans, the Ottomans became a significant power in Asia Minor, then the Balkans, where in 1389, they defeated Christian armies at Kosovo.

C. In 1453, the last remnant of the Byzantine Empire, Constantinople, fell. The Ottomans began an expansion that spread from North Africa to Hungary. They got as far as Vienna, which they repeatedly sought to conquer.

D. The Ottomans saw themselves as the embodiment of the Islamic ideal of the *ghazi,* the warrior for the faith. One of their duties was to rid the world of infidels through wars of conquest.

III. The Ottomans were much like the Romans in their approach to governing their vast empire.

A. The Ottomans were not an exclusive group. Anyone could become a member of the ruling elite by learning the Turkish language and Ottoman customs. In fact, the Ottomans ensured a constant infusion of new life by *devshirme*, the practice of kidnapping Christian boys from the Balkans and raising them to be Turkish Muslims.

B. These boys became the core of the Janissaries, the ferocious wing of the Ottoman army, whose soldiers swore an oath to spread the faith. In the 15th and 16th centuries, this army was technologically superior to those in Europe.

C. The Ottomans, from the founder of their dynasty, Osman, to the sultan Suleiman the Magnificent (r. 1520–1566), produced generations of outstanding leaders, who were capable administrators and warriors. Under Suleiman, the empire reached its greatest extent.

IV. As had previous empires, the Ottomans fought on many fronts, from Europe to the Middle East. Iran, which the Ottomans never ruled, was a major threat and drain on resources. The Ottomans also campaigned every year in the Balkans to conquer and put down insurgencies.

A. The Ottomans believed that the best way to rule ethnic groups was not by assimilating their subjects or imposing Turkish values. In fact, the later sultans lost some enthusiasm for proselytization because Christians paid taxes, which many sultans preferred to converts.

B. The Ottoman rulers did not impose the Turkish language but encouraged local languages to be spoken and ethnic groups to govern themselves. The only requirement under Turkish rule was to accept the foreign policy and lead of the Ottomans.

C. Christians and other minority groups could practice their own religion, but they were heavily oppressed. The Turks were arrogant and cruel, and any insurgency was met with ruthless destruction. Such treatment stirred up feelings of nationalism in the Balkans.

V. The Ottoman Empire declined by the 18th century to become "the sick man of Europe," but it was still a formidable force. Among its rivals were Russia on the Black Sea, Austria in the Balkans, and Venice.

A. During a series of wars, the Ottoman Empire shrank, and by 1914, it seemed to be on the verge of destruction. The Balkan states had broken away. The once-great empire in Europe was a tiny area near the Greek border.

B. The Ottomans still reigned in Asia Minor, including Lebanon, Syria, Palestine, and Iraq. (Egypt was a British protectorate.)

C. In 1914, the nationalist Young Turks began to revitalize the Ottoman Empire with a vision of a true Turkish nation-state. They made a secret alliance with Germany, which brought them into World War I in the fall of 1914.

VI. By late 1915, Britain was searching for a new strategy to justify its earlier losses in the war and to prompt capitulation of the central powers. Winston Churchill came up with the idea of attacking the Ottoman Empire.

A. The Turks were rivals to the British in the Middle East and sought to assault the Suez Canal, Britain's lifeline to India. A defeat of Turkey would give Russia, an ally of Britain, a reason to stay in the war. Britain promised that if Constantinople were captured, Russia or Greece would get it.

B. In February 1915, Britain launched a military campaign in the Dardanelles. About 250,000 British troops landed on the beaches of Gallipoli. The British had already begun to bombard the area, and the Turkish forts began to collapse.

C. It looked as though the Ottoman Empire would fall. Communications were down, and the Turkish troops, under German officers, had no idea what was happening.

D. A young officer named Mustafa Kemal—later known to history as Kemal Ataturk, the father of the Turks—took command. He saw his Turkish soldiers fleeing and ordered them to stop, fight, and wait for more troops.

E. All summer long, the trench warfare continued at Gallipoli. Many soldiers on both sides died. By December, the British gave up. When the last British troops withdrew in January 1916, Turkey had a new hero, Mustafa Kemal.

VII. Gradually, the Ottoman Empire was shorn away. Jerusalem was captured, and Arabia revolted. By the time the armistice was signed on November 11, 1918, the Allies were eager to carve up the Middle East.

A. Italy got southern Anatolia and southern Asia Minor. France got Syria. Britain got Palestine and Iraq, and Greece got Constantinople.

B. The Allied armies began to march into the interior of the empire. The sultan offered no resistance, but Mustafa Kemal rallied the Turks to fight back. Instead of conquering Turkey, the Allies suffered one of the most disastrous retreats in modern history.

C. The Turks forced the Allies to sign a new peace treaty, one that recognized them as a nation.

D. As dictator and president, Mustafa Kemal began a program of Westernization. He himself took the western-style surname name of Ataturk and required all Turks to take surnames in the Western style. This was part of a series of reforms, including substituting the Roman for the Arabic alphabet, a Western calendar, and giving women the right to vote.

E. Kemal Ataturk began to build a secular, Westernized nation-state called Turkey. He made treaties with the Soviet Union and the Balkan states.

VIII. This nation-building continued until Ataturk's death in 1938.

A. He left Turkey under strong but wise authoritarian rule. During World War II, Turkey was thought to be friendly by both Germany and the Allies, and it became a firm U.S. ally during the Korean War.

B. Turkey became the most stable and prosperous nation in the Middle East because of one man, Kemal Ataturk, who built upon the legacy of history to transform his nation.

Essential Reading:

Lewis, *Emergence of Modern Turkey*.

Supplementary Reading:

Gelvin, *The Modern Middle East*.

Inalcik, *Social and Economic History of the Ottoman Empire*.

Lewis, *From Babel to Dragomans*.

Questions to Consider:

1. Does Ataturk show the way to viable solutions for nations in the Middle East today?

2. Discuss the Ottoman concept of governing through autonomous ethnic groups as a model for nations in the Middle East today.

Lecture Nineteen—Transcript
The Ottoman Empire and Turkey

In our last lecture we explored the legacy of the Roman Empire and the fact that the greatest legacy of the Roman Empire would be one that the emperor Augustus never could have imagined—that it would be Islam and Christianity, these two world religions, that arose in the Roman Empire, and whose spread was made possible by the economic, cultural social and political unity of the Roman Empire. We saw how similar these two religions were, illustrating our seventh law of history—that religion is among the most powerful motivating forces in all of history. If we are to be successful in the world today, we simply must deal with the fact that throughout much of history, there has been no separation of church and state, and the Christian and Islamic faiths were both rooted in the idea of a complete assimilation of church and state.

We saw that Islam recognized its debt to Christianity and Muhammad's only problem was why the Christians would not understand that he was the last and final revelation of God. Both taught one God; both taught a fundamental ethical system of doing good to others, and yet from the time Islam arose in the early 7th century, it has been at war with Christianity. We carried our story right on down to 1453, the struggle between Islam and Christianity in the Middle East and the capture of the city of Constantinople, Constantine's own city, built as a testimony to his Christian faith and to the deep Roman involvement in the Middle East. We saw that the capture of Constantinople was something that Edward Gibbon would have been proud to have us study because he carried his *Decline and Fall of the Roman* Empire right down to this momentous event, which he said continued to reverberate through history.

Now the fall of the Roman Empire, in schoolbooks, is always said to be 476 A.D., and there's nothing wrong with that date. That is when there ceased to be a Roman Empire in the West. That is to say that Rome itself was under the leadership of the Pope, and the whole of the Roman Empire still existed, in theory united. But there was need for only one ruler, and that was in Constantinople. That empire in Constantinople did not fall until 1453. The Ottomans, the Turks, were the successors to the long struggle between Christianity and Islam in the Middle East. The Ottoman Empire deserves our attention—one, because it illustrates our interest in the rise and fall of empires, and that they rise and fall because of individual decisions by outstanding leaders, and two, it illustrates—to continue our theme of the motivating force of religion—because the Ottoman Empire was the most successful of all of the Islamic empires devoted to *jihad*, to the holy war.

Moreover, it was a superpower, and from the capture of Constantinople in 1453 to the final retreat of the Ottoman armies from Vienna in 1683, it dominated much of the political history of Europe. And for those of us interested in the lessons for today, the Middle East, as we have it right now, was very much shaped by the long centuries of the Ottoman rule. It also gives us in the 20th century, in the nation-state of Turkey, a remarkable illustration of how you can successfully nation-build and can create a republic in the Middle East. So the Ottoman Empire is rife with examples for us, but who were the Ottomans? Who were the Turks? The Turks are another noble and ancient race. They stretched, in their beginnings, over much of Central Asia. They have always taken pride in their nomadic heritage and, linguistically, there is a close bond between the Turks and the Mongols. In fact, recognizing this close association, it was one of the goals of Genghis Khan to bring all the Turkic people under his control.

They appeared in Europe early on, and the Huns, who swept into the Roman Empire in the 5th century A.D. under Attila, reaching all the way to the walls of Rome, are a Turkic-type people, a nomadic people and are ferocious warriors using mainly mounted archers. In the 11th century, the Turks became a major factor in Asia Minor. One of these Turkish groups that solidified itself under its warlords, fighting against the Byzantines along their frontier in Asia Minor, were the followers of the war chief Osman—or Uthman, as the early Europeans called him—which gives us our name, the Ottomans. Under the early sultans, they first became a power in Asia Minor, then spread into the Balkans, where on June the 20th, 1389 the Ottoman Turks delivered the decisive defeat of the armies of Christendom that had gathered at Kosovo, the Field of the Blackbirds. June the 20th, 1389, a defeat that still resounds throughout the Balkans and shapes Balkan history.

From that time onward, Constantinople was doomed. In 1453, the last remnant of the Byzantine Empire fell, and the Ottomans began a career of expansion that would carry them all across North Africa.

Ottoman ships sailed out from the ports of Tunis—Egypt was under their domination—and carried them all the way to Hungary, where in 1526 the Ottoman armies delivered a decisive defeat to the king of Hungary and occupied Hungary; and finally all the way up to the walls of Vienna, which they repeatedly sought to conquer. The Ottomans saw themselves as the embodiment of the Islamic ideal of the *ghazi*, the warrior for the faith. The proudest title they could take on their tombs when they were buried was that Muhammad was the *ghazi* of God in battle, spreading the faith. One of their duties is to rid the world of the infidel. In pursuit of this task, they carried out their wars of conquest.

The Ottomans were in no sense a nation-state. In fact, they were much more like the Romans in their approach to governing their vast empire. The Osmanlis were not an exclusive group. Anyone could be a member of the ruling elite by learning Turkish, learning Turkish ways and the various customs of the Ottomans. In fact, the Ottomans ensured a constant infusion of new vital life by their practice of the *devshirme*, which meant that they went all through the Balkans, and they literally kidnapped young Christian children, Christian boys— from Serbia, from Bulgaria, from Albania, from all parts of their Balkan Empire—brought them back to Constantinople at a very early age, reared them to be Muslims, reared them to speak Turkish, and tried to have them forget any ties that they had to their native land.

That became the core of the Janissaries, those most ferocious of armies that terrified Europe—infantrymen carrying in their little soft caps a spoon, a wooden spoon, which was a symbol of the fact that the sultan fed them, and whenever they were angry, they would overturn their soup kettles; that was the sign of their revolt. They could not marry, and they swore an absolute oath to the sultan and to the spread of the faith. They were the core of the Ottoman army, but the Ottoman army also had a superb cavalry. But more than that, in the 15th and 16th centuries, it was technologically superior to the European armies it faced—above all by its heavy artillery, frequently manned and molded for them by mercenaries who came from Christian Europe, particularly Germans and Hungarians would come into the Ottoman Empire to serve in their engineering corps.

So it was a most formidable army, and the Ottomans, from the founder of their dynasty, Uthman, right on down through Suleiman the Magnificent—from 1520 to 1566, sultan of this empire—

generation after generation, produced outstanding leaders who were both capable administrators and warriors. The sultan had an enormous harem, and thus produced a number of sons. Essentially, when a new ruler came to the throne, his first task was to strangle all of his brothers. This ensured that the best of them all would come to the throne, and in these early years it did do just that. Suleiman the Magnificent, under whom the empire reached its greatest extent, was one of the true heroic figures of the 16th century. That was a great age—the age of Ivan the Terrible, of Elizabeth of England, of Charles the Holy Roman Emperor, the age of Martin Luther and it was the age of Suleiman the Magnificent. No ruler was more feared or more influential throughout the world, than Suleiman.

Their wars against the Christians were only one of the fronts, however, on which the Ottomans had to fight because they, too, were faced with the problem of the Middle East. In point of fact, the Ottomans never successfully extended their rule into Iran. From the 16th century onward in Iran, the Ottomans faced a major threat. Just as often as they campaigned in Europe, they campaigned against the Iranians, their fellow Muslims, but followers of the Shiite faith. But every year, the campaign drums would begin, the great huge kettle drums, and the Ottoman armies would move out through the Balkans in further conquest of breaking and putting down insurgencies, and we want to come back to my geopolitical idea. Remember, geopolitics is understanding politics through geography.

I have said that the Middle East extended from Pakistan and Afghanistan all the way through what we consider the Middle East—through Israel, Lebanon, Syria and Turkey—northward to the Danube River, and all the way out to the Pillars of Hercules. We saw that Alexander the Great extended his rule, before he ever invaded Persia, to the Danube. He went all the way out to Pakistan and then turned back and was planning his next expedition to conquer Carthage and extend his power to the Atlantic. The power of Suleiman the Magnificent ran along that same course—Budapest, the Danube and the constant attempt to conquer Iran, which drained the Ottomans' money and manpower.

The Ottomans believed that the best way to rule the Balkans and the Middle East was by not trying to assimilate those they ruled over or even by imposing their Ottoman Turkish values. In fact, the later sultans lost some of their enthusiasm for spreading the faith because those who were Christians paid taxes to have that privilege, and many of the Ottoman sultans preferred to have the taxes rather than the converts. Also, they did not attempt to impose the Turkish language. In fact, they encouraged the local languages to be spoken, and they most liked to have the individual groups they ruled over govern themselves. So they had a number of ethnic groups—as in Greece, as among the Serbs and the Bulgars—and let them keep their religion, let them pay taxes, let them even have schools in their native language to keep them divided. This is how they also operated in Lebanon, where the Christians, the Druze—a group that broke off from Islam in the 11th century—and the Muslims were all governed individually unto themselves. The only important thing was that they had to accept the foreign policy and lead of the Ottomans.

There has been some tendency—since the Second World War, and more recently in the 1990s when it became clear how difficult the political situation in the Balkans remained—to look back with nostalgia upon the Ottoman Empire as having brought a certain degree of peace and prosperity to these areas. The founders of our country did not see it that way, and to them the Ottoman Empire of the 18th century was the very epitome of tyranny. The rulers were capricious. No matter how wealthy you were, one day you might just be brought home [to meet] the grand vizier. You might have come home, found the Janissaries there to arrest you then be strangled with a bowstring. In fact, sultans by the 17th and 18th century liked to promote grand viziers very, very rapidly, give those grand viziers—in other words, their second in command, the real administrator of the empire—absolute immunity to carry out all kinds of corruption and pillage, let them amass a huge personal fortune, then strangle them, confiscate that and appoint some other fool to be the grand vizier. It's an interesting statement of how human nature never changes; you always find people to take those jobs.

Minority groups like the Christians were certainly given the right to practice their own religion, but they were heavily oppressed. Turks were enormously arrogant, cruel, and any insurgency was met with absolute ruthless destruction. The Turkish riders, the irregular troops that they used to put down insurgencies, became a byword for terror in the Balkans. Moreover, they succeeded only in stirring up feelings of nationalism among the people of the Balkans, who never forgot their ancient defeat at Kosovo, and never forgot their allegiance to

Christianity. The founders used to say do you want to see what tyranny does as compared to freedom? Under the freedom of Rome, Asia Minor, Turkey and the Middle East flourished with cities.

They didn't need to take tours, the founders, to see those great ruins of the Roman Empire. They knew it had been a flourishing area—agriculture had flourished—and they said now look what it is like under the Turks. It is almost a desert. So the Turks were the example of oppression, of capricious government, of tyranny as being the desire of one man to put his own interest and well being above that of millions. The Ottoman Empire, from the great age of Suleiman, declined by the 18th century to being "the sick man of Europe," but it was still a most formidable force. Around the Black Sea it had Russia as its rival. In the Balkans it now had Austria, almost a crusading empire, fighting to spread the faith of Christianity back into the Balkans.

And the Ottoman Empire carried out a long series of wars against Venice, another sometime superpower that we forget, that ruled an empire in the Middle East. In the course of the wars between Venice and the Ottoman Empire the Parthenon was blown up. The Venetian ships shelled it. It was a powder magazine for the Ottoman governor. In the course of those long wars, the Ottoman Empire shrunk ever more until, by 1914, it seemed as though the Ottoman Empire was on the verge of destruction. The Balkan states had broken away in a series of wars. The Ottoman Empire in Europe, once so great, was now only a tiny little area near the Greek border. It still had its empire, though, in Asia Minor—stretching out to Baghdad—Lebanon, Syria, Palestine and all the way out to Iraq, where Baghdad was one of the provinces of the Ottoman Empire. Egypt, of course, was a British protectorate.

So the Ottoman Empire came to 1914, and the Ottomans had begun to be revitalized by nationalists. The Young Turks—Enver Pasha is one of their most important figures—believed that the Ottoman Empire could be saved by making the Turks into a true nation-state revitalized by nationalism. The Young Turks were cruel. They carried out genocide against the Armenians in order to make Turkey what they saw as a completely homogenous nation-state. In particular they admired Enver Pasha, who was almost a dictator of these Young Turks. The sultan was still there as a figurehead, but they guided policy, and they admired Germany tremendously. In

August of 1914, the Turks made an alliance with Germany, a secret alliance, and it brought them into this war, already in the fall of 1914, on the side of Germany and the Austro-Hungarian Empire. They were absolutely convinced that the Central Powers would triumph.

By the early winter of 1915, the deadlock we have spoken of had fallen across the western front. The British Cabinet was searching for a bold new way, and a new strategy, to justify all the losses they had already incurred in the first months of the war, and to bring about a capitulation of the central powers. The heated brain of Winston Churchill—you know how much I admire him—came up with this idea of an attack upon the Turkish Empire, and it made a great deal of sense. The Turks were real rivals to the British in the Middle East. The Turks were attempting an assault upon the Suez Canal, which was the lifeline of Britain to its empire in India, and a defeat of Turkey and the capture of Constantinople would give Russia a means and a reason to stay in the war.

And so promises were made, apparently both to the Russians and to the Greeks, that if Constantinople were captured, Russia would have it or the Greeks would have it, depending on whatever meeting you were in. Thus was launched, starting in February 1915, the great campaign against the Dardanelles, or the Gallipoli Campaign—Winston Churchill's idea, but as he later said, they never gave his plan a real chance. It was much altered by the generals, some of them who want to undermine Churchill himself; others simply in the righteous conviction that the real war had to be won in France, that this was just a sideshow. It wasn't a sideshow to the men who disembarked there. Some 250,000 British troops landed on the beaches of Gallipoli, in places like Anzac Cove, forever named to honor the brave Australian and New Zealand army corps numbers who landed there.

But it seemed to be an easy task. In fact, in February, the British had already begun their bombardment, and the forts along the Dardanelles began to collapse. The British ships were just about to push through to Constantinople, and the Turks were in such terror that they were loading up their archives, but then the navy withdrew. Some of its ships hit mines, and they withdrew, and the troops had to be landed in April, including these Australian and New Zealand troops, and on that one day in April, the 25th, it looked as though the

Ottoman Empire would fall. The Turkish troops under German officers had no real idea what was happening—communications were down—and the British only had to push forward over the hills and ravines of the Gallipoli Peninsula to arrive at Constantinople.

But there was a man of destiny, Mustafa Kemal. We know him in history as Kemal Ataturk, the father of the Turks, and he was the father of the Turkish nation, a young officer—he had broken with the Young Turks—but a strong Turkish nationalist. And while their German officers dithered around, Kemal Ataturk—or Mustafa Kemal, as he was known then—took command. The very name Mustafa, of course, is an Arabic name, but Kemal means perfect; that is what one of his schoolteachers had named him. With fierce blue eyes, a domineering personality, he saw his Turkish soldiers fleeing from the Allied troops, and he asked, where are you going? And they said, we're defeated. He said, no, attack. I do not order you to attack; in fact, I order you to die. But in the time it takes us to die, more troops will come up, and we will stop them. So they did, that day, and the long siege at Gallipoli began, and Mustafa Kemal became a national hero.

All through the long summer, the trench warfare continued there at Gallipoli, and the British and French soldiers, the Australian and New Zealand soldiers, the Turkish soldiers, died. They died in artillery barrages; they died in frontal assaults; they died of dysentery, until by the winter, by December 1915, the British gave up. When the last British troop withdrew in January of 1916, the British had suffered 250,000 casualties, and Turkey had a new hero. The Turkish army on the whole continued to lose during the war. Though frequently the Turks fought with bravery, they were misled by some of their German generals. Thus the sweep into Jerusalem was greatly facilitated by the incompetence of the German general commanding the Turks, which gave the Turks another view that they were just as good as the Westerners and just as brave.

But their empire was shorn away, Jerusalem was captured, Arabia was up in revolt, and by the time the peace terms were signed, or the Armistice was signed, on November the 11th, 1918, the Allies were just waiting to carve up the Middle East. This was the final triumph, don't you see, of all that the Allies had been striving for, in fact, going all the way back to Herodotus. Many of those men who fought at Gallipoli carried their Herodotus and their Homer with them, to sing the story of this ancient war in which Europe had triumphed over the values of the East. Now the Allies were going to gobble up the sick man of Europe. The Italians had cut off their portion of southern Anatolia and southern Asia Minor. The French were going to have their share; they were going to have Damascus and Syria. The British were going to have Palestine and Iraq, and the Greeks were finally going to have even Constantinople.

The Greek army landed; French troops landed; Italian troops landed, and they began to march into the interior. The sultan offered no resistance. The Turkish army seemed defeated and dispirited, and once again Mustafa Kemal rallied them. He proclaimed to the Turks, as the Allies seemed invincible, we stand, we fight, we conquer, or we die, and they rallied behind him. They began to drive the Allies out, Fierce cavalry attacks, heavy artillery barrages, led always by the personality of Mustafa Kemal, until instead of conquering Turkey, the Allies watched as the French army was stopped, the Italian army began to withdraw, and the Greek army utterly routed. It was one of the most disastrous retreats in modern history, and the Turks took the ancient city of Smyrna—Izmir, as they would rename it—the very center of Hellenism in Turkey, and burned it to the ground during a massacre.

They forced the Allies to sign a new peace treaty with Turkey, one that recognized them as a nation, which still gave them a little territory in Europe, and Mustafa Kemal began to build a nation-state. If you want an example that, in the Middle East, a nation-state can be built, it is Turkey, and it is the creation of this one man of destiny. It is with good reason that you go into any restaurant anywhere in Turkey, and there is a portrait of Kemal Ataturk staring down at you with his riding breeches and his crop under his arm, still guiding the Turks. First of all, it is Turkey; they renamed themselves. They were no longer the Ottoman Empire; they were the Turks, the land of the Turks. In fact, to be a Turk had been something like being called a peasant in the old Ottoman Empire; now it became a sign of pride.

Turks, after all, had not only ruled an empire, but the Turkish language was spoken all the way into Central Asia, and Turkey had a long border with Russia—Russia, in the grip of the Bolsheviks, almost a pariah of Europe. Mustafa Kemal, Kemal Ataturk, made a treaty with the Soviet Union and began to collaborate with them. He made treaties with the Allies. He made treaties with the Balkan states, and he began to make Turkey into a European nation. The Turkish language was written in the Arabic script—one fell decree, boom, we now use the Latin alphabet. The language began to be purged of Persian and Arabic words, and real Turkish words were used. They even avoided Western words. Let's come up with a Turkish word for all of these new things that come to us from the West—such as DNA and so on—let's come up with new words for them.

And every Turk under the age of 40 was required to learn to write in the Latin alphabet, and they were sent to school to learn to do so. Clothes were changed. If you go to much of the Middle East today and go off of the main streets, you see people dressed just the way they were in the Middle Ages; not so in the Turkey of Mustafa Kemal. They were forced to wear coats, hats, dress just like Westerners, and to take Western names. He was voted the name Kemal Ataturk, the father of the Turks, and his generals took names from the great victories they had won. Turkey became a republic. He, as president, had enormous powers, but it was a republic, and women voted. Yes, they had the right to vote. He even allowed one opposition party late in his life.

So in less than about a15-year period, from 1922 down until his death in 1938, he carried out the nation building of Turkey, and when he died, he left Turkey stable—still under a strong authoritarian rule in the after years, but wise enough to guide its way between the terrors of the Second World War, being both thought to be friendly by Germany as well as by the Allies, to become a very firm ally of America at the time of Korean War—to be the most stable and prosperous nation in the Middle East. That is due to this one man, Mustafa Kemal, who built upon the legacy of history to transform his nation.

Lecture Twenty
The Spanish Empire and Latin America

Scope:

Despite its proximity to the United States, its vast resources, and its industrious population, Latin America has never developed enduring institutions of democracy. As with China, Russia, and the Middle East, the answer lies in history. The Native American cultures were as creative as those of the ancient Middle East, but there was no concept of freedom. Quite the opposite, the Aztec Empire was one of the most despotic regimes in history. The Spanish conquest brought with it twin engines of despotism, the centralized autocracy of the Spanish kings and the Catholic Inquisition. The Inquisition is one of the most notable examples of Lord Acton's maxim that "all power tends to corrupt." Christianity began in the ideal of freedom of conscience. In the Inquisition, it became the great prototype for totalitarian repression. The wisdom of history teaches that the propinquity of freedom does not ensure its spread to alien soil.

Outline

I. As we have noted, religion is one of the most powerful forces in human history. It is seen in the struggle between Islam and Christianity from 312, when Christianity became the official religion of the Roman Empire, to Muhammad's death in 632 and the subsequent expansion of the Islamic empire into the Middle East and Europe.

   A. The Ottoman Empire arose to spread Islam by *jihad* all the way to Vienna in 1683. There was no national or individual freedom in this empire. The various national groups were conquered and ruled as subjects.

   B. Kemal Ataturk led the reforms that created post-World War I Turkey after the British, French, Italians, and Greeks intervened in its affairs. But the study of the Middle East raises the question: Is freedom a universal value? In fact, freedom has never existed in the Middle East. Islam is not a religion of freedom; it is a religion of submission.

C. At the end of World War I, the League of Nations required France to establish a protectorate over Syria. The British received a mandate to establish protectorates in Palestine and Iraq. None of these areas, which had been part of the Ottoman Empire, had a national heritage or a tradition of unity.

    1. The French and the British both failed to establish democratic governments.

    2. France set up a constitutional government in Syria in the early 1920s, but elected politicians were assassinated, and insurgencies broke out. The French military could not force democracy on Syria.

    3. Britain had no more success in Iraq or Palestine, due in part to the Ottoman Empire's lack of nationalism and ethnic hatred between groups.

II. Latin America is another part of the world where freedom has been difficult to plant. The prime influence here was that of Spain, which undertook to bring Catholicism to the New World.

A. Catholics and Muslims battled in the Crusades in Europe and the Middle East. One crusading nation was Spain, whose monarchy dominated the 16th and 17th centuries as one of the world's superpowers.

B. Islamic armies swept across northern Africa and, by 711, crossed into Spain, defeating the Germanic Visigoths there and conquering almost all of the Iberian Peninsula. The Catholic kingdoms, including Castile and Aragon, hung on in the far north.

C. Moorish civilization in Spain, admired by later generations, was tolerant, but it was not Christian. The small Catholic kingdoms began to push south against the Moorish kingdoms.

D. By 1492, the last of the Moorish kingdoms in Spain fell to Ferdinand, whose marriage to Isabella joined the kingdoms of Aragon and Castile and united Spain. According to Machiavelli, Ferdinand wrapped himself in a pious cloak as "the most Catholic king," yet he was a master at double-dealing, lying, and every form of statecraft that Machiavelli admired.

E. Ferdinand was a fervent Catholic who believed that God had placed him in the position of king to spread the true faith around the world.

III. Ferdinand's Spain was the first centralized monarchy in Europe, a forerunner, in a way, of 20th-century totalitarian states. Ferdinand sought to control the economy of Spain and, later, the New World. He also wanted absolute homogeneity and orthodoxy.

A. Christopher Columbus's voyage to the New World sought wealth, power, and the spread of Christianity. Along with the great conquistadors went the priests to convert the native populations, by persuasion if possible and by force if necessary.

B. Ferdinand used two tools, the Inquisition and centralized monarchy, to obtain and hold power and to impose Catholicism in the Spanish Empire.

    1. As we mentioned, the Catholic Church at the time was concerned with orthodoxy. Being Christian was not enough; one had to adhere to the doctrine taught by the Church.

    2. The Church fought not only Muslims but heretics, such as the Albigensians in southern Spain. To combat them, the Church created a bureaucratic instrument, the Inquisition, that sent priests to towns and villages to listen to complaints, question suspects, and bring people to trial.

IV. Ferdinand's control of the Spanish Inquisition, formally established in 1478, gave him an instrument to impose absolute religious conformity.

A. The Inquisition questioned the loyalty to the faith of Islamic and Jewish converts. Were they true Christians?

B. The Inquisition operated by arriving in small towns in Spain and offering those who were suspect a 30-day grace period to admit heresy and promise to become Christians. After 30 days, a suspect might still be called to face a tribunal.

    1. The rules for the Inquisition were carefully laid out. The accused was allowed to identify possible accusers who were his enemies, but he might have been denounced by a friend.

2. The basic means of interrogation was torture. The Inquisition worked under Roman law, which considered evidence extracted by torture more valid than evidence voluntarily given. A confession resulted in a sentence to be burned alive in the public square.

3. Citizens were required to attend these so-called acts of faith. Even those who professed Christian beliefs as they were tied to the stake were still burned.

C. That is how the Inquisition flourished in Spain and served as a vehicle for despotism in the New World. It was a force of control, a force to shape the will of humans. The Inquisition and Ferdinand's despotism were the Spanish Empire's legacy to Latin America.

V. The Spanish Empire was a superpower. The heir of Ferdinand and Isabella, Charles, was king of Spain and Holy Roman Emperor from 1520 to 1556.

A. Next came Philip II, another fervent Catholic determined to continue spreading the word of God in the New World and to conquer Protestantism. In 1588, he unsuccessfully launched an armada against Britain.

B. Spain continued to decline through the 17th century, but it retained its colonial empire.

VI. Latin America's legacy includes not only the Inquisition and Spanish totalitarianism, but the brutality of its own Native American empires. The Aztec Empire that Cortes conquered in 1518–1519 rested on centralized power, a belief in a god-king, a priesthood, and human sacrifice. It ruled by terror in Mexico, much as Ferdinand and Isabella had ruled by terror in Spain.

A. Freedom has been hard to plant in Latin America. For a long time, this group of nations has had proximity to the model of the United States, yet freedom there has never flourished.

B. Inspired by the American Revolution, Latin American nations had their own revolutions, overthrowing the Spanish in the early 19th century. New republican governments were founded with liberal principles and constitutions.

C. Yet the history of Latin America has too often been the story of one dictator followed by another. Mexico, for example, had nine governments within the first 10 years of independence from Spain. The legacy of Spain to Latin America may be comparable to the legacy of the Ottomans to the Middle East.

Essential Reading:

Bakewell, *History of Latin America.*

Elliott, *Empires of the Atlantic World.*

Supplementary Reading:

Burns and Charlip, *Latin America.*

Homza, *Spanish Inquisition.*

Questions to Consider:

1. Do you believe that the social and economic problems of Latin America are the causes or the consequences of the failure of freedom to take root in that area?

2. Discuss the idea that the Inquisition was one of the prototypes for the totalitarianism of 20th-century despotisms, such as Stalin's Soviet Union.

Lecture Twenty—Transcript
The Spanish Empire and Latin America

We continue in this lecture to explore the question of religion as one of the most powerful motivating forces in human history. We have looked at the struggle between Islam and Christianity that dominated the period from the rise of Christianity—its establishment as the official religion of the Roman Empire in 312—and the rise of Islam, the life of Muhammad, and the expansion after his death in 632 of the empire of Islam all over the Middle East and into Europe. We examined the Ottoman Empire as the most successful example of an Islamic empire of the faith. You might almost want to call it a Crusader empire, but they didn't take the cross, they took the crescent. It is an empire of the faith, an empire that arose as a means of spreading the faith by the *jihad*, the holy war, and indeed spread the faith all the way up to the walls of Vienna in 1683.

We also looked at 20th-century Turkey, the creation of Mustafa Kemal—Kemal Ataturk—as one example of a successful nation-building enterprise in the Middle East. It has been pointed out that this was not done by outside pressure or intervention. In fact, it was the very intervention of the British, French, Italians and Greeks into the life of Turkey at the end of World War I that spurred the nationalism that enabled Mustafa Kemal to carry out his great reforms. The whole study of Turkey and the Middle East raises also the question for us, is freedom a universal value? All through our course, we have come back again and again to the Middle East and the fact that freedom has never existed in the Middle East. Islam itself is not a religion of freedom; it is a religion of submission.

The Ottoman Empire is a splendid example of a government structure that is the absolute negation of freedom. There was no national freedom under the Ottoman Empire. The various national groups were conquered and ruled as subject people. There was no political freedom; the sultan was chosen by whomever could be the strongest among the brothers in strangling all the rest. There was no legitimate process of changing the sultan. The Janissaries would revolt, overthrow him, kill him and put another in his place. There was no individual freedom; neither property nor ideas were safe in the Ottoman Empire. The successor states of the Ottoman Empire, with the exception of Turkey, continue this sad story of the inability to establish freedom in the Middle East, and are, at the same time, a lesson in the failure of superpowers to impose their will upon the Middle East.

At the end of World War I, while Turkey was creating itself into a nation, France received a mandate from the League of Nations to establish a protectorate over Syria. The British received a mandate to establish protectorates in Palestine and Iraq, all of which had been part of the Ottoman Empire. None of these areas—Syria, Palestine or Iraq—was a nation-state. None of them had a national heritage and tradition of unity. They were artificial areas, administrative areas, of the Ottoman Empire that brought together large numbers of very different people. The French and the British failed miserably in the anti war years to establish democratic governments and nation build. That is what both said they wanted to do.

The French came with a legal mandate from the League of Nations. They set up a constitutional government in the early '20s. Elections were held, and the politicians who were elected found themselves assassinated. Insurgencies broke out in Damascus and Aleppo. The French would put down one insurgency, only to have another break out. The French used the Foreign Legion, but then nobody much cared whether those boys ever went home or not. Still, with bombardments, aerial attacks and the Foreign Legion, the French could not bring democracy to Syria. In fact, all it did was to so weaken the morale of France that it played a role in why France collapsed before Germany in 1940. Britain had no more success in Iraq or in Palestine. Freedom is a very difficult plant to grow in the Middle East. Part of the legacy of the Ottoman Empire has been the division, the lack of national feeling, and the ethnic suspicion and hatred among the groups of the Middle East.

Another part of the world where freedom has been very difficult to plant is Latin America. Latin America, like the Middle East, takes us back to two competing empires of the faith. One is the Ottoman Empire and its legacy in the Middle East and the other is the Spanish Empire and the vast task it undertook to bring the Catholic religion to a whole New World that had been discovered. The Catholic religion and the Islamic faith found themselves in this tremendous struggle, the Crusades. One of the crusading nations of Europe, though it did not send troops to Jerusalem, was Spain. The Spanish monarchy that dominated the 16th and 17th century was one of the superpowers of all time. The Spanish monarchy grew up as a Crusader state.

We talked about how Islam swept across North Africa and, by 711, was able to cross into Spain, defeating the Germanic kingdom there, the Visigoths, and rapidly conquering almost all of the Iberian Peninsula. The Christian kingdoms like Castile and Aragon hung on only in the far northern tip of Spain. The very name of the little Kingdom of Castile, the land of the castles, spoke to the constant warfare among Muslims and the remaining Christian kingdoms. Divided and weak, these kingdoms hung on and gradually began to assume the offensive against the Moors of Spain, as they were called.

Moorish civilization in Spain has aroused the admiration of later generations. It was a tolerant civilization. The Moorish land of Spain was called the country of the three languages, where Arabic, Hebrew and Latin existed side by side,; where Jews found a tolerance they did not find in Christian Europe; where Jewish scholars could translate the writings of Aristotle from Arabic into Latin and see that they passed on to the medieval universities of Christian Europe. It was a land of poets and artistic beauty in terms of its architecture, but it was not Christian, and the Catholic kings of Spain were going to have nothing of it. Relentlessly, they pushed ever farther south. The Moorish kingdoms of Spain were badly divided among themselves. They began to lose the martial vigor that had once brought them from North Africa.

By 1492, the last of the Moorish kingdoms in Spain, the beautiful city of Granada, would fall. Its conqueror was Ferdinand, King of Castile and Aragon, the husband of Isabella, who had been Queen of Castile. Their marriage brought together these two kingdoms of Aragon and Castile, and united the whole of Spain. Ferdinand of Aragon and Castile, 1479-1516, also was one of those titanic figures of the 16th century, like Suliman the Magnificent, Ivan the Terrible, or Queen Elizabeth I of England. His title was the Most Catholic Christian King. He was admired by Machiavelli as the perfect example of a prince, of a leader.

Machiavelli talked about how Ferdinand always had huge on-going projects, and bringing them to success, such as the reconquest of Spain, or ultimately the founding of the New World. He said that Ferdinand wrapped himself in a pious cloak, "the most Catholic king," yet he was a master at double dealing, lying and every form of state craft that Machiavelli admired—understanding, as Machiavelli did, that it would be wonderful if the whole world acted according to the golden rule, but it does not. The goal of Ferdinand was to have power, but it was more than that. It was not just power to be king; it was the power to do things. He was, as was his wife, a fervent Catholic. He believed that God had placed him in this position to spread the True Faith all over the world. The first step had been to drive the last Moorish king from Spain in 1492.

The Spain that Ferdinand created was perhaps the first of the true centralized monarchies in Europe. It was a forerunner, in its own way, of the totalitarian states of the 20th century. Ferdinand sought to control not only the whole economy of Spain, and of the vast New World that would be discovered, but he also sought to control the minds of Spaniards. He wanted absolute homogeneity and orthodoxy in his Spain. That was the duty that God had given him. In 1492, the great expedition of Columbus sailed out under imperial patronage. Columbus, as we saw, was actually looking for a route to China, and instead stumbled upon an entire new world, as far as the Europeans were concerned. Lord Acton once said that the mistake of Columbus was better than all the wisdom in the universities of Christendom. There he found his new world.

Part of the reason for exploiting this new world was certainly wealth and power, but it was also to spread the Christian faith. With the great conquistadors like Pizarro and Cortes went the priests of the Catholic faith to spread the word and the religion, and to convert by persuasion if possible, by force if necessary. God wanted these converts one way or the other. But the centralized Spanish monarchy of Ferdinand was not just a unified power that broke the old traditions of the various regions of Spain, which really dispensed with any efficient parliamentary government; though Spain had a tradition of parliamentary government. It also sought religious conformity through the Inquisition. The Inquisition and centralized monarchy were the two tools of Ferdinand, King of Spain.

From very early on, the Church, as we have seen, was very concerned with orthodoxy. It was not enough just to be a Christian. It was not enough just to say I believe in Jesus; I believe that he is the Son of God, he died, was buried, was resurrected and now sits at the right hand of God the Father and can give me salvation. You had to have the right doctrine all the way along the line. The Church was the means of enforcing that doctrine. To have a false view, let us say, of the nature of Christ—how his divinity and his humanity were joined into one—was to lose your soul. The Church taught you what the correct view was. There were dangers to the Church, such as people sitting down and reading the Bible by themselves because that's how most heretics were born. It was not just the Bible, but the teachings of the Church—and the Church fathers like Augustine and Jerome—that were crucial in the shaping.

In Christianity, there were always heretics. In the Middle Ages, the Church found itself forced not only to fight against the Muslims, but against even more perfidious enemies within, such as the Albigensians in the south of Spain. It was to combat them that the Inquisition first began to develop, being formally recognized in 1233 B.C. These Albigensians, whose name came from the little town of Albi, didn't believe in a clergy. They believed that God was not so cruel as to send people to everlasting fiery punishment in hell. If you didn't believe in Christianity, the worst that could happen to you was that you'd be reborn and live in the south of France, which is not a bad fate at all. They had to be rooted out, and they were when a savage Crusade—that is what it was called—was launched against these heretics. To extirpate the Albigensians, the Church created a huge bureaucratic instrument, the Inquisition. Those were the priests who went into each town and village, listened to complaints, questioned, and brought people up on trial.

Having created such huge bureaucratic machinery, it must not be allowed to fall into rust. In fact, that is one of the characteristics of a bureaucrat. Once the purpose for which their agency has been created is gone, they must find a new purpose. That purpose was fulfilled to its height in Spain. The Inquisition was formally established there in 1478, and Ferdinand took it under his control. Unlike the Inquisition in other parts of Europe, this Inquisition was not under the immediate control of the Pope, but of Ferdinand himself, of the king. This gave him an instrument to impose absolute religious, and thus intellectual, conformity over all of Spain. In 1492, the Moors were driven from Spain. Perhaps as many as 200,000 intelligent, industrious people, who would have been perfectly willing to be loyal subjects of Ferdinand, were expelled. That was he price that the Church exacted from the willing Ferdinand in order o support him in his vast plans.

Then the Inquisition began to pose other questions. Are there not many people who have converted from Islam to Christianity? What about another group of infidels among us, playing an important role in the intellectual and commercial life of Spain, the Jews? The Jews were then expelled. But the question also remained, are there not many Jewish people who converted, and are thus living as Spaniards, whom we did not expel? Are they really true Christians? The Inquisition began its work in Spain. Picture yourself in a small town in Spain. Your family was of Moorish descent at one time—the same way that later on in Germany, good Germans who had fought in the trenches of World War I and won the Iron Cross, whose grandparents perhaps had converted from Judaism, were not only suspect, but carried off to the camps just for being who they were.

Without any crime being against you, one day the Inquisition arrived. The Inquisition, all dressed in black, looked very much like a medieval form of the Gestapo. They came into a town, and they gave everyone a 30-day grace period to recant, to say yes, I am a heretic. Yes, I am still a practicing Jew, but I now will become a Christian. Even to admit that, then, was to incur further suspicion, so you just kept silent. All your good neighbors were there; they were not going to say anything against you. At the end of that 30-day period, you were simply pulled out of your house the same way, in the 1930s, a rap on the door would take a father away from his home. You were brought into the Inquisition. Let us say it's about the year 1518, when Cortes was carrying out his great expedition against Mexico, and the Spanish Empire was spreading over the whole world by the will of God.

There sat before you a tribunal, and their faces were shrouded; you really couldn't see much about them. The word came out to you—we understand that you still practice Jewish rites. No, I am not a practicing Jew; I'm a Christian. We have three statements by witnesses that you will not eat pork. I just don't like pork. Who are these people? We cannot tell you that. The rules for the Inquisition were very carefully laid out. You could demand to be allowed to ask who your enemies were. But I would certainly not like, under the pressure of a tribunal, knowing what the fate was, to try to think of everybody who was an enemy of mine. That would have been hard.

You name three or four, but there were a lot of people you thought were your friends, and they were the ones who have most denounced you. Maybe you had a little piece of property they hoped to gain. Maybe they were just envious of your success and good luck.

At any rate, you stood accused of being a Jew. The most basic means of interrogation was torture; again, just as in the Third Reich or in the old Soviet Union. In fact, the Inquisition worked under Roman law, which meant evidence extracted by torture was more valid than evidence voluntarily given. There were two ways of looking at this. If somebody was torturing you, you could tell the truth to make them stop. That was a perfectly valid way of looking at it. Another valid way was saying that if they were torturing you, you would say anything they wanted to make it stop. Roman law said torture was the best way, so you were being tortured. The tortures were very imaginative indeed; particularly the one where they tied you up by your hands and let you drop until your bones felt as though they were breaking. Or you were put on the rack and twisted until the joints came apart. Are you not really Jewish? Do you not practice Judaism? Yes, you finally said. I am so glad you have come clean, my son or my daughter. Now you will be burned alive in the public square.

The citizens were required to attend these acts of faith, as they were called, to watch the heretic, the Moor, the Jewish person or just someone who believed a little bit differently about the Church. Maybe they had said once, just to you, thinking you were a friend, isn't it amazing that Jesus said selling all you have and giving it to the poor is the way to gain heaven, and our church acts just the opposite—look at those gold ceilings. That's enough. You have, under torture, admitted your heresy. There you were at the stake. The inquisitor came out to lay the flames in front of you, and he gave you a final chance to recant. You said I am a good Christian. I accept all the Church says. That is good, my son. Now you will be burned still at the stake—you have to be—but you will go to heaven. That was how the Inquisition flourished all over Spain, bringing its mechanism, its vehicle for despotism, to the New World. It was a force of control, a force to shape the will of humans. Secretive, relentless, with all the power of the state behind it, this Inquisition and the totalitarian despotism of Ferdinand were the legacy of the Spanish Empire to Latin America.

The Spanish Empire was a superpower. The heir of Ferdinand and Isabella, King Charles, the emperor of the Holy Roman Empire, of that vast political array of some 365 political units, including Belgium and Austria, was also king of Spain, ruling from 1520 until he just wore himself out finally and abdicated in 1556, ruled over this more than half the world, the domains in Spain, the New World and the whole Holy Roman Empire. Then Philip II, who from a tiny little study in the great palace he built north of Madrid, El Escorial—shaped like a gridiron because his patron saint was Lawrence, the martyr who had been roasted alive by the Romans during the persecutions—when he looked up at the Roman tormentors, and they asked him how he was doing, gleefully smiled, he smiled up at them with just a lovely heavenly look and said I think I'm done on this one side, turn me over to the other. That was the patron saint of Philip.

He brought all of that same grand determination not only to continue to spread the word of God in the New World, but also to conquer Protestantism. In 1588, he launched his armada, the most Catholic armada, against Britain, and it collapsed utterly. The decline of Spain would continue on through the 17th century, but it retained its colonial empire. A legacy of Latin America today is not only the Inquisition and the totalitarianism of Spain, but it was also the brutality of the Native American empires in Latin America. The Aztec Empire that Cortes conquered in his heroic expedition of 1518 to 1519 was one of the most brutal empires in history. It was the heir of empires like the Maya Empire, and it rested upon a centralized power, a belief in a god-king, a priesthood, and human sacrifice. It ruled as much by terror in Mexico as Ferdinand and Isabella had ruled by terror in the Spain of their day.

We ask tell ourselves it is not only in the Middle East that freedom has been so very hard to plant, but it has also been in Latin America. Whenever I am told that all you have to do is to begin freedom is establish a democratic government, and people will want freedom—that in fact the very propinquity of freedom, having it in the neighborhood, in the region, will serve as a beacon to everyone else in the region—and freedom will thus flourish, I ask well, what about Latin America? You see, propinquity is that the Latin Americans—this industrious, intelligent, vital set of nations—has had for a very long time the model of the United States, and yet freedom has never flourished in Latin America.

They, too, went through their revolutions, very much inspired by our own revolution, and the first part of the 19th century saw the overthrow of the Spanish Colonial Empire throughout most of Latin America. Republics arose. Brave and heroic soldiers like Simon Bolivar and Bernardo Higgins led armies to victory, and new governments were founded upon liberal principles and upon liberal constitutions. Yet the history of Latin America has been all too often the tragic story of dictator after dictator after dictator. George Washington stepped down after eight years. The great dictators of Latin America did not follow that example. Their countries needed them too much. Our Constitution of 1787 still gives us liberty under law today. How many Latin American constitutions can we name that are 200 years old?

Instead, a country like Mexico, with an industrious, intelligent, hardworking population, a great tradition of Native American culture—one of the places where the first university in the New World was founded—within the first about ten years of its independence from Spain, would have some nine governments. It would have an emperor, and it would have a tin-pot dictator of the first order named Santa Anna, and be shorn of one of its wealthiest provinces, the great land of Texas. So ponder the legacy of the Latin Americans from Spain as we ponder the legacy of the Ottomans to the Middle East.

Lecture Twenty-One
Napoleon's Liberal Empire

Scope:

Napoleon saw himself as a combination of Alexander the Great and Julius Caesar. Napoleon arose out of the democratic excesses of the French Revolution. His career illustrated for contemporaries the classical view that tyranny is the end result of radical democracy. These same contemporaries regarded Napoleon as a multifaceted genius. He sought to transform Europe into his vision of a liberal, enlightened successor of the Roman Empire under himself as the new Caesar and benevolent despot. He failed. His career attests to the enduring lesson of *hybris*, that outrageous arrogance that leads tyrants to cause their own downfall. But Napoleon also illustrates the danger of preemptive wars in the name of liberal and democratic ideals.

Outline

I. The wisdom of history includes the lessons of empire. We have examined empires of faith, that is, empires motivated by strong religious views. Now we turn to four empires—France, Britain, Russia, and China—focused on religion in a larger sense, a comprehensive worldview. We start with the Napoleonic Empire of France.

II. In June of 1812, a Grand Army of 600,000 men, the largest army ever mustered on European soil, crossed the frontier into Russia. It was led by the military genius and emperor Napoleon Bonaparte, age 43.

   A. Napoleon's army was a wonder to behold, with massive artillery, cavalry, and infantry. Riding alongside him were troops from Poland, Prussia, and Austria. What had brought Napoleon to attempt the conquest of Russia? He would say destiny; others would say opportunism.

   B. Born in 1769 in Corsica, then part of France, Napoleon was educated at French military academies. He had some trouble with authority as a schoolboy but performed well, particularly in mathematics.

C. After graduation, he was commissioned as an officer in the artillery. He was just 20 years old when the French Revolution began in May 1789. France overthrew its feudal past and proclaimed a universal declaration of the rights of man.

   1. In this new democracy, man is born free and must remain free. All are equal under the law. Citizens can live as they choose as long as they don't harm others, and the majority decides the law.

   2. Liberty, equality, and fraternity were the messages of the French Revolution.

III. In seeking to export their ideas, the French revolutionaries became embroiled in wars with their neighbors and in their own internal struggles. Civil war in France led to the Reign of Terror and the deaths of some 40,000 aristocrats and other "enemies of the state." By 1799, the French wanted order, and that was Napoleon's duty.

   A. Napoleon dreamed of being a new Alexander the Great. He left his army in Egypt and returned to France in 1799 to become the first consul of the French republic. Within five years, he had transformed France into an empire and was crowned by the pope himself; like Charlemagne, Napoleon reached out to take the crown and put it on his own head.

   B. Napoleon embodied the values of the French Revolution, casting away the constraints of the past. Everything that was old and feudal, including Christianity, had to go.

   C. John Adams correctly predicted that the French Revolution would end in tyranny. Napoleon was a tyrant by ancient definitions—he rose to power by nonconstitutional means, but like the dictators of the 20th century, he was fond of plebiscites.

   1. The title he assumed could be traced back to Julius Caesar. When his soldiers marched into battle, they carried standards bearing eagles, as the Romans had.

   2. Like Julius Caesar, Napoleon saw Europe as one great empire, all equal under his rule. He codified the law of France, just as the Roman emperor Justinian had codified the law of Rome.

V. Napoleon's goal of bringing liberal ideas to Europe led him to march into Russia in 1812, but he was distracted by his failure to control Britain, with which he was almost constantly at war.

A. To bring Britain to its knees, Napoleon created the Continental System, an economic union in which the nations of his empire were forbidden to trade with Britain and, instead, were to develop their own industries.

B. Napoleon's empire stretched from Spain and Portugal to France, Belgium, Holland, Switzerland, and Italy. Much of Germany was either part of his confederation directly or, like Austria and Prussia, allied with him. The only place in Europe where his power did not reach in 1809 was the Balkans.

C. In 1810, the Russian czar declared that he would no longer refuse to trade with Britain. As Napoleon's economic sanctions against Britain began to fail, he decided to invade Russia.

V. Another problem for Napoleon was Spain, whose Bourbon monarchy was one of the most corrupt in Europe. Intrigue was rife, Spain's economy and empire were in shambles. The tentacles of the Catholic Church stretched everywhere.

A. Napoleon came to Spain to liberate its peasants from the shackles of despotism and religion. In 1808, he tricked the Spanish king and his heir to abdicate and put his brother on the throne.

B. Napoleon thought the Spaniards would welcome his takeover, but they fought him determinedly. The Spanish army proved surprisingly resilient. The British saw their chance and sent an army under a general, the future duke of Wellington.

C. From 1808 to 1812, Napoleon fought down multiple insurgencies in Spain, with growing atrocities on both sides, captured in the paintings of Goya. In 1812, Napoleon put this war aside to invade Russia.

VI. Napoleon was a student of history, especially military history. He learned a great deal from Julius Caesar about battlefield command, but he was an innovator, as well.

A. Napoleon did not encumber his marches with large wagon trains carrying food; his army lived off the land.

B. Napoleon was an innovator in the use of artillery. His preferred strategy was to bunch artillery in massive quantities, bombard the enemy, and have his infantry rush the enemy line. Then his cavalry would sweep through the hole and roll up the enemy's lines.

C. So dynamic was Napoleon as a military innovator that his books were among the standard textbooks at West Point. U.S. Civil War generals, such as Robert E. Lee, admired Napoleon and tried to follow his tactics.

VII. Diplomat, strategist, and bearer of liberal ideas of the French Revolution, Napoleon marched into Russia. He should have learned from the lessons of history.

A. About a century earlier, King Charles XII of Sweden had led a Swedish army into Russia and met a devastating defeat. His army froze in Russia, and Charles fled to the Turks.

B. In ancient Greece, Herodotus told the story of Darius marching into Russia to conquer the Scythians, who withdrew and led him farther and farther into Russia until his army perished in the cold steppes.

C. But Napoleon saw himself as a man of destiny, a "world historical figure" who would propel history to a new level.

D. One of Napoleon's masterstrokes of warfare was to always bring the enemy to battle. But the Russians continually withdrew, leading Napoleon's enormous army farther and farther into Russia.

1. The Russians burned their crops as they retreated, leaving little food. They set aflame whole villages. A bloody battle fought near Moscow didn't go the way Napoleon had planned. He won, but the cost in manpower and casualties was terrible.

2. The Russian army withdrew beyond Moscow, and Napoleon entered the city in triumph. Almost immediately, a fire set by the Russians broke out and burned for four days. When it ended, little food remained for the French troops.

E. Czar Alexander had no intention of negotiating with Napoleon, for he knew of his unbounded ambition. This autocrat was also fearful of liberal ideas spreading into Russia.

F. Napoleon began to retreat. The bitter weather had begun, and his soldiers began to freeze and starve. As they made their way back, they were attacked by Cossacks on horseback, the very people Napoleon had thought would welcome him.

   1. The Cossacks preferred the czar's authoritarian rule. Napoleon's men tried to fight, but the Cossacks attacked and galloped away.

   2. The only survivors were scroungers of stolen food. In the midst of this horror, as the weather got worse, Napoleon deserted his army and returned to Paris, drawn in a carriage, wrapped in furs, and drinking Burgundy wine.

   3. Of the 600,000 men Napoleon led into Russia, perhaps 100,000 made their way back to France.

VIII. With this preemptive war against Russia—a war that did not need to be fought—Napoleon had aroused an alliance that included Britain, Prussia, Russia, and Austria against him. He also began to lose something of his military genius. By the time he fought the Battle of the Nations in 1813 near Leipzig, the whole of Europe was arrayed against him.

A. Defeated in battle, Napoleon quit and accepted exile on the island of Elba, close to his native Corsica. The old line of French kings was restored to the throne. The revolution seemed officially at an end.

B. On March 1, 1815, Napoleon escaped Elba and landed in France. The troops sent by the king to suppress him instead embraced him, for he was their emperor. The French loved him.

C. He lasted only 100 days, defeated by the British and the Prussians at the Battle of Waterloo on June 28, 1815. Once again, he abdicated and, this time, was exiled to St. Helena, a dismal island in the South Atlantic from which escape was impossible. He died there in 1821.

D. Why did Napoleon fail? An ancient Greek would blame his outrageous arrogance (*hybris*)—above all, his decision to invade Russia. Instead of arousing a universal love of liberty in Europe, Napoleon aroused a universal loathing of France and spurred the fires of nationalism.

Essential Reading:

England, *Napoleon*.

Palmer, *Age of Democratic Revolutions*.

Supplementary Reading:

Segue, *Napoleon's Russian Campaign*.

Rose, *Life of Napoleon I*.

Questions to Consider:

1. Why do you think the Russians, with bad governments, nonetheless fought so savagely against both Napoleon and Hitler?

2. Napoleon saw himself as the embodiment of all that is best in benevolent autocracy. Do you agree?

Lecture Twenty-One—Transcript
Napoleon's Liberal Empire

We continue to explore the wisdom of history with a focus on the lessons of empire. In our last four lectures we examined what we might call empires of faith, that is, empires that were motivated by a strong religious view. We looked at Christianity and Islam, how they arose within the framework of the Roman Empire; and then at the Ottoman Empire, and at the empire of Spain, the legacy of the Ottoman Empire, which was an empire that arose as a means of spreading the faith. The early Ottoman sultans took pride in the name of being a *ghazi*, a warrior for the faith, determined to rid the world of the infidels; and the empire of Spain that arose out of the crusade against Islam in the Spanish Peninsula, and the legacy of both these empires to the Middle East and to Latin America.

Now we turn to four more empires, which also were based upon faith, if we are willing to take a larger view of what we mean by religion—not focused on God, but focused on a world view. That is how I define a religion. It is a means for providing a comprehensive world view. So we look now at the empires of France, of Britain, of Russia and China, and their lessons for us today. To do this, let us be taken away from where we are right now, and go back to June 22, 1812. We are crossing the frontier into Russia, marching with the Grand Army, some 600,000 men, a true European coalition led by the military genius and emperor, Napoleon. He is still in his early 40s, 43 years of age, and he is leading the largest army ever mustered on the continent of Europe.

Picture that display. It's the early 19th century, the golden age of uniforms—Hussars in bright green jackets with their cloaks flung casually over their shoulders, their high hats with plumes on top, their tight breeches and high jackboots; the French troops splendid in their blue uniforms; and in the center of all of this, Napoleon himself, a master of war, and truly at home when he is in the saddle, the man on horseback. The peasants come out to watch this glorious display of awe and splendor, the massive artillery of Napoleon, the cavalry, the infantry. Riding alongside him are troops from Poland. In fact, some 90,000 Poles will march with Napoleon, for he has restored their country. The Grand Duchy of Warsaw is one of his creations to spread the ideals of liberty, equality and fraternity all across Europe, and then all across the world.

Why, forces from Prussia march alongside, as do the troops of Austria, the troops of his father-in-law, the emperor of Austria, for he has now married into the highest nobility of Europe. His wife of some three years, 21 years of age now, is the daughter of the emperor of Austria. He refers solemnly to his *père*, his father, the emperor. What has brought him to this task, the conquest of Russia? He would say that he was a man of destiny. He follows his star. Others see him as an opportunist, but he has made the best of his opportunity. He was barely 20 years of age when the French Revolution broke out in 1789. He was born in Corsica, which was part of France when he was born, but as Hitler and Stalin, people like to point out that he wasn't really a Frenchman. Well, he had a certain degree of Corsican nationalism, and for awhile Corsica had dreamed, under its great patriot, Paoli, of becoming independent.

Napoleon was thoroughly French. He had been educated in the French military academies. As did Hitler and Stalin, he had a little bit of trouble with authority as a schoolboy, but he performed well, particularly in mathematics where he won prizes, and when he graduated from the military academy, he was commissioned as an officer in the artillery. He was also a good dancer, and dancing was part of their military training. He was 20 years of age when the revolution broke out, those glorious days in May of 1789 when in one fell swoop, France sought to overthrow all the shackles of its feudal past, and gave to the world a universal declaration of the rights of man—that man is, in all places and in all times, born and must remain free and equal; that all are equal under the law; that you can live as you choose as long as you harm no one else. That is the definition of freedom, but it is the majority who decides when you break the law and harm others; so it is democratic, it is egalitarian, and it is free. Liberty, equality and fraternity—these were the messages of the French Revolution.

The revolution sought to export its ideas, and almost from the beginning the revolution found itself embroiled in wars with its neighbors, such as the Prussians, and it found itself embroiled in its own internal struggles—civil war within France, and ultimately by 1793, from July of 1793 to July of 1794, a terror in which the revolution turned in upon itself, and one became suspected of counterrevolutionary activities. In this age of democracy everybody was a citizen and aristocrats somehow stood outside that fold. So people were put to death just for who they were, for being aristocrats. Now by the standards of the 20th century, it was a small affair, but some 40,000 Frenchmen were put to death under the Terror, including the instigator of it, Robespierre. By 1799, it became clear that the French wanted, above all, order, and that was Napoleon's duty.

He was already something of a schemer. He had led the army of France to Egypt, and he would continually dream of an empire in the east where he could be a new Alexander the Great. Alexander was one of his models, Julius Caesar the other. But being frustrated by the British, he left his army, as he would do again, and came back to France in 1799. A new government was established with Napoleon bearing the proud Roman title of consul, first consul of the French republic. Within five years, he had transformed it into an empire and was crowned on December 2 by the Pope himself, and like Charlemagne before him, reached out to take the crown from the Pope and put it on his own head.

He was in his own eyes, and the eyes of many who have studied him, the embodiment of the values of the French Revolution. He was its culmination. John Adams, with the wisdom of history behind him, said when the French Revolution began, it would end with a tyrant. The French, he said, were like drunken sailors on a spree, and they were riding their horse so hard they would fall off of it. The French had cast away all real constraints of the past. They wanted to change the calendar. They wanted to change the way that years were dated. Christianity was under terrible attack; monasteries were seized and clerics were under severe pressure. Everything that was old and feudal was to go, and it was a new age. John Adams said, "If you abolish the lessons of the past, you will fail."

Napoleon was a tyrant by ancient definitions, that is to say, he rose to power by non-constitutional means, but like the dictators of the 20th century, he was very fond of plebiscites. About 99% of French voters in a plebiscite were said to have approved of his assumption of the imperial title. It was an emperor who looked back to Rome, and the very title that he took, emperor, went back to Julius Caesar. His soldiers, when they marched into battle, carried eagles as the Romans had. The very name, legionnaire, was a statement of his devotion to the idea of Rome. Like Julius Caesar, he saw all of Europe as one huge empire, all equal under the rule of Napoleon. He codified the law of France, just as Justinian, the Roman emperor, had codified the law of Rome, and everyone was equal before that law, just as they had been in Rome.

Moreover, there was equality of opportunity, and it was his proud boast that every private carried a marshal's baton in his knapsack. He was served by administrators and generals who rose from some of the lowest ranks of society. It was an empire that rested upon commerce, and he found many of his most devoted admirers among the businessmen of the day. He professed liberal ideas. It brought those liberal ideas to Europe that led him on this march into Russia. He had some distractions as he marched in 1812. The most enduring distraction was Britain. He simply could not understand why he could not bring Britain to its knees. However, as Churchill would later say, that storm-tossed line of battered ships alone stood between Britain and the continental despot and his goal of absolute rule.

He had been almost constantly at war with Britain during his time as emperor. The British, they were so old-fashioned. Why, the French Revolution was far more liberal. France had universal male suffrage, not so in Britain. In fact, Britain was a fairly closed aristocracy, and they were, Napoleon said, a nation of shopkeepers. All they really cared about was business. They were his distraction, and it was to bring Britain to its knees that Napoleon had created a new economic union for Europe, a union which he called his Continental System, in which everyone within his empire—and it was a vast empire—was forbidden to trade with Britain and was instead to develop its own industries.

His empire stretched from Spain and Portugal, through France, Belgium, and Holland. Switzerland was the Helvetian Republic. The Italians were particularly enthusiastic about the institutions of liberty that Napoleon had brought to the Italian Peninsula. Much of Germany was either part of his confederation directly, or was with Austria and Prussia, which were allied to him. The only place in Europe where his power did not reach in 1809, when he married the daughter of the Austrian emperor, was down into the Balkans, the land of the Turks, but by 1812, Russia had left this Continental System, and the czar, in 1810, declared that he would no longer refuse to trade with Britain.

Napoleon had economic sanctions, and as these economic sanctions began to fail against Britain, he decided upon a preemptive war, and that was the invasion of Russia. But he had another distraction, and this was even more puzzling because Britain's policy since the 16th century, its foreign policy, was based upon maintaining a balance in Europe, a balance of powers, and they would certainly stand up to Napoleon. But Spain, that was the curious matter. He had come to Spain bringing them the most liberal ideas, and he would certainly be welcomed as a liberator. Spain had one of the most corrupt monarchies in all of Europe, the Bourbon monarchy of the Spaniards. Intrigue was rife. It was an economic basket case. Its empire was in shambles, and the ordinary Spanish peasant was one of the most oppressed people in Europe. The Catholic Church stretched everywhere its tentacles everywhere. Its drain upon the economy of Spain was enormous—the large numbers of monks, the monasteries.

He came to Spain to liberate the Spanish from the shackles of despotism and religion. Instead, in 1808 when he had made, by his means, the most reasonable of choices and put his brother upon the throne of Spain, by tricking the Spanish king and his heir to abdicate, it should have been absolutely clear that the Spaniards would welcome this, but they didn't. They fought him tooth and nail. The Spanish army proved surprisingly resilient. The Spanish peasants died in insurgency after insurgency against Napoleon. Of course, those British—they saw their chance, and they sent an army under a general who would one day rival Napoleon in the field of battle, the man who would become the Duke of Wellington, and the British hung on there in Spain.

But once he had started, Napoleon had to stay the course in Spain, so from 1808 to 1812, he had fought down insurgency after insurgency with growing atrocities on both sides. Yes, he brought liberal ideas, but if the Spaniards were going to fight him, he would have to put down their insurgencies. The paintings of Goya would capture the brutality of this civil war that broke out in Spain—for example, the one of the shootings in May of the Spanish peasant, with his arms held out like a crucified Jesus, a crucified Spain, and the men of Napoleon, his legionnaires, standing anonymously in their rows, shooting down those patriots. In 1812, this war still dragged on, but he put that aside, and you would have put it aside too if you had seen the splendor of this army marching into Russia.

Napoleon was a student of history. In fact, he's one of the best commentators ever on Julius Caesar. Unlike modern scholars, Napoleon actually knew what it was to lead an army into battle, and he learned a great deal from Caesar about battlefield command, but he was an innovator as well. His army traveled on its stomach, literally; that is to say he did not believe in large wagon trains carrying food. His army lived off the land. He was an innovator in the use of artillery, and as a former officer of artillery, he understood its uses in modern war. He liked to bunch his artillery in massive quantities, carry out a bombardment of the enemy, then with his infantry, rush into the enemy line and punch through. Then his cavalry would sweep through the hole and roll up the enemy's lines. It had happened again and again in glowing victories such as Austerlitz.

In fact, so dynamic was Napoleon as a military innovator that his books are still the standard textbooks—books about the Napoleonic campaigns—at West Point. When you talk about the terrible frontal assaults in the Civil War, it was because all of these generals wanted to be a new Napoleon. In fact, one of the few books that we know Robert E. Lee checked out of the Academy library, when he was commandant of West Point, was the four-volume *Campaigns of Napoleon*. At Gettysburg, he tried to carry out a new Napoleonic victory. Men who understood war admired Napoleon.

Diplomat, then, strategist, bearer of the liberal ideas of the French Revolution, he marched into Russia. However, had he been a little wiser in his study of history, he would have reflected more seriously on King Charles of Sweden, Charles IX who, just about a century earlier, had led a Swedish army that had been invincible into Russia and which met a devastating defeat. His army froze in Russia, and then King Charles fled ignominiously to the Turks. Or even going back to the Greeks that Napoleon admired so much, Herodotus told the story of Darius marching into Russia to conquer the Scythians and of the Scythians who simply withdrew—withdrew and lead him farther and farther into Russia until his army perished in the cold of the steppes.

But they were not men of destiny, were they? He was a man of destiny. The term "world historical figure" was invented for Napoleon. In fact, the philosopher Hegel, having seen Napoleon after the great victory over the Prussian army at Jena, said, "I have seen the Weltgeist," the spirit that drives the history of the world on horseback. He was that man who would propel history, the whole world, to a new level. "As long as my star is in the ascent," he said, "nothing can stop me; and when my destiny is over, an atom will suffice to shatter me." As he might have suspected from history, the Russian army refused to fight him. It was, again, one of his masterstrokes of warfare always to be able to bring the enemy to battle. That is what Julius Caesar could do so well—make the enemy fight the battle on your ground. But no, the Russians just withdrew and withdrew and withdrew, and he went farther and farther into Russia with this enormous army—again, living off the land.

This became more difficult because the Russians burned their crops as they retreated. Whole villages were put to the flame by the Russians as they withdrew. His army was already on scant rations, and the Russian army suddenly turned at Borodino on the River Moscow, not too far from Moscow itself, and an enormous bloody battle was fought. It didn't go the way Napoleon wanted it to. His artillery was scattered instead of bunched up, and he always tried to concentrate his maximum force at the enemy's weak point. It didn't work out that way either. He won, but the cost in manpower and casualties was terrible, and the Russian army simply withdrew beyond Moscow. So he entered the city of Moscow in triumph, and almost immediately fire broke out, certainly set by the Russians themselves. For four day the city of Moscow burned. When the fire had come to an end, Napoleon was stuck in a burned-out city with little food for his troops.

He had already written Czar Alexander asking to negotiate, but Alexander had no intention whatsoever of negotiating. He had negotiated with Napoleon before, and he knew the ambition of Napoleon was unbounded and Napoleon would never keep his word. But beyond that, Alexander was already fearful of those liberal ideas that were spreading into Russia, for he was autocrat of all the Russians. So he simply refused to negotiate, and Napoleon was faced with, what do I do? The Russians won't fight me again. I've captured Moscow. He turned and began to retreat, and the bitter weather began on October 19. By November, it was terrifying. The cold, along with the bravery of the Russian soldier and the size of that vast land, have always been its best allies. His soldiers began to freeze and to starve.

As they made their way back, slipping and sliding in the falling snow, they were attacked on either side by hard-riding Cossacks. They were the very people who Napoleon thought would welcome his liberal ideas, but no, they liked the czar; they liked the authoritarian rule of the czar. They darted in and cut and slashed. Napoleon's men tried to form and fight them, but they galloped away. The very peasants that Napoleon had come to liberate from the tyranny of the czar, from the backward religion of Russia, mutilated the soldiers that were left behind. So, there they were, marching along, nothing to eat for two or three days. They knew if they fell behind, the peasants would come out and torture them to death, or the wolves would feast upon them as they lay there starving.

So their very existence would depend on maybe five or six potatoes that they stole, so each one kept them for himself. Yes, there's your comrade lying beside you, and that comrade lying beside you and you can barely sleep because of his moaning from the agonies of hunger. But you eat that one potato quietly, and then you have one for the next day, and one for the next day, and so you go. It was these men, the scroungers, who would come back from Moscow. In the midst of all this horror, as the weather grew worse, Napoleon deserted his army. How historians can admire Napoleon, who deserted his army, baffles me. Can you picture George Washington at Valley Forge deserting his army? Can you picture Robert E. Lee deserting his army as they staggered along from the retreat out of Petersburg? No.

But Napoleon abandoned his army and rushed back in record time to Paris, drawn in a carriage, like a sled, and very warm, wrapped up in all kinds of heavy furs, and drinking Burgundy wine—that was always his favorite—Burgundy and mutton and chicken; he found the beef in Russia that they gave him a little too tough, so mutton and chicken—and they would always ask of the emperor at each meal, would you like rice, *Monsieur l'Empereur*, or would you like beans tonight? So he made his way back to Paris, but of those 600,000 men that he led into Russia, maybe 100,000 ever made their way back. They died in rivers, they were destroyed by the ever-more vigorous

Russian army, or were killed by the peasants, or just fell by the wayside, never to rise again.

Now Napoleon, with his preemptive war against Russia—a war that did not need to have been fought—aroused a whole alliance against him. Prussia and Austria, even his father-in-law broke with him, and Britain then became the head of an alliance of Russia, Prussia and Austria to grind him into the dirt. He also began to lose something of his military genius. He once said, "Never entrust command to someone over 40," and he was already 43 when he led his army to that disaster in Russia. By the time he fought the Battle of the Nations in 1813 near Leipzig, the whole of Europe was truly arrayed against him. The tactics that had done so well in the past failed him again. He was defeated, and he abdicated. He quit. He just quit and agreed to accept exile on the little island of Elba. The old line of the French kings was restored to the throne of France. In a way, the revolution seemed officially at an end. All those ideals that he had proclaimed, he didn't think were worth fighting for.

He was exiled to Elba. It was almost as though the allies who exiled him there were taunting him because it was too close to Europe, too close to Italy, not far from his native Corsica. On March 1, he escaped—March 1, 1815—and landed in France. The emperor was back. The troops that were sent by the king to suppress him melted away and went over to his side, embraced him, for he was their emperor, a little older now, a little fatter. Yes, he liked meat. He was a large meat eater, and he was quite corpulent, as a matter of fact. He was even more corpulent now, and they rushed and hugged him and embraced him, and Paris fell at his feet, for he was back, and the French loved him.

Well, he lasted 100 days. The allies were not going to give up. Under the Duke of Wellington at the Battle of Waterloo on June 28, 1815, Napoleon's army gave everything that it could. At the end, his old guard failed to break the British square. Wellington prayed for either darkness to fall to put an end to the battle, or for the Prussians under General Blucher to arrive. The Prussians arrived, and Napoleon's army was defeated. Once again, he abdicated, but now no Elba for him, but St. Helena, a dismal island in the South Atlantic from which escape was impossible. Like an eagle in a cage, the great Napoleon would drag out his last six years there in that dismal place, watched over by a malevolent English governor who put petty restrictions upon the man who had once ruled Europe. The only solace for Napoleon during those days was to dictate his memoirs, to explain to the world what he had really wanted to do, and to drink wine. "It helps me sleep," he would say, but his stomach pains grew worse and worse and he began to suspect that the English governor was poisoning him with little bits of arsenic. He died in 1821.

Why had he failed? Well, a Greek would come back and tell you it was *hybris*; it was outrageous arrogance, and above all, his decision to invade Russia. It was in not knowing his limits, and it was in attempting to impose values upon other nations that they did not want. In fact, all he did was arouse, not a universal love of liberty in Europe, but a universal loathing of the French and spurred the fires of nationalism—along with the sense that their country was unique—which would consume Europe in the 20th century.

Lecture Twenty-Two
The British Empire in India

Scope:

European history from Louis XIV (1638–1715) until Napoleon was dominated by the struggle for empire between France and England. The triumph of Britain and the British Empire of the 19th century left behind a legacy that still shapes our world. The British of the great age of empire believed that they were combining liberty and empire, bringing the benefits of law and civilization to a large part of the world, from Canada to India and Australia. But for many of the subjects of this great empire, Britain simply illustrated the lesson that the lust for power—not the love of freedom—is the motivating force of history. The British experience in India illustrated the lesson of the "imponderables" of history and the power of ideas and religion. Who could have imagined that a frail Indian barrister could—without violence—bring the greatest empire in the world to its knees?

Outline

I. Britain was the heir to France's failure to sustain its empire. The two countries had fought since the 17th century.

   A. The duke of Marlborough, Churchill's ancestor, helped block France's King Louis XIV from becoming the absolute master of Europe.

   B. From 1756 to 1763, France and Britain fought in Europe, India, and North America. In the end, France lost out entirely in India and North America. As a result, we Americans are heirs of the British Empire, not the French.

II. The British, along with the Romans, were the most successful imperialists in history. Their empire reached its height after World War I, stretching over lands so vast that the Sun literally never set on them. Australia, New Zealand, Canada, and the Persian Gulf—all were under the flag and law of the British Empire.

   A. Britain believed that its empire would bring freedom to the world. During World War II, Winston Churchill rallied the

British by telling them that the British Empire would not survive unless Germany was conquered.

B. India was the jewel in the crown of the British Empire, lauded by the writer Rudyard Kipling. The young Churchill went to India as a lieutenant in 1894 and remained, to the end of his days, a firm believer in the linkage of empire and democracy.

C. Oxford scholar Alfred Zimmern was another strong believer in the destiny of empire and democracy. His 1906 book *The Greek Commonwealth* compared the ancient Athenian democracy to the British Empire, with both laboring to bring freedom to the world.

D. A sense of racial superiority pervaded British rule. The British claimed that they could rule a vast land such as India because of their "moral fiber," enhanced by their study of classics. For all their education, though, the colonizers did not understand Indian civilization well. In South Africa, which was also under British control, ruthless racial divisions existed.

III. The man who would be known as Mahatma Gandhi (Mohandas Gandhi) would stare down the greatest empire of its day through the sheer force of his moral authority.

A. Gandhi studied law in London, where he tried to dress and eat like an Englishman. He came to understand that he was different, that India was different. India was his nation, his culture. The seed of independence was planted.

B. Gandhi practiced law in South Africa, where he experienced firsthand the racist side of British society. He was thrown off a train because he insisted on riding in the first-class compartment. From that point on, Gandhi began to fight for the right of Indian workers in South Africa to enjoy what the queen had proclaimed, equal rights for all of her subjects.

IV. By 1911, Gandhi returned to India, at first traveling throughout the country to learn more about it.

A. When World War I started, Gandhi urged Indians to support Britain, believing that Britain would return the favor with self-government. During the war, he realized that this outcome this would never occur. In the 1920s, he began his nonviolent resistance to British rule. He called on Indians to unite as a culture and as a nation.

B. This resistance seemed strange to the British, who were used to political agitators who were more "British." Gandhi dressed in the Indian fashion. He urged Indians to discard British-made cloth and make their own.

C. Gandhi told his followers that they would meet injustice every day, but that they must stand up to it.

D. Gandhi was jailed repeatedly for leading protests against British control. In response, he fasted, in accordance with Hindu tradition. He received enormous attention from the world press.

E. For all the injustice of the British Empire, it did believe in law, and Gandhi was treated with all the equity provided by English law.

V. By the 1930s, the British Empire was dying. The economic and human costs of World War I had left Britain almost bankrupt and strained its ability to run an expanded empire. In addition, many Britons, including politicians, no longer wanted an empire.

A. This feeling was not universal. Among conservatives, the most outspoken opponent of freedom for India or even dominion status—a self-governing unit under the British sovereign—was Churchill. He believed that if Britain left India, civil war would result.

B. During World War II, Britain began to dismantle its empire, aided by the United States. By the end of the war, Britain, in severe financial straits, decided to cut India loose.

C. But India was badly divided between Muslims and Hindus. Part of Gandhi's mission was to make these two groups understand that they both worshiped the same God. He encouraged Muslims to become familiar with the Hindu religion and Hindus to read the Koran. He wanted a united India.

D. India was ultimately split into a Hindu India and a Muslim Pakistan. As Churchill had foreseen, savage sectarian riots broke out. Gandhi traveled from town to town, trying to make peace. When the riots continued, he began to fast.

    E. A Hindu fanatic assassinated Gandhi in January 1948. Gandhi's last word was "Ram!" ("God!"), for he believed that the souls of those who die with the word of God on their lips will go straight to heaven.

    F. Gandhi taught national freedom based on the enduring moral values of India—courage, justice, moderation, and wisdom—values he believed could be found in every society in the world.

VI. The British Empire continued to divest itself of colonies, leaving its legacy around the world.

    A. Its greatest success story is the United States. We have carried the English language throughout the world and have shouldered the burden of the empire in many areas.

    B. India is another success story. The British Empire's legacy is evident in the prevalence of English, the education system, a free-market economy, and a working democracy.

    C. Other areas have been less successful. Many former British colonies in Africa have failed to find liberty under law and have seen terrible suffering. Nor is the Middle East a bastion of democracy.

    D. During World War I, Britain proclaimed that it would support the creation of a Jewish state in Palestine. But during the 1930s, as Jews tried to leave Germany and other parts of Europe to escape the Nazis, the British turned back their ships. In 1948, the United States, not Britain, was the first country to recognize the new state of Israel.

    E. Though the British Empire was flawed in serious ways, it left behind the greatest legacy for good among all the empires of the 19th and early 20th centuries. But it is an instructive example that a democracy cannot, over the long run, rule an empire.

    F. It was only after World War I, when Britain's electoral base began to expand beyond the aristocracy, that the empire began to fade. The more democratic Britain grew, the less imperial it became.

Essential Reading:

Ferguson, *Empire*.

Huxtable, *Empires of the Atlantic World*.

Supplementary Reading:

Brown, *Gandhi*.

Gandhi, *Autobiography*.

Questions to Consider:

1. Taken in the balance, was the British Empire a force for good?

2. Did the rapid dismantling of the British and French colonial empires after World War II reflect the wisdom of history?

Lecture Twenty-Two—Transcript
The British Empire in India

In our last lecture we explored the rise and fall of the empire of Napoleon, and we saw at the end that a Greek would have told us this was one more instance of *hybris*, of the outrageous arrogance. Even looked at from our modern point of view, we must continue to believe that power is certainly the constant in history, not the love of freedom. And, as Lord Acton said, "All power tends to corrupt, and absolute power corrupts absolutely." The Napoleon who marched into Russia is a very good instance of the growth of power, of ever-greater absolutism, and of the fact that a tyrant, for that is what he was—a tyrant with many good ideas, perhaps, but a tyrant—who believed, as Winston Churchill defined a tyrant, "A tyrant is one who believes his own desires and ambitions and pleasures are worth the suffering of millions." That is exactly what Napoleon believed, and he was able to build a consensus with the French people to follow him in this desire.

Napoleon's empire fell because of the mistakes he made—the unnecessary war against Russia, the attempt to impose the liberal values of the French Revolution upon Spain, and his inability to bring Britain to its knees. Perhaps, had he negotiated with Britain—perhaps, had he given Britain its desire for more free trade—history would have been different. I frequently ponder what would have happened if the French had been as successful as empire builders as the British. Britain was the real heir to the French failure to build an empire. Britain had fought against France since the 17th century.

Churchill's ancestor, the Duke of Marlborough, had followed the lead of a collation of powers to block Louis XIV from becoming absolute master of Europe. From 1756 to 1763, France and Britain had fought, literally, a world war in Europe, in India and in North America. At the end, by 1763, France had lost out entirely in North America and had lost out entirely in India, but had the French been more successful, we might be giving these lectures in French. The Code of Napoleon might be the law all through our country. We might have perhaps a better sense of good taste in food than we do, good taste in wine, perhaps live life a little more casually than we do. But we are not; we are the heirs of the British Empire. The British were the most successful imperial people, along with the Romans.

To understand the British Empire and its legacy to us, let us go to the spring of 1930. We are not in Britain; we are in India, and we are making our way, with an ever-growing crowd of Indians, with a huge number of journalists from all over the world, to the sea, where we're going to boil sea water to make salt. The leader of this crowd of people is a frail, 61-year-old lawyer; the man who would be known to history as Mahatma Gandhi—Mohandas Gandhi or Mahatma Gandhi, the great-souled one. He's so tiny and frail, draped in traditional Indian garb with only a walking stick and sandals. And yet he tells the young men beside him, I can walk any one of you into the ground, so he does. He can also stare down the greatest empire of its day. This man, Gandhi, through the sheer force of his moral authority, will bring down the British Empire in India.

Let's picture Britain, the empire, at its height. Indeed, it was at its height after World War I in terms of the amount of territory it covered. It stretched in those days over lands so far flung that the sun never set, literally, on the British Empire. Whether you were in Australia or New Zealand, whether you were in the forest of Saskatchewan, or in the blue Pacific, or in the Persian Gulf, you were under the flag and law of the British Empire. How large is the island of Britain? It is about the size of the state of Colorado, and yet that small nation ruled that vast empire. It believed it ruled that vast empire with law and freedom, and that the British Empire was bringing freedom to the world, so that in the most critical time of World War II, Winston Churchill would rally the British people by telling them that unless they conquered the Germans, without victory, there would be no survival for the British Empire and all that empire stood for. It stood, in Churchill's view, for all the good things that freedom brings—the British Empire, of which India was the jewel in the crown.

The Britons were a proud, imperial people, but one also conscious of history and destiny. The poet of empire was Rudyard Kipling. Much admired in his own day, he fell out of favor during much of the 20th century. He's come back in favor a bit more now as people find, in the words of the modern literary critics, texture and nuance in Kipling. But he sang in *Recessional* of the British Empire:

> God of our fathers known of old—lord of our far-flung battle line, beneath whose awful hand we hold dominion over palm and pine—Lord God of hosts, be with us yet, lest we

forget—lest we forget!…Far-called, our navies melt away; on dune and headland sinks the fire. Lo, all our pomp of yesterday is one with Nineveh and Tyre! Judge of the Nations, spare us yet, lest we forget—lest we forget!

So he sang of the British Empire, calling the Britons to understand that one day their empire would to, pass away. But that seemed a distant day in the 1890s and 1900, a distant time when the young Winston Churchill went out to India as a lieutenant in 1894. Churchill would remain, to the end of his days, a firm believer in the linkage of empire and democracy.

Another strong believer in the destiny of empire and democracy was Alfred Zimmern. He was a scholar at Oxford, but he went on to play a major role in the League of Nations. In 1906, he published a book on the Athenian commonwealth, *The Greek Commonwealth*, in which he clearly compared the Athenian democracy, as an empire, to the British Empire. He talked about the Athenians laboring in pursuit of bringing freedom to the entire world. James Bryce, who would write one of the most insightful books on the Athenian democracy, held a chair in law at Oxford. He would write a parallel between the Roman Empire and the British Empire, both of which, he said, had as their task to rule a large portion of the world under freedom and under law.

The 19th century was an age of racial feelings with a sense of racial superiority. Along with their belief in the freedom that they were bringing to the people of the empire, the British also had a very keen sense of their superiority. Indeed, they used to say that a small number of British can rule over a vast land like India because of their moral fiber. That moral fiber was enhanced by their study of the classics. There has never been a better educated, classically trained group of administrators than the British who ruled this empire. That's what they studied at Oxford and at Cambridge. Even their civil service examinations presumed that they had understood the lessons of Greece and Rome, could even write Latin poetry or Greek poetry.

They came out to India to govern it with very little understanding of the Indians and very little sense of the special qualities, the uniqueness, of Indian civilization. But the British were capable of learning, and Alfred Zimmern, the same scholar and administrator who wrote *The Greek Commonwealth*, pointed out that there were stages in the growth of the British Empire. The first British Empire, he said, came to an end with the American Revolution, and the British learned from the American Revolution. They learned how gradually to expand freedom to their imperial possessions. So by the 1930s, Canada, Australia, New Zealand and South Africa had achieved dominion status. Though you will note all of these were white, in South Africa the most ruthless kind of division of the races existed.

As it did also in India, and it was this exclusion of the Indians from the rights that a white Englishman had that drove Gandhi from being a lawyer to being a foe of the British Empire. He'd first experienced this when he had gone out to South Africa. He had been sent to school in London and studied law, and tried to be an Englishman. He dressed like an Englishman, and in fact, he arrived in Southampton dressed in the white suit that the British always wore in India, with a little pith helmet. He came down, and of course it was the middle of the winter, and everybody laughed at him. He went away immediately to buy a new suit of clothes and went to a tailor who sold him a tuxedo, which he then walked down the street in. He tried eating meat because the Indians believed that it was eating so much red meat that must somehow make the British strong. He said it was as though he had a little baby goat inside him, bleating to get out.

He came to understand already, when he was studying in England, that he was different, that India was different. When he was in a vegetarian restaurant in London, a group of men and women came up to him, English men and women, and they said would you please teach us to read Sanskrit, for we are reading the *Bhagavad-Gita*—we think it is a noble book of religion—but we would like to read it in the original Sanskrit. He said I don't know Sanskrit. We didn't learn that in school; we learned English. Together, they sat down and read it in English, and Gandhi began to understand that yes, the Bible is a great work of literature, but so too is India. India was his nation, his culture. With Gandhi, we see the importance of the idea of national freedom and the idea that you are nationally distinct.

His goal became to understand, first, India. He went to South Africa, where he practiced law for a short time, but even there he experienced first hand that Britain had a very racial society. He was riding on a train just after he'd arrived in South Africa, and he was sitting in the first-class compartment when the conductor came in. The conductor grabbed him and said get out of this first-class compartment. Gandhi said, but I have a ticket to the first-class compartment. He said, colored—that was the word he used; he was trying to be polite—do not ride in the first class. You go to third class. Gandhi said, I have paid for a first-class ticket.—Get out now, or I'll throw you off.

Gandhi refused to move. He said, I am a lawyer, and the conductor said, there are no colored lawyers in South Africa. Gandhi pulled out a piece of paper, which was his commission from the Queen to be a lawyer, and he said, well, since I have this paper showing I'm a lawyer, and which in your words I am colored, there must be at least one colored lawyer in South Africa. He was promptly thrown off the train, and his luggage pitched after him. There he sat, shivering. He began to fight simply for the right of the Indian workers in South Africa to enjoy what the Queen had proclaimed, equal rights for all of her subjects, quality under the law.

By 1911, he had made enough progress that he felt good about going back to India. He spent some time just traveling through India to learn about India. At first, when the Great War came, he urged Indians to at least support the British effort, believing still that the British Empire would bring freedom to India and that if India contributed enough, Britian would reward it with self-government. But in the course of the war, he realized this would never come, and in the 1920s he began his passive resistance to British rule. He did not like the term "passive resistance." It was not passive, but it did not believe in violence. He believed you can be just as strong, indeed stronger, without violence. He believed in calling the Indians back to their unity as a nation and to the unity of their culture.

This all seemed strange to the British because they were used, indeed, to political agitators in India, but they dressed like Britishers and tried to take British ways. Not here, no, no, no. Gandhi dressed in the Indian fashion. Gandhi would take a little spinning wheel, which was both the symbol of the unity of life, and at the same time called the Indians to discard British-made cloth. You produce cotton. You let it go to Britain. They make it into shoddy cotton goods and send it back, and you pay a high price for it. Be independent. I don't hate machines, Gandhi said, but I do hate the tyranny they exercise over human beings. Do you suppose Gandhi today would use a

©2007 The Teaching Company.

computer and have e-mail? I ponder that frequently. I despise the tyranny that they exercise over humans.

Every day, he would say, you will meet injustice today. Stand up to it. Do harm to no one, but let no one do harm to you. So he took his crowds into the salt works because the British had a monopoly on the production of salt. This was against the law, and they threw him in jail, the British did, as they did so many times. Time and time again, he would go on a hunger fast. That was right out of the Hindu tradition. If a man outraged you, treated you wrongly, you would go and sit on his doorstep in your village and begin to fast. Gandhi awakened an enormous interest in the world press. American and British newspaper people followed him all the time, this small, frail little man. The British courts didn't really know what to do with him. Yes, he was breaking the law, but he was so polite in court.

You would have to ask what would have happened to Gandhi in Germany in the 1930s. We would probably not have a lecture on him. Nobody would ever know what happened to him, but not in Britain. For all the injustice of the British Empire, it did believe in law, and Gandhi was treated with all the equality that English law could give out, all the equity that English law could give out. But there was more to the British Empire in India by the 1930s. It was clearly dying. The Great War, while it had expanded the size of the British Empire, had strained its will to be great. The cost of the war in manpower—one million British subjects were killed in this war of 1914 to 1918—the economic cost that left Britain almost bankrupt. As Churchill said, it was a victory that had been bought at a price so large as to be almost indistinguishable from defeat.

But there was even more. The will of Britain to hold this empire together was dwindling. Perhaps the British were right to believe that their empire rested upon the moral fiber, for the Britons no longer wanted empire. Even the Conservative governments began to try to figure out ways to be rid of India, and yet at the same time not outrage the business opinion that was so crucial to their political survival. Of the Conservatives, the most outspoken opponent of freedom for India, or even dominion status—of raising it to the ranks of Canada, for example, as a self-governing, independent unit under the British sovereign and following British foreign policy—was Winston Churchill himself. Until 1947, he was bitterly opposed to India's independence and bitterly opposed to Gandhi himself.

When the viceroy of India invited Gandhi to come to the viceregal palace to discuss and negotiate, Churchill rose in Parliament and said the sight of this half-nude fakir—that's what he called Gandhi, a F-A-K-I-R, fakir, charlatan—striding up the steps of the viceregal palace is enough to disgust any Englishman. He believed that if Britain left India, it would result in civil war on a massive scale, and he also simply believed—dead wrong, of course—that the Indians did not understand freedom. They might one day be educated to it, but they did not understand it still by the 1930s. Then the second Great War came, and Britain once again survived, it began to dismantle its empire, aided in this dismantling by the Americans. Time and time again during the war, Roosevelt would explode when one of Churchill's schemes for an invasion, say of Greece, came before him, "We are not fighting this World War—the Second World War—to make the British Empire bigger. We're not fighting it to enable the British Empire to survive." President Eisenhower would oversee, from 1952 to 1960, with glee, Britain's empire dismantled.

By the end of the Second World War, Britain, in severe financial straits, decided just to cut India loose. The problem was that India was badly divided between Muslims and Hindus. Part of Gandhi's mission had been to make them understand they all worshiped the same God. "Many roads hast thou fashioned; all of them lead to the Light"; that is what Gandhi believed. He tried to encourage Muslims to become familiar with the Hindu religion, and Hindus to read the Koran, so they would understand that there was one God who loved them all, and no religion had a monopoly on the truth. He wanted a united India; that is what he strove for. But he had served his purpose; he had fulfilled his destiny. The British were leaving, and then cleverer politicians began to scheme in India. The final decision was to split India into two nations, one the Hindu India and the other Pakistan. It was a bitter disappointment to Gandhi.

But in London, visited by a group of Indian politicians at the time when India was becoming independent, Winston Churchill was asked by them, what do you think of this? Churchill said simply, "I wish you all the best and I want you, in ten years, to be able to sit down with me and say that the ordinary Indian is better off now than he was when the British were here." As Churchill had foreseen, savage riots broke out, killing on a massive scale between Hindus and Muslims, attempts to change the borders and women and children massacred. Once again, Gandhi went from town to town, city to city, village to village, alone, with his little staff, going into Hindu houses where the riots had been most savage, with Muslim crowds surrounding him saying we're going to kill you, and talking to the Hindus, and saying you must forgive these who have killed in your village. With a little Hindu child without parents, Gandhi would turn to a Muslim and say were you part of the crowd that killed this family? The Muslim would say yes, yes, I did; it was wrong.

Such was the force of Gandhi that he would say yes, yes, I understand that. Then I want you to take this child and rear him in the religion of his parents. When Muslims and Hindus refused to give up these riots, Gandhi again began one of his fasts. Day after day, he refused to eat, and it seemed as though he was going to die this time. But Hindu and Muslim came together, begged him to eat, and said that they would try to put an end to the violence. So he'd take a little bit of bread, a little bit of orange juice. He would finally be assassinated by a fanatic, a Hindu fanatic, in 1948, in January. His last words were "*Ram*!"—God!—for he believed in the *Bhagavad-Gita*, this great work of Hindu religion, that if you die with the word of God upon your lips, your soul will go straight to heaven. He taught national freedom based on the enduring moral values of India, which he believed were indeed courage, and justice, and moderation and wisdom—values he believed you found in every society in the world if you looked for them.

The British Empire continued to dismantle itself, leaving a legacy throughout the world. In some ways, the greatest success story of the British Empire was the United States. We, after all, taught them the lesson of not oppressing too much. We have carried their language to the far corners of the world. We have shouldered the burden of their empire in many parts of the world. But India is another success story. It still has trouble with Pakistan. It has had periods of authoritarian rule, but English is the common language of India. The education system of India is profoundly influenced by the English system. It is a land of science and technology and of a free market economy and has a working democracy. Churchill, I believe, would understand that the ordinary Indian is better off now than they were under British rule, and that is all he had ever wanted.

So Britain had its success stories. There were other areas that have been less successful. Like the French Empire in Africa, the states that were carved out in Africa from the colonial heritage of Britain have failed to find liberty under law in so many cases, and have been the scene of the most terrible kind of suffering. Britain left a legacy in the Middle East that is with us still today. The British Empire, during World War I, had proclaimed in the Balfour document that Britian would support the creation of a Jewish state in Palestine, as long as the rights of the other inhabitants of Palestine were not outraged. One of the strongest supporters of this was Winston Churchill.

But all during the 1930s, as Jewish people tried to leave Germany, or as they tried to leave parts of Europe that they knew would fall under Nazi control unless something was stopped, time and time again their ships were turned back by the British. The British thought that their need for oil was more important than the most basic humanitarian actions. In 1948, it would not be Britain, who simply sought to wash its hands of the whole Palestinian matter, but the United States that would be the very first to recognize Israel. George Marshall told Harry Truman that this would embitter our relations with the Arabs for years to come. But Truman was guided, one, by a deep humanitarian sense; and two, by the Old Testament and his conviction that God had willed a new Zion.

The British Empire showed us an empire that grew into its mission; that became wiser, more just, was flawed in very serious ways, but grew to its mission. Of all the empires of the 19th and early 20th century, it left behind the greatest legacy for good, and yet it is also an instructive example that a democracy cannot, over the long run, rule an empire. I want you to ponder this. The British government that created the empire was one of the most closely controlled aristocracies in history. Right down until 1900, the electoral base in England was very, very small. It had a commercial aristocracy that educated itself for empire. After World War I, when Britain started on the road of a broad electoral base, when the Labor Party became so important in Britain, the empire began to be dismantled. The more democratic Britain became the less imperial it became. So we still ask the question, can a democracy rule an empire?

Lecture Twenty-Three
Russia and Empire

Scope:

In the 20th century in both Russia and China, democratic revolutions would end in savage tyrannies. The wisdom of history teaches us that this is not an accident. It was the predictable result of the historical development of both countries. From its misty origins as a Viking nation until Vladimir Putin, Russia has never known freedom and democracy in the American sense. Russia was shaped by the heritage of Byzantium, Orthodox Christianity, and the Mongol conquest. Political and individual freedom were utterly subordinate to the ideal of a God-chosen absolute ruler, with total power over state and church. Ivan the Terrible, Peter the Great, and Stalin and his Gulag were all testaments to the propensity of mankind to choose despotism over freedom.

Outline

I. In the past two lectures, we've studied empires of faith that provided a comprehensive worldview. For the British and French, the view was that all people want liberty, equality, and democracy. In the next two lectures, we'll explore two more empires of faith: the Russian empire (the Soviet Union) and the Chinese empire of Mao Tse-tung (Mao Zedong). Both were based on Communism as a worldview.

II. The father of Communism is Karl Marx, a German. His *Communist Manifesto* of 1848 called on workers of the world to unite. By the end of his life, he saw completion of *Das Kapital* as his great task.

    A. Marx would not have been surprised if a visitor from the future had told him that millions of people would view his ideas as a revelation of truth, his *Das Kapital* their Bible.

    B. Marx regarded *Das Kapital* as a volume of scientific truth, based on what he saw as indisputable laws of history and economics. Its doctrine is that workers will destroy the capitalism that oppresses them.

1. To Marx, every society reflects its economic system, especially its mode of production. Greece and Rome had slaves and were, thus, slave societies. The Middle Ages had serfs and was a feudal society. The 18th-century mode of production was based on laborers exploited by capitalists.

2. Moved by the world's suffering, Marx sought salvation in the end of capitalism. In his view, the capitalist profits by exploiting workers, paying them the lowest possible wages. With plenty of available workers, the capitalist can cut wages while increasing his profit.

3. But Marx believed that, according to the laws of economics, capitalism is self-destroying. He shows how the growing disparity between a worker's wages and a capitalist's profits would force workers to revolt and destroy capitalism.

III. *Das Kapital* shaped the history of the 20th century, of Russia in particular. In 1917, Russia was in a state of near collapse. The czar's government had fallen, and the Russian Parliament had proclaimed a constitutional government based on liberal ideas.

A. The government felt obligated to stay in World War I, but the Russian army and the Russian people had had enough. The Russians wanted peace, bread, and a redistribution of land.

B. On November 7, the Bolsheviks (Communists) were determined to take power. Their leader, Vladimir Lenin, was a devoted follower of Marx. Lenin believed that Marx was the thinker, but that men of action must create revolution. Leon Trotsky and Joseph Stalin urged Lenin on.

C. The Bolsheviks struck. The leader of the constitutional government, Aleksandr Kerensky, tried but failed to put down the coup.

D. From 1918 to 1922, the Bolsheviks under Lenin waged a relentless war of terror against all who opposed the establishment of Communism. By 1929, Russia was the Soviet Union, ruled by the totalitarian dictator Stalin.

E. Russia is a sobering example that freedom is not universally valued. Russia has never wanted freedom, from its beginnings as a Viking state to today's Vladimir Putin.

IV. Russia shares some of the same historical currents as Britain. Both began with the arrival of Vikings. In 1066, the Norseman (those Vikings called the Normans by the French and English) conquered England. Already in 9th-century Russia, the Vikings exploited the political disunity of the Slavic tribes, but they also incorporated Russia into their trade network and established the city of Kiev.

A. Another influence was Christianity from Constantinople, which became Russian Orthodox Christianity. In Latin (Roman Catholic) Christianity, the pope is above the king or the emperor, who rules only the secular world. This idea does not exist in Russian Orthodox Christianity, which unites the roles of chief priest and emperor. From the beginning, the kings and, later, the czars of Russia were popes, as well.

B. Russia has also been shaped by struggle. Almost from the outset, Russia faced two threats, expansion from Germany and the Mongols, and was forced to choose which threat to address. The constant need to keep alien forces at bay has shaped the Russian character.

V. Tyranny has been another dominant force in Russia, homeland of some of the most ferocious tyrants of all time. This legacy came from Rome. When Constantinople fell in 1453, the prince of Moscow, Ivan the Great, married the niece of the last emperor of Byzantium. In the theology of the Russian Orthodox Church, Russia became the heir of Rome.

A. Ivan took the title *czar*, a word that, like *kaiser*, comes from *Caesar*. The double-headed eagle, the symbol of the Roman emperor's power, decorated the czar's coat of arms.

B. In 1547, 14-year-old Ivan, known as "the Terrible" in the West, though a better translation might be "Stern and Just," became czar, one of a series of despots who reformed Russia in the most brutal possible fashion.

1. Ivan largely wiped out the landed class and created his own army and bureaucracy. His brand of terror, characterized by men in black riding black horses, rooted out anyone suspected of disloyalty to the czar.

2. Ivan understood that the Russians did not want freedom but a stern master who would protect them. Ivan's reign saw the beginning of Russia's enormous expansion into Asia.

C. Peter the Great, an 18th-century czar, was a benevolent despot who based his idea of government on an all-powerful ruler. Peter traveled to the West and set out to reform Russian institutions.

1. He reformed the Russian Church. Those who refused to adapt were burned alive. The Russian alphabet was reorganized to make it clearer. The Russian army was transformed into a modern European army.

2. The cost was enormous, but Peter Westernized Russia to compete with the great powers of Europe. Russia grew throughout the 18th century and into the 19th.

VI. In 1917, Russia had an opportunity for freedom, but it chose instead to follow Communism. It broke with its own religious tradition, accepting the new religion of tyranny with the fervor of the convert.

A. Stalin had the support of millions as he arrested, imprisoned, and killed millions more of his own people. In theaters, people saw historical plays that depicted cruel but just rulers saving Russia from invaders, providing leadership in times of crisis.

B. Adolf Hitler believed that when he invaded Russia, the Soviet people would rise up and drive out the Bolsheviks and that Russia would collapse. Instead, the Soviets rallied to Stalin as the only man strong enough to defeat the Germans.

1. As the German armies approached Moscow, Stalin refused all advice to flee. Instead, he called the Russians to follow in the path of their ancestors who had prevailed against the Swedes, the Mongols, and the French.

2. The Germans were beaten back from Moscow. Stalin turned Hitler's preemptive war into the greatest victory

in Russian history. He would not negotiate; he fought the war to the end on the steppes of Russia.

C. When Stalin died in 1953, he had transformed the backward nation of Russia into the greatest empire in the world. When the Soviet Empire collapsed in 1990, instead of entering a new age of freedom, it drifted to a new tyrant.

Essential Reading:

Riasanovsky, *A History of Russia*.

Supplementary Reading:

Conquest, *Stalin*.

Solzhenitsyn, *The Gulag Archipelago*, vol. I.

Questions to Consider:

1. Can the Vikings—who arrived in both Britain and Russia—be called one of the most seminal forces in history?

2. Do you think the United States should have gone into Russia with a contemporary equivalent of the Marshall Plan after the fall of Communism?

Lecture Twenty-Three—Transcript
Russia and Empire

In our last two lectures we explored the lessons of history from the French Empire of Napoleon and the British Empire of Winston Churchill. It's interesting that Churchill, who liked to surround himself with memorabilia of great men, had a particular fondness for Napoleon. His study at Chartwell was filled with things that refer to Napoleon—portraits of Napoleon, books about Napoleon. We saw in both the empire of Napoleon and in the British Empire, which Winston Churchill loved so much, statements of the idea that an empire can bring liberty to the world. We called both of these empires "empires of faith," in the sense that the liberal belief that liberty and equality and democracy are wanted by all people, in all places and in all times, is much like a religion. It provides a comprehensive world view. In fact, in the 19th century, the view that liberty was the destiny of history pervaded the teachings of Hegel, the most influential philosopher of history of the period. The idea that liberty is the universal value was fundamental to both the empires of France and of Britain.

In these next two lectures we're going to explore two more empires of faith—the Russian Empire, the Soviet Union, and the Chinese Empire of Mao Tse-tung, for they are equally based upon a religious belief; Communism as an all-pervasive world view, upon which these empires were erected, and which, 50 years ago, dominated half the world in land mass and in terms of population. To understand this legacy of empire, this lesson of history, we shift our minds back to a June day in 1882. It could be almost any working day in 1882, and we are at the British Museum. At his accustomed desk, with books piled all around him, scribbling away is a very dark-haired man, rather short. If we were to interrupt him to ask him a question, he would have a very Teutonic accent; it is Karl Marx.

He has been a failure through most of his life. He is an academic failure, one of those who had a Ph.D., but could never find a position because, he would have told you, his views were too liberal, and he was excluded from any position at a German university. He has been an educator, and his *Communist Manifesto*, published in 1848, still resounds with its words calling the workers of the world to unite. They have nothing to lose but their chains. But his dreams of an early expansion of his ideas into political reality have begun to vanish. He now sees his great task as completing his volumes, what we will call *Das Kapital*.

He would not be surprised at all if you were to say I am from the future, and I've come back to tell you that your book will have, for many people all through the 20ᵗʰ century, the same validity that others hold with the Bible; that your book will be taught in hundreds of thousands of schools, that millions of people will look upon it as a revelation of truth. In fact, your book will be their bible, and you, in a way, will be their St. Paul, bringing to them the truth that saves. This would not surprise him because the work that he is writing, *Das Kapital*, is a volume of scientific truth. It is based on the indisputable, he would say, laws of history and of economics. It is a scientific book, hard to read, filled with long footnotes—Marx has the passion of a German scholar for footnotes—lots of economic calculations, but references to history as a whole. Its view, its doctrine, its gospel, is that the worker will be saved, and the worker will be saved from the clutches of an all-destroying capitalism.

Marx holds that other thinkers have completely failed to understand the simple fact that everything is based on economics. He had learned from the great Hegel that ideas make history; that the idea of freedom is what makes history. No, ideas are made by economics, and every society will reflect the kind of economics it has, above all, its mode of production. Labor is everything. In the days of Greece and Rome, the mode of production was slavery, and these were slave societies. They were then replaced in the Middle Ages by a mode of production resting upon serfs, and these were feudal societies. The 18ᵗʰ century had seen the feudal nobility lose its power to the bourgeois, to the capitalist. Now the whole mode of production is labor that rests upon its exploitation by the capitalist.

As much as St. Paul, Marx is moved by the suffering that he sees in the world, and the need to bring salvation, that salvation comes in the worker understanding why capitalism must come to an end because it's all very simple, don't you see? The capitalist's whole profit rests upon exploiting the worker. The worker has his wage, and the capitalist pays him the lowest possible wage. On the basis of that, the capitalist makes his profits. The children of the worker will ensure that there will always be plenty of workers to go around. There will always be nine people for every job that is available; hence the capitalist can continue to cut their wages while increasing his own profits. But capitalism is self-destroying by the laws of economics, and Marx shows how each generation of capitalist increased the number of monopolies, driving out each other with fierce competition—what the people of his day called Darwinism—until ultimately, there will reach such a disparity between the wages that the worker receives and the profits that the capitalist makes, that the workers will rise up and revolt and tear down the capitalist. This will happen; you cannot avoid it.

This is what he was writing here in his book, *Das Kapital*, and it will go on to shape the history of the 20th century. Indeed, if we were teaching our course in the year 1980, we would say that Communism and Karl Marx were just as influential in world history as Christianity. We must always avoid thinking that an idea like Communism is gone, never to appear again. After all, it is still the teaching of one of the great empires of our day, China. But to understand how it came to shape the 20th century, we shift forward to November the 7th, 1917. We are in Petrograd. It was once called St. Petersburg, and will be called that again, but now it is called Petrograd. Its name has been changed because of its Germanic tones during this Great War that has gone on between the Allies and Germany and Austria-Hungary.

Russia is in a state of almost collapse. There had been great hopes in March of that year, 1917, when, literally, the czar's government had collapsed, and the Russian Parliament had proclaimed a constitutional government based on liberal ideas—constitution, quality before the law, a bill of rights—but all through that long summer of 1917, the events are of control of the constitutionally minded government. Above all, they feel deeply indebted, for money as well as honor, as it is said, to stay in the war. The Russian army and the Russian people have had enough of this bloody war. In fact, the losses of Russia will equal those of Germany in the course of this huge Great War. The Russian people want bread, they want a redistribution of the land, and they want peace.

In this constitutional government, all varieties of opinion are allowed to flourish, including those that are determined to destroy this constitutional government. On November the 7th, the Bolsheviks, Communists, have determined to take power by force. They are going to seize control of the newspapers and power plants. The navy, deeply loyal to these Communist ideas, will train its guns upon the

Winter Palace, and revolution will sweep Russia. The leader of this Bolshevik party is a most unlikely figure, almost as unlikely as Marx, Lenin. He has grown up in a very middle class society, but his brother was vaguely associated with a conspiracy to assassinate the czar, and he'd been hanged. Lenin found ways to a better career closed to him, so he has become the devoted follower of Karl Marx, and he has become the leader of the Marxist party in Russia.

They still are a minority. They are even a minority among the Communists in Russia. But at one meeting, they were the largest group there, and they became the Bolsheviks, the majority party and have clung to that title. Lenin believes that Marx was the thinker, but it takes men of action to create a revolution. The time is ripe, and the worker must be called to this class struggle to wipe out the capitalist, to create a classless society, by a hard core of party members—men like himself, men like Leon Trotsky, men like Joseph Stalin. In the face of much opposition, it is Stalin and Trotsky who urge Lenin to go on this bold course of seizing power this night.

The Bolsheviks strike, and the leader of the constitutional government, Aleksandr Kerensky, a fiery orator, believes that he can still rally the Russian army to put down this coup. He drives all around the suburbs of St. Petersburg, stopping to try to harangue the army, and nobody will listen to him. He will fade into history, coming to the United States, where he will live out a long life, telling everybody how, if he had just had the real support from the Allies, he could have prevented the tragedy of a Communist Russia, but his day is gone.

The Bolsheviks seized power, and from 1918 to 1922 under the head of Lenin, they waged a relentless war and a terror against all who oppose the establishment of Communism. It is a terror without precedent in human history. Millions will die, as compared to the 40,000 we saw die in the French terror. By 1929, Lenin having died in 1924, Russia will be not only the Soviet Union but the repository of the most absolute totalitarian dictator that has ever existed in history, Joseph Stalin. Russia will be a sobering example to us that freedom is not a universal value, that people, in all places and in all times, may not want freedom. Russia is a land that has never wanted freedom. From its misty beginnings as a Viking state, right down to Vladimir Putin, Russia has avoided, again and again, freedom. What are the currents that have shaped Russia? I agree with those like

Dostoevsky or Alexander Solzhenitzyn that Russia is a brilliant civilization, but one fundamentally different than Western Europe. Dostoevsky said, "The Russian soul is a dark place."

Russia began with some of the same historical currents as Britain. In fact, it is most interesting; two of the most successful nations of the 20th century, and two of the greatest empires, Britain and Russia, began with the influence and the arrival of Vikings, Norsemen—first the Anglo-Saxons and then the Normans of William the Conqueror. In Russia, the various Slavic nations along the great rivers of Russia, the various Slavic tribes fighting amongst themselves, asked, in the 9th century, Vikings to come to their aid—the Rus', the Norsemen. These Vikings arrived and found a land ripe for conquest, rich, and they began to exploit the political disunity of the Slavic tribes, but also the trade, carrying fur and amber and slaves all the way to Constantinople, down the highways of the Russian rivers, and bringing back gold, establishing the city of Kiev, Kiev the Golden. Rurik would be looked back to as the first of the rulers of Russia, the Viking chieftain.

In 988, Vladimir would accept Christianity from Constantinople. One current is the Vikings; the second is Russian Orthodox Christianity, the Christianity of Constantinople. That Christianity differed in one fundamental political aspect from Latin Christianity. That is to say in Latin Christianity, the Pope, as ruler of the sphere of God, was above the king or the emperor, who ruled only the secular. The Pope could excommunicate emperors, they could excommunicate kings, and the Pope placed the king under the law of God. In Russia, that idea would not exist. Byzantine Christianity rested upon the absolute identification of the chief priest with the emperor, and Russia took this in. From the beginning, the kings, and later the czars, of Russia were pope and ruler as well. This idea of government under the law did not exist.

The next current shaping Russia was struggle. Almost from the outset, the Russians had been faced by wars on two fronts, the expansion of Germany and the Mongols. The greatest of Russian heroes in these misty days of the Middle Ages—like Alexander Nevsky, who conquered the Teutonic knights in a bold battle in 1242 on the frozen ice [the battle of Lake Peipus]—had been forced to set their priorities. Already in 1223, Genghis Khan's armies invaded Russia, and by 1240, they had captured the golden city of Kiev—

burned it to the ground amidst a horrible massacre of skulls piled up outside its walls. Down until 1480, the little princes of Russia were forced to pay tribute to the Mongols. It was always a choice between fighting the Germans or fighting the Mongols. Nevsky himself had to pay tribute to the Mongols in order to free up his forces to defeat the Germans. This constant struggle and the need to survive against alien forces have shaped the Russian soul.

Then tyranny—Russia has been the homeland of some of the most ferocious tyrants in all of history. With that tyranny came a legacy from Rome, for when Constantinople fell in 1453, the ruler of Moscow, the prince of Moscow—Ivan the Great, as he is called—married the niece of the last emperor of Byzantium. He married Zoe, the niece of Constantine XI, who died in battle fighting the Turks. In the theology of the Russian Orthodox Church, Russia became the heir of Rome. Rome has fallen two times, it was said—once when it fell, and the Coliseum is the symbol of it and once again when Constantinople fell in 1453. There will not be a third time, was the proud boast. The prince of Moscow took over the title *czar*. Just like *kaiser*, czar goes back to the word *Caesar*. The double-headed eagle of Byzantium, the symbol of the power of the emperor of Rome, now became the coat of arms of the Czar of all the Russias.

In 1547, only 14 years of age, Ivan—known as Ivan Terrible in the West, though a better translation of it might be the one who is stern and just—became Czar of all the Russias. He would be one of a series of Russian despots who set about to reform that land in the most brutal possible fashion. He largely wiped out the landed class, who was the people at court. He created his own army. He created his own bureaucracy and his own terror. These were men in black outfits riding only black horses, who would strike into a village and root out anybody suspected of disloyalty to the czar—killing even his own son—and the prototype in movies for Joseph Stalin, who loved to watch movies about Ivan the Terrible. He understood that the Russians did not want freedom; they wanted a stern master who would protect them. Ivan the Terrible's reign saw the beginning of the enormous expansion of Russia, becoming a major Asiatic power. In fact, the Cossacks under Ivan would ride all the way out into Siberia and bring him back furs, establishing frontier posts throughout that vast land.

Another current shaping Russia has been the frontier, this vast expanse to the east. Peter the Great, the 18th-century example of a benevolent despot, which was the idea that the best form of government was to have an all-powerful ruler. That's even what George III was trying to do in our country—to be one who took care of efficiency, put aside old-fashioned ideas. But in Russia, it took a very different turn with Peter the Great—traveling to the West, learning the ways in which the West was superior to Russia, and then bringing them back. St. Petersburg was his window on the West, and it was built on the bones of thousands of laborers. The Russian Church was reformed, and those who refused to go along with its modern ways, the old believers, were persecuted, burned alive. The Russian alphabet was reorganized to make it clearer, and the Russian army was transformed into a modern European army.

The cost was enormous, but he made Russia western so that it could compete with the great powers of Europe. It was Peter the Great and his reformed army that destroyed Charles XII and the army of Sweden at the Battle of Poltova in 1709—remember, the battle I told you that Napoleon should have remembered. All through the 18th century, Russia grew and expanded on into the 19th century. The czar, Alexander, was the catalyst and the foundation of the alliance that brought Napoleon down. He rode in triumph through Paris, and his soldiers threw down before his feet the conquered battle standards of Napoleon's army. This was the Russia that Lenin and Stalin inherited.

In 1917, Russia had its opportunity for freedom. It chose instead to follow one of the most bizarre economic theories ever postulated because Communism simply has never worked, but it was imported wholesale into Russia. They chose to break with their Russian tradition of religion, accepting this new religion with the fervor of converts. The great churches of Russia, with their magnificent domes and icons, were turned into museums of Atheism. They accepted tyranny without equal. Do you believe that Joseph Stalin, in the 1930s, on his own, arrested these millions who went out to the Gulag—perhaps 20 million of them perishing there? Do you believe that on his own he drove the trains that took them to the Gulag; that on his own he ferreted out all of these counterrevolutionary figures, these saboteurs, as they were called? Absolutely not—he had the support of millions of Russians. In the theaters they saw *Ivan the*

Terrible and *Alexander Nevsky* and saw how again and again, Russia had to be saved from its invaders by yes, cruel, but just and stern rulers who gave the leadership that was necessary in a time of crisis.

The Nazis and Adolf Hitler believed that when they invaded Russia—and remember Hitler invaded Russia on June the 22nd, 1941, intentionally choosing the date that Napoleon had chosen—that the Soviet people would rise up and drive out the Bolsheviks and that Russia would collapse like a house of cards. Instead, the Soviets rallied to Stalin. He himself was overwhelmed by surprise at Hitler's invasion, and for several days, he was almost incoherent, but he refused to leave Moscow. The Russians believed he was the only man cruel enough, mean enough and strong enough to defeat the Germans, and so Comrade Stalin rallied the nation.

As the Russians saw the German armies approach Moscow, as the German Panzer units could see the spires of Moscow rising up in the enclosing winter weather, Stalin had refused all advice to flee to the Urals. Instead, he called the Russians to follow in the path of Alexander Nevsky, to follow in the path of Dmitry, who defeated the Mongols on the Don, to follow in the path of Ivan, and to follow in the path of the conquerors of Napoleon. We are Russian, he said, and we will conquer. And so the Germans were beaten back from Moscow. Stalin never trusted anybody; he is the perfect example of somebody who is paranoid. He believed that paranoia is just good thinking when everybody is after you, so you stop them first. So he took this preemptive war by Hitler and turned it into the greatest victory in Russian history.

He was told by all of his military advisors that he must keep large numbers of troops in Siberia because Japan was going to attack him at the same time that the Germans were attacking him. Only one source of information told him differently, Richard Sorge, a German-born, devoted Communist journalist in Tokyo. He gave the astounding news that the Americans are going to be attacked by the Japanese on December the 7th. Stalin believed it. He brought back his crack units from Siberia, and they drove the Germans from the walls of Moscow. He would not negotiate; he would fight that war to the end. And there on the steppes of Russia, the German army was crushed by men who would go over the top in places like Stalingrad cheering for the party, for Comrade Stalin and for the motherland. When Hitler had been broken, and the Russian army marched in triumph through Berlin and was brought back to Moscow for their great victory parade, the soldiers threw down the battle standards of the Nazis with their swastikas at the feet of the new Czar of all the Russias.

Joseph Stalin found his people still exhausted from the civil war, many of them using wooden plows, a pariah of Europe cordoned off like a germ from Europe. When he died in 1953, he had the greatest empire in the world, and his people were in the nuclear age. This man kept Machiavelli by his table, and he understood that people didn't want freedom in Russia; they wanted stern rule. And so when the Soviet Empire collapsed in 1990, instead of there being a new age of freedom, we have seen a society drift right for a new Stalin or a new Ivan the Terrible.

Lecture Twenty-Four
China and Empire

Scope:

Civilization arose in China independently from the birth of civilization in the Middle East. But like the Middle East, China, throughout its history, has chosen despotism over freedom. Classical Chinese civilization was defined by Confucius. Order, not freedom, was his ideal, and he believed that order must flow down from above. The ruler is a benevolent despot, whose character and virtue make him worthy of obedience. This ideal still pervades China. Thus, in 1912, China could have a revolution aimed at establishing democracy, but the result would be Mao Tse-tung and despotism more total than anything imaginable to an emperor of the Han or Ming Dynasty.

Outline

I. We turn now to a second Communist empire, China, still a major power in the 21st century. To understand the Chinese empire, we begin in November 1950, during the Korean War, as the U.S. army pushes deep into North Korea.

    A. At headquarters, General Douglas MacArthur rejects any suggestion that Chinese troops are about to attack. But they do attack, dealing American forces a stunning defeat.

    B. It took more than two long, bloody years to reach a stalemate in this struggle on the Korean peninsula. The legacy of that struggle between China and the United States is still with us.

    C. China emerged as a world power. The United States—which had triumphed five years earlier in World War II—found itself on the brink of nuclear disaster with the Soviet Union and facing danger from China.

II. What does China tell us about the law of history that freedom is not a universal value? It's a mistake to base foreign policy on the belief that all people in all times want freedom. China, like Russia, has never chosen freedom during its long history.

A. China's long, glorious civilization began around 1700 B.C. As in Mesopotamia and Egypt, the growth of civilization seemed to stem from climatic change and the need for a central power to control the flooding of the Yangtze River.

B. From the beginning, China was ruled by despots. Initially, a king headed an elaborate bureaucracy. The Chinese were willing to accept the absolute rule of this king, whom they believed the gods had chosen and through whom the gods would channel all necessary knowledge.

C. The Chinese king and his court lived well under the mandate of heaven, supported by commoners' taxes.

D. But the mandate of heaven was a challenge. If the king did not rule with justice, if he was not humane, then the gods would revoke their mandate from the son of heaven, and he would fall.

E. Early China was ruled by a series of dynasties, each coming to power in a time of turmoil, ruling for two or three generations, then falling into stagnation and corruption, so that they oppressed the people rather than governing with justice.

III. Confucius (552–479 B.C.) has long influenced the Chinese attitude toward government (see *Books That Have Made History: Books That Can Change Your Life* from The Teaching Company). Along with Socrates, Jesus, and Buddha, he was one of the greatest teachers who ever lived. Unsuccessful in a bureaucratic career, he took as his mission educating students, who could bring his precepts into Chinese government.

A. Confucius developed his ideas, collected in the *Analects*. Confucius was an older contemporary of the great poet Aeschylus and only slightly older than Socrates. But the freedom that was so central to Greece played no role in the thought of Confucius.

B. His concern was order, not freedom. A ruler justified his absolute power by the exercise of moral virtue. For Confucius, the universal values were wisdom, moderation, justice, and courage. The ruler who saw only to his own pleasures and had no concern for the people would fail.

C. The ideas of Confucius set the mark for Chinese civilization until 1949. In the dynasties that rose and fell in China, the bureaucracy was staffed by those trained in Confucian thought.

D. Confucius did not deny the existence of the gods but thought that humans could not understand them. He believed, however, that religion and proper tribute to the gods played a fundamental role in holding society together.

E. The family was the essential element in Chinese society. Sons respected their fathers, who treated them with justice and kindness.

IV. The first emperor to unite China, Ch'in Shih Huang-ti (Qin Shi Huangdi), and his son ruled from 221 to 206 B.C. This emperor broke with the tradition of Confucius and instituted a new bureaucracy. He buried alive 700 Confucian scholars and confiscated and burned ancient books.

   A. Ch'in Shih Huang-ti's ambitions led him to multiple conquests and expansion. Thousands died in the construction of his great monuments.

   B. The emperor sent servants across the empire for various herbs to make him immortal. He believed that black was the color of immortality, and that the number six was a key to immortality. He forced all of China to carry out his wishes, no matter how irrational.

   C. Ch'in Shih Huang-ti began to build his tomb, surrounded by 7,000 life-sized terracotta soldiers to guard him in death. After he died, the Chinese said that his dynasty fell because it was not humane. His arrogance and power had corrupted him.

V. Like the Russians, the Chinese faced potential conquerors in the Huns and the Mongols. Genghis Khan invaded China, and his grandson, Kubla Khan, became the emperor.

   A. The Chinese have had a remarkable ability to assimilate conquerors. The foreign barbarians who took over China became more Chinese than the Chinese themselves. Kubla Khan took a Chinese imperial name, and his descendants ruled as full Chinese.

B. China's long, continuous civilization and its ability to assimilate foreigners have enabled the country to rise from disunity and chaos to power repeatedly. The Chinese know nothing of political or individual freedom, but national freedom has always been key.

VI. In 1911, the last Manchu emperor fell from power, and China was thought to be entering a new age of democracy and freedom. The most important figure of this revolution was Sun Yat-sen, a doctor who tried to adapt Western ideas to China.

A. Sun's ideal of the new China embraced the principles of democracy, nationalism, and prosperity but from a Chinese perspective.

B. Nationalism was the key to the new China. The Chinese must understand that they were one nation with a great civilization. Their brand of democracy was not based on America's individual freedom. It was a communal democracy guided by the general will of the Chinese people, to which individuals were subordinate.

C. As for prosperity, Sun did not want capitalism. An admirer of Lenin, he believed that Chinese society as a whole should control the mechanisms of productivity—a socialistic economy.

D. The West looked on with terror as China endured civil war in the late 1920s and 1930s. Warlords ruled entire areas of China. No continuous government could establish itself. China seemed hopelessly old-fashioned and weak.

VII. Torn apart by civil war, China was ripe for another invasion. Japan seized Manchuria and attempted to conquer all of China.

A. The threat of Japanese conquest brought together the two main factions fighting for control in China: the Nationalists, led by Chiang Kai-shek, and the Communists, led by a former assistant librarian, Mao Tse-tung (Mao Zedong).

B. Though Mao's father had been a poor peasant, Mao was educated. As a librarian, he began to learn about Karl Marx and became one of the first members of China's Communist Party. Mao's genius was to understand that Communism would flourish with rural peasants, not Marx's urban factory workers.

C. The Nationalists and Communists united to defeat Japan but fought each other during World War II. The United States at first believed that democracy would prevail, but it later realized that the Nationalist forces had no support and the Communists would win.

D. In 1949, Chiang Kai-shek and his battered army withdrew to Taiwan. In Beijing, Mao Tse-tung and the Communists took power. Mao set out to create Soviet-style despotism and stamp out all that had come before him.

VIII. The Chinese Communist Party became the sole source of truth, and Mao would add his legacy to those of Marx, Engels, Stalin, and Lenin. He put his wisdom about human nature and politics into a little red book of quotations.

A. Mao first led China to fight the United States to a standstill in North Korea.

B. He then carried out a massive collectivization of farms. He proposed five-year plans, just as Stalin had, by which China would be industrialized and food production would increase. But thousands, perhaps millions, of Chinese starved to death in famines.

C. Mao began to fear in the early 1960s that the people were losing their revolutionary fervor. He felt that a new generation had to be educated in the ways of Communism.

1. He began a campaign to root out nonbelievers, unleashing the Cultural Revolution.

2. Throughout China, young people locked up and beat their teachers. Intellectuals were sent into the fields to learn with their hands what Communism was about. Opponents were jailed and killed.

IX. Some Westerners think that China's free-market economy will one day bring freedom, but history teaches us that capitalism is compatible with despotism.

Essential Reading:

Confucius, *Analects*.

Wright, *The History of China*.

Supplementary Reading:

Fears, *Books That Have Made History: Books That Can Change Your Life*, Lecture Twenty-Three.

Roberts, *A Concise History of China*.

Questions to Consider:

1. Do you see a conflict between the absence of political freedom in China and the fact that the free-market economy has flourished in many epochs of China's past?

2. Confucius used the family model for order and good government in the highest political sphere. Discuss.

Lecture Twenty-Four—Transcript
China and Empire

We turn now to the second of our empires of Communism, one that is still a major power in the 21st century. To understand China as an empire, the destiny of empire in China, I'd ask you to put yourself back to November of the year 1950; you are with the American army, pushing deeply into North Korea, approaching the Yalu River. You are not going to be home by Christmas, probably, but it won't be long after that, you're quite convinced. You're even having turkey and dressing brought in to you in the frigid temperatures of North Korea, where the temperature can plunge down to 40 below zero and the winds come down from Siberia.

In headquarters, General Douglas MacArthur is persistently rejecting any suggestion that large numbers of Chinese troops are about to attack. In fact, he has carried out a very bold strategy, which hearkens back to Napoleon. After his brilliantly successful landing at Inchon, he has now divided his army into three columns, just the way Napoleon did—widely separated, even cut off by the terrain. To any suggestion that the Chinese are about to enter, he says no, there may be a few volunteers, but there is no major Chinese force about to attack us. That is when the great horns begin to blow, and the well clothed, well armed Chinese army comes out of the freezing winter weather to strike the Americans, dealing American forces one of the worst defeats in our history during that retreat, which would become forever known as the heroic march from the Chosin Reservoir.

It would take more than two long, bloody years to reach a stalemate in this struggle on the Korean Peninsula, and the legacy of that struggle between China and the United States is still with us in North Korea today. China had emerged on the world stage as a major power, and America, which five years before had been utterly triumphant over both Japan and Germany, sole possessor of the atomic bomb and one of the largest and the best-equipped army the world had ever seen, now would find itself on the brink of nuclear disaster with the Soviet Union, on down until 1990, and would still be faced with major danger from China.

How did it come about that America squandered this position of supremacy? And more important, what does China tell us about our basic law of history—that freedom is not a universal value, and that we make a major mistake when we base our foreign policy on the belief that all people in all times want freedom, and freedom will grow naturally? China, like Russia, is an example of a nation that has never chosen freedom during its long history—the product of a long and glorious civilization; that is China. Civilization came to China later than it did to Egypt and to Mesopotamia. We saw the birth of civilization around 3000 B.C. in Mesopotamia and Egypt, and we characterize that birth of civilization by the development of complex government structures, monumental architecture, writing and the use of the metal bronze.

This would not occur until around 1700 in China. As in Mesopotamia and Egypt, it seems to be due to climatic change, and above all, the need to have a well organized central power to control the flooding of the great river, the Yangtze, and to build dikes and to cultivate the land. From the moment it emerges as a civilization, China has despotism, ruled by a king with an elaborate court ceremonial, and with a number of nobles as his experts. Our earliest record of Chinese civilization is writing found on tortoise shells and bones. Thousands of these have been found, some 25,000, and they are oracles. The question was posed to the gods about weather in particular, or about dynastic policy, and the bones were then heated after they had been inscribed with these early Chinese characters. The way they broke told you the answer the gods had given you.

Now obviously you need a group of experts to tell you this, don't you? That is how the Chinese bureaucracy and its priests arose, and the king was at the apex of this, experts who could tell you about the weather and give you the necessary solid advice so that you did not starve. The Chinese were willing to accept the absolute rule of a king who they believed had the mandate of heaven, had been chosen by the gods to rule over them, and through whom the gods would channel all the knowledge that was needed. Another element of Chinese civilization was magnificent vessels of bronze because, as in Egypt, the pharaohs had built their pyramids with elaborate interior decorations of gold and elaborate relief sculptures. In China, the experts and the king lived well, and part of your duty in accepting the mandate of heaven as a subject of the king was to pay the tax and the tribute that enabled them to have a luxurious lifestyle.

But the mandate of heaven was a challenge, and if the king did not rule with justice, if he did not rule in the best interest of the people as a whole, if he was not humane, then the gods would take away their mandate from the son of heaven, as the emperor was called, and he would fall. So the Chinese have seen their history as the rise and fall of a series of dynasties, each one coming to power in a time of turmoil and chaos by a god-chosen ruler, ruling for two or three generations, perhaps well and wisely, then beginning to stagnate, and finally to allow the power to corrupt them so that they oppressed the people rather than governing with justice.

The prime statement of the Chinese attitude toward government, one that is still decisive in China, is the views of Confucius. In our course on books that have made history, books that can change your life, we saw Confucius as one of the most seminal thinkers in all of history. He lived from 552 to 479. He was, along with Socrates and Jesus and Buddha, one of the greatest teachers who ever lived, and that is what he was, a teacher. He had not been successful in an attempt at a bureaucratic career. Instead he took it as his mission to wander through a divided China—by that time the old imperial unity had broken up, and China was in the time of the warring states in the 6th century B.C.—and to give his advice to the rulers, and to try to educate students who could then bring his precepts, his teaching, into the governing of China.

Like Jesus and Socrates and Buddha, he never wrote a book. The *Analects of Confucius* are the sayings that he gave to his students, which were then collected. Now Confucius is developing his ideas at the same time that freedom is growing in Greece. He is a contemporary of the great poet Aeschylus. He is only a little older than Socrates, whom you'll remember died in 399. Now for Aeschylus, for Socrates, for Herodotus, for the Greeks who fought at Marathon in 490 and at Plataea in 479, freedom was fundamental, and freedom was the most precious of possessions. In the Athenian democracy, national freedom, individual freedom and political freedom achieved balance.

So the freedom that was so central to Greece played no role whatsoever in the thoughts of Confucius. His concern was order, an order that flowed down from the top. He assumed a ruler, and a ruler who had absolute power, but who justified that absolute power by his exercise of moral virtue. The good man that Confucius tried to educate was good in that he brought his moral qualities to bear by making the lives of those he governed better. Confucius taught that wisdom, moderation, justice and courage were the universal values—the same values that Socrates taught, wisdom, justice, courage and moderation. What we call the cardinal virtues of Socrates were taught by Confucius. He compared the people to grass, and the wind of a good ruler should ruffle them, rule over them. The ruler who saw only to his own pleasures, who took no concern for the people, would bring only misery and war, and would fail. The people were not to be free. They were to have order and justice.

The ideas of Confucius would set the mark for Chinese civilization right on until 1949. In the dynasties that rose and fell in China, the bureaucracy was staffed by those trained in Confucian ways. Early on, the Chinese developed a system of credentials very similar to ours today. They had a baccalaureate degree based on the mastery of fundamental principles of Confucian thought, and the reading of the classics that he put in place, the book of odes, the poems and the study of history. History was fundamental to Confucius's idea of a good man, in the education of a good man. He edited the historical work from the early period of China, the *Spring and Autumn* chronicles, and the knowledge of music and the knowledge of ritual.

Confucius did not talk much about the gods. In fact, one of the things the master would never talk about was evil and the gods. He didn't deny the existence of the gods, but human wisdom could not understand them, so let us understand what we can, and that is men. He believed, however, that religion and the proper tribute to the gods played a fundamental element in holding society together. So his model was not a free republic, it was the family. Time and time again Confucius returned to the family as the fundamental element in Chinese society, the respect that sons had for their father, and in return, that the father treated his son with justice and kindness and was worthy of their respect.

There was one break with Confucius under the first emperor to unite all of China, Cheng Shi Huang Di—it means the "first emperor." From 221 to 206 B.C., he achieved unification of China, which maintained very briefly under his son. But he broke with the tradition of Confucius, and he even had 700 scholars of Confucian thought buried alive because one of them had come and said what you're doing is not in concert with the precepts of the master. So he said fine, I will just bury all of you alive. But even more, I'm going to destroy all of these books of Confucius. So all through China there vent out an order—it was a cultural revolution, don't you see—to confiscate all the ancient books, particularly books of history that might show examples of good rulers from the past, and these were burned. It became a crime to study them. A whole new bureaucracy was put in place, and the first emperor set out to rule with the sternness he thought China needed.

His great plans and ambitions led him to conquest after conquest after conquest. He is credited with building the Great Wall of China, but I am told now that modern scholars have proved this to be false, that he may have done some repair of different earthworks that existed against the northern barbarians, the Huns and later people, but the Great Wall of China dates largely from the 17th century. And I am told that the Great Wall cannot be seen from the Moon. In the tourist literature, you might still read that it is the one human building on Earth that can be seen from the Moon, but I am told that that is not true. I've never been to the Moon, so I can't say that for sure. But that was the impression he made upon his age—great buildings and great structures that thousands would die to put in place—that was what he was.

As his life went on, he became ever more concerned with immortality, and he sent all over the empire for various herbs that could be brought to him to make him immortal. He was also much concerned with the elements and with the fact that water could conquer fire. He believed that black was the color of immortality and the number six was a key to immortality. So these became fundamental to all calculations, for example, and all court dress. In other words, he could force all of China to do what he wanted to do, no matter how irrational it was. He became utterly convinced from his chemist that mercury—the ingestion of small amounts of mercury—would make him immortal.

Nonetheless, he began to build his tomb, and there 7,000 magnificent life-sized terracotta figures of soldiers—that were uncovered a number of years ago—guarded him even in death. There they were placed, and we are told that he had a huge lake of mercury there inside his tomb in the belief that it would reinvigorate him and bring him back. But when he died, his son very rapidly collapsed, and the Chinese who looked back on the fall of that dynasty said they fell because it was not humane. Not that it was authoritarian but that it was not humane, and because of the outrageous arrogance of this first emperor, the *hybris* of the Greeks, that his outrageous arrogance and that power corrupted him. Cheng Shi Huang Di—he would be recreated in the 20th century.

The Chinese have this deep sense of humaneness and the order of the universe tied up with an absolute ruler. Like the Russians, they had been faced by potential conquerors, and what the Mongols were for Russia in the Middle Ages, the northern barbarians, as the Chinese called them—we know them in European history under names such as the Huns—had been, a constant danger time and time again, not only invading China, but on more than one occasion conquering China. So the Mongol conquest of Genghis Khan had its first real outside expansion out of Mongolia into China. His grandson, Kubla Khan, would become the ruler of China, the emperor of China.

But the Chinese have a remarkable ability in their civilization to assimilate the conqueror. The foreign barbarians who have taken over China have become more Chinese than the Chinese themselves. So Kubla Khan might build his capital at what the west would call Xanadu, but he took a Chinese imperial name, and his descendants ruled as full Chinese, and are even accepted by the Chinese as one of the imperial dynasties. So, too, the Manchus, who conquered China in the 17th century, coming like the Mongols from Manchuria and Mongolia, would very rapidly be assimilated to China. That is the power of its civilization. You see, Chinese civilization is one of the most long-lived continuous civilizations in all of history.

It's worth pondering. Egypt had a long civilization, but no one speaks Egyptian today, and their religion is gone. Greece—there have been Greeks living in Greece as long as the Chinese have had a civilization. They still speak the Greek tongue. Greek has a very long continuous civilization. Iran, we have learned in this course, has a very long continuous civilization, even speaking the same language back to the 18th century B.C. So, too, does China. That long civilization, and their ability to assimilate the foreigner, has enabled them time and time again to rise from disunity and chaos and become a great power again. The Chinese know nothing of political freedom or of individual freedom, at least in Confucius, but national freedom has always been key to China. National freedom in China, as in Russia, has taken the form of xenophobia. The foreigner is always the barbarian, and China the very center of the world.

So it was that the last of these imperial dynasties ran its course, and in 1911, the last Manchu emperor fell from power. China was thought to be entering a new age of democracy and freedom. The most important figure of that revolution was Sun Yat-sen. He had been educated in Hawaii. He was a doctor, and very deeply imbued with Western ideas, which he thought must be adapted to China. His principles of the new China—which he wrote from a series of lectures that he gave in the United States, where he came to lecture to Chinese communities to gain money for the revolution—embraced the principles of democracy, nationalism and prosperity, but he saw them in very Chinese ways. That is to say, that nationalism was the key to the new China.

The Chinese must be made to understand that they were a unified nation, that they had a great civilization and then democracy. But democracy was not the individual freedom that he had observed in America. He believed that democracy must be communal, that what mattered was the whole family of the Chinese nation, and that the general will of the Chinese people must guide the democracy, not individuals. Finally, prosperity—here he did not want capitalism in China. He greatly admired Lenin, and Lenin was a bulwark to him in the early 1920s. He believed that China must be organized in such a fashion that society as a whole controlled the mechanisms of productivity—a socialistic economy with a democracy based upon the subordination of the individual to the will of the whole, and finally to a deep national call to greatness.

China wasn't ready for any of this, and the West looked on with terror, and a certain degree of amusement even, as China, all through the late 1920s and 1930s engaged in a terrible civil war, with warlords ruling whole parts of China and no government able to establish itself with any continuity. Hollywood made film after film during the 1930s about the warlords of China, movies like *The General Died at Dawn*. It seemed as though China was hopelessly old fashioned and hopelessly weak, and that is exactly what the Japanese believed when they began their invasion of China, seizing Manchuria and then attempting to conquer the whole of China for its valuable natural resources, simply as an expansion of the Empire of Japan.

This threat of Japanese conquest brought together the elements fighting for control in China, those who still followed the principles of Sun Yat-sen, but these had taken a very different turn under the leadership of Chiang Kai-shek, the Nationalist Party, and those who followed Communism. It was a former assistant librarian, Mao Tse-tung, who would become the head of the Communist Party in China. His father had been a poor peasant at one time, but Mao had received an education. And it was from his head librarian that he first began to learn about Karl Marx, and was one of the early members of the infinite Communist Party in China.

Marx would never have imagined that Communism would come to China, not even to Russia, because they did not have the workers. They did not have a real large proletariat, an industrial base. But Mao's genius was to understand that it was in the peasants that Communism would flourish. From the outset, it was a determination to win the peasants; not the industrial cities over, but the peasants. So he fought. He made some alliances with the Nationalists to defeat the Japanese. He made as much use as he could of American weapons. But the Nationalist forces under Chiang Kai-shek, and the Communists, fought each other during World War II as much as they fought the Japanese. When the Japanese had finally been conquered, then they turned upon one another.

It seemed again clear to American foreign policy that China would go this route of, yes, a strong leader, Chiang Kai-shek, but one that would be based on democracy. We began to believe that China really was ours. Well, General Marshall came back from China, after a visit there in 1947, to say China was lost. The Nationalist forces have no support whatsoever, and the Communists are going to rule that country, and so they would. In 1949, Chiang Kai-shek and his battered army withdrew to ancient Formosa, Taiwan. In Beijing, near the site of the first Chinese capital, Mao Tse-tung and the Communists would take power. They weren't even resisted as they captured Beijing. Mao set out, under the guidance of Joseph Stalin at first, to create just as absolute a despotism as existed in the Soviet Union, and in his own way, to create the same kind of despotism as the emperor—the first emperor, as he called himself—who sought to stamp out all vestiges of what had gone before.

The Chinese Communist Party became the sole source of truth, and Mao added his legacy to that of Karl Marx, Friedrich Engels and Joseph Stalin and Lenin. He put his wisdom about human nature and about politics, including the phrase that revolution really comes from the barrel of a gun, into a little pocket set of quotations bound in red. Stalin, too, had written such a set of quotations, *The Principles of Communism*, and it had been read all over the Soviet Union. Mao led China first to fight the United States to a standstill in North Korea, and then brought a massive collectivization of the farms—brought the farms together in huge collectives—and the cost did not matter. Five-year plans were proposed, just as they were by Stalin, by which China would be industrialized and food production would go up. The Chinese peasant had always wanted the land for himself, but now in those collective farms, as in Russia, it failed. So thousands, and then perhaps even millions, would starve to death in enormous famines that struck China, but still the progress of despotism and of Communism went ahead.

Mao began to fear, in the early 1960s, that the Chinese were losing their revolutionary fervor. He felt that a new generation had to be educated in the never-ending cycle of revolution. There was always somebody out there a little suspect, somebody who was a counter revolutionary in his heart, or somebody who was a capitalist in his heart, or maybe who just wanted a little plot of garden for himself and they must be rooted out. So he unleashed the Cultural Revolution. He began it just as Stalin frequently had, by saying this is a new age; we want 100 flowers to flourish, but as soon as you jumped forward and began to "flourish your flower" a little bit, he— Mao—then stepped in because you had betrayed yourself.

All over China fiery young people took their teachers and locked them in closets, bringing them out from time to time to beat them. Intellectuals were sent out into the fields to toil and learn with their own hands what Communism was about. And Mao, still vigorous in the eyes of his people, was growing fatter; but when anybody questioned his power of mind and his power of body, he swam the river, floating nine miles down. He left a legacy that is still with us today. It's a most interesting concept, the idea that if China admits capitalism and a free market economy, the very establishment of that free market economy will change the entire millennia of Chinese history. Except for the time of the Communists, the Chinese have always been very good capitalists and had a free market economy. In fact, one of the greatest of the capitalists was Kubla Khan. China will test the thesis—a free market economy brings true freedom with it. It is still a question mark.

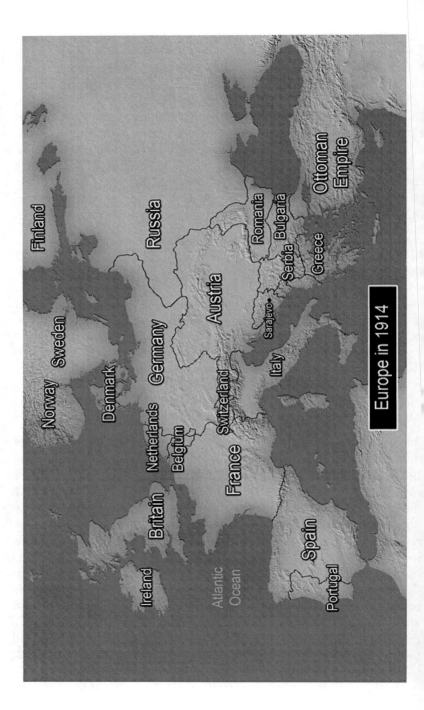

Europe in 1914

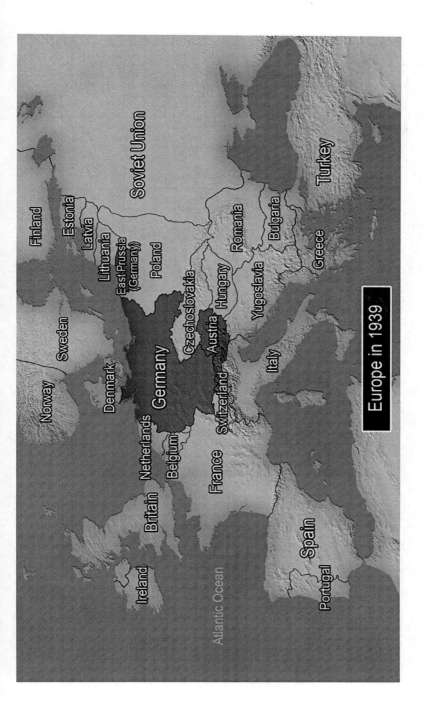

Europe in 1939

Aegean World, 13th Century B.C.

Hittite Empire
Hattusha

Canaan

Egypt

(Anatolia)

Mediterranean Sea

Troy

Greek Cities
Delphi
Aulis
Athens
Corinth
Mycenae
Pylos · Sparta

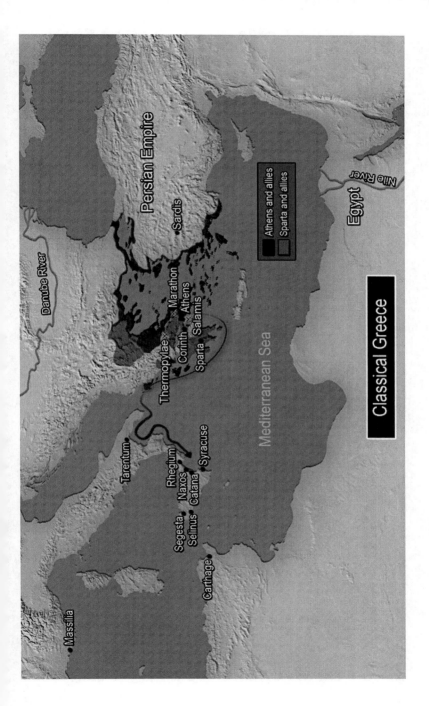

Classical Greece

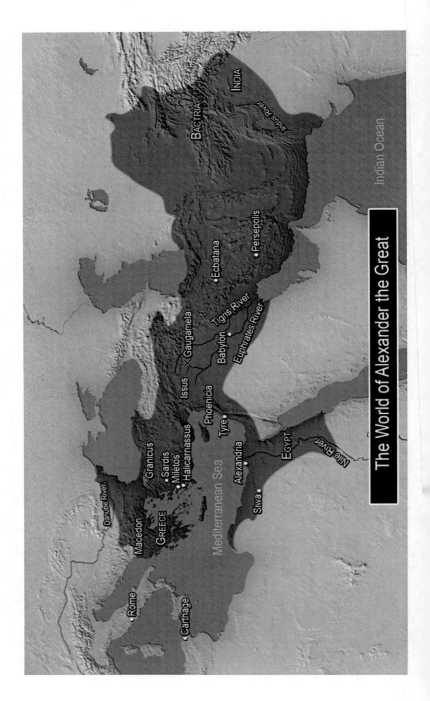

The World of Alexander the Great

©2007 The Teaching Company.

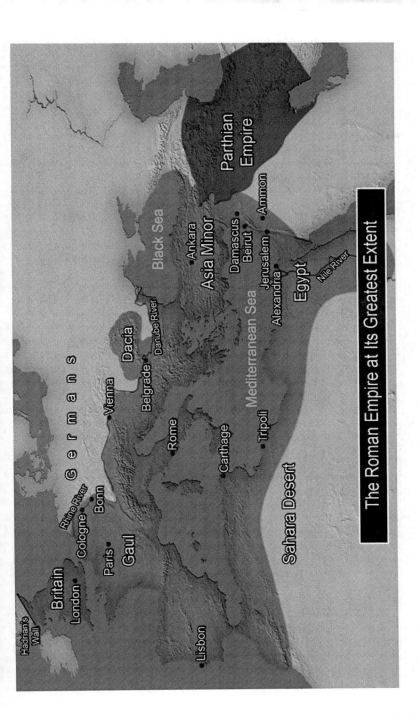

The Roman Empire at Its Greatest Extent

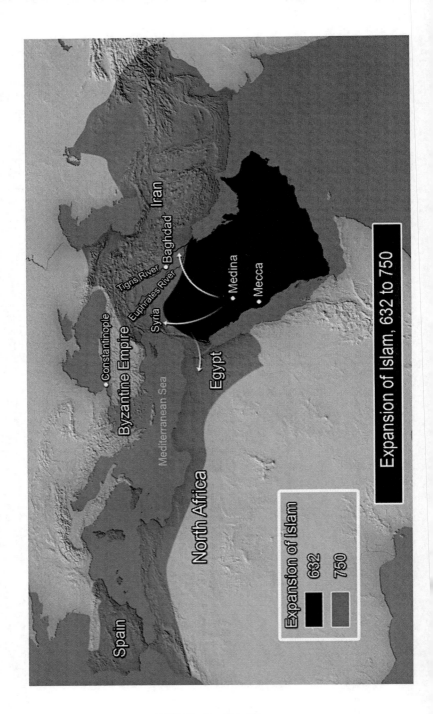

Expansion of Islam, 632 to 750

Expansion of Islam
632
750

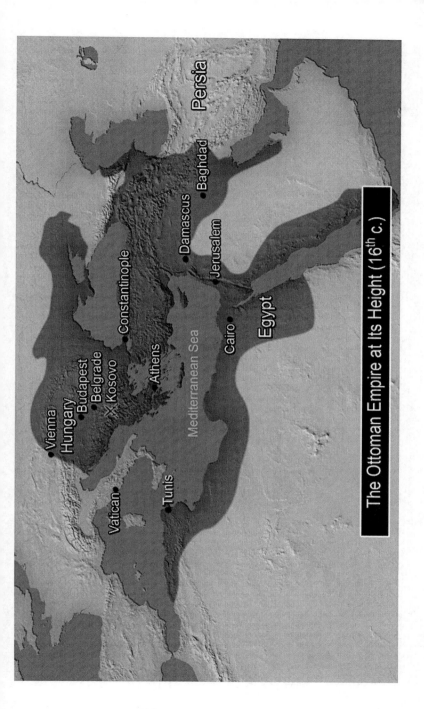

The Ottoman Empire at Its Height (16th c.)

Persia

Baghdad

Damascus

Jerusalem

Constantinople

Egypt

Cairo

Athens

Budapest
Belgrade
X Kosovo

Mediterranean Sea

Vienna
Hungary

Tunis

Vatican

The British Empire at Its Height (after World War I)

©2007 The Teaching Company.

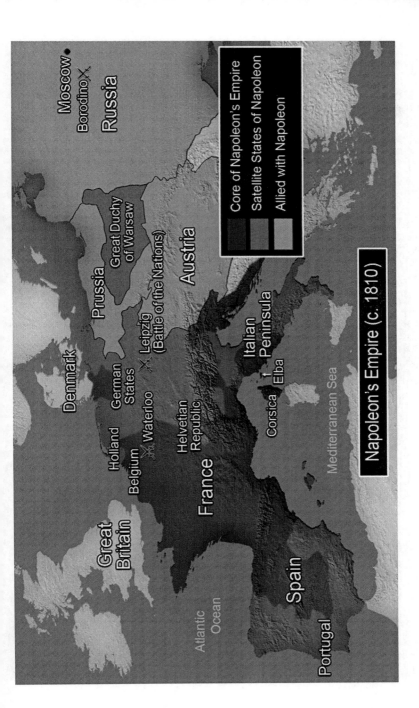

Napoleon's Empire (c. 1810)

- Core of Napoleon's Empire
- Satellite States of Napoleon
- Allied with Napoleon

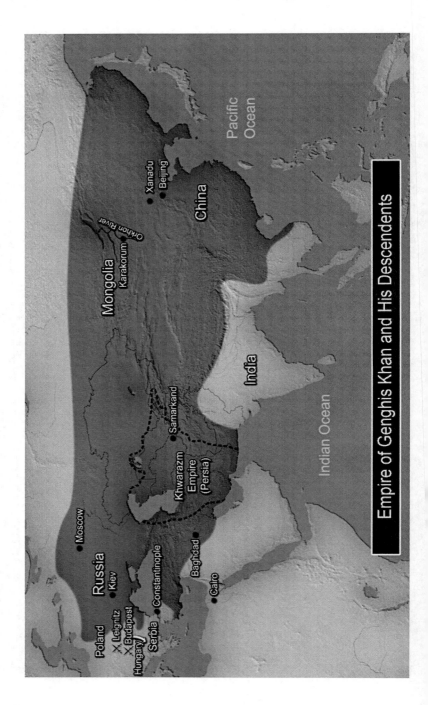

Empire of Genghis Khan and His Descendents

The Lewis and Clark Expedition

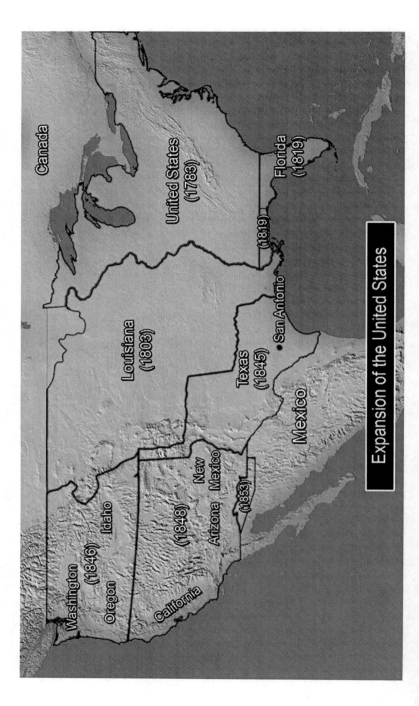

Expansion of the United States

Timeline

B.C.

3000	Birth of civilization in Egypt and the Near East
2500	Pyramids of Giza in Egypt; Indus Valley civilization in India
2000	Stonehenge
1760	Shang Dynasty in China, first historical dynasty in China with writing and bronze artworks
1295–1225	Ramses II, pharaoh of Egypt; historical context for the Exodus
1250–1240	Trojan War
1027–256.	Zhou Dynasty in China
1000	Beginning of Sanskrit literature
563–483	Buddha
551–479	Confucius
546–330	Persian Empire conquers and rules the Middle East
490–404	Golden age of Athenian democracy
336–323	Alexander the Great
259–209	Ch'in Shih Huang-ti, first true emperor of all China
218–146	Rise of the Roman Empire
48–31	Julius Caesar and Augustus establish monarchy in the Roman Empire
31 B.C.–180 A.D.	Golden age of the Roman Empire

A.D.

6	Birth of Jesus
312	Conversion of the Roman emperor Constantine to Christianity, which becomes the official religion of the empire
476	Fall of the Roman Empire in Western Europe
622	Hegira of Muhammad
800	Charlemagne establishes what will become the Holy Roman Empire of the German nation
988	Russia converts to Greek Orthodox Christianity
1066	Norman Conquest of England
1096–1272	Crusades
1194–1500	Gothic art and architecture dominate Europe
1215	Magna Charta
1155–1227	Genghis Khan
1304–1527	Renaissance
1440–1521	Golden age of the Aztec Empire in Mexico
1453–1683	Golden age of the Ottoman Empire
1492	Columbus reaches the New World
1517–1648	Reformation
1558–1603	Queen Elizabeth I of England
1648–1789	Age of the Enlightenment
1775–1789	American Revolution and Constitution—the Founding

1789–1815 .... French Revolution and Napoleon

1804–1806 .... Lewis and Clark expedition

1804–1824 .... Liberation of Latin America from colonial rule

1816–1914 .... Golden age of the British Empire

1861–1865 .... American Civil War

1914–1918 .... World War I

1929–1953 .... Joseph Stalin rules the Soviet Union

1933–1945 .... Adolf Hitler rules Germany

1939–1945 .... World War II

1945– .... Scientific and technological revolution

1948–1976 .... Mao Tse-tung (Mao Zedong) rules China

1990– .... United States as world's only superpower

Glossary

Bactria: Ancient name for the modern country of Afghanistan.

balanced constitution: The ideal form of government in the view of Classical thinkers, such as Aristotle, Cicero, and Polybius. The balanced constitution was achieved by a proper mixture of the main elements of government: the need for strong leadership (monarchy), the need for advice by a small group of experts (aristocracy), and a broad base of popular support (democracy). The balanced constitution also brought about a proper set of checks and balances among the executive, judicial, and legislative functions.

birth of civilization: Rise of complex governmental structures, writing, monumental architecture, and the use of metal. These developments occurred simultaneously in Egypt and Mesopotamia around 3000 B.C.

Communism: A system of ideas and government which maintains that society should be organized so that the means of production and subsistence should be held in common and labor organized for the benefit of all. As a political system, Communism has resulted in the creation of a totalitarian state and party apparatus to subordinate all facets of the individual, society, and economy to the control of the state.

consul: The chief magistrate of the Roman Republic. Two consuls were elected annually. The consul was commander-in-chief of the Roman army once war had been declared by the assembly of all Roman citizens.

democracy: Etymologically, *democracy* and *republic* both mean the same thing: the power of the people. *Democracy* is derived from the Greek *demos* ("people") and *kratia* ("power"). *Republic* is derived from the Latin *res publica*, the "people's thing" or "commonwealth." Today, the terms are used almost synonymously by many who speak of the United States as a democracy and a republic or a democratic republic. Some of the Founders, such as James Madison, made a distinction. Madison defined a democracy as "a society consisting of a small number of citizens who assemble and administer the government in person." A republic, according to Madison, differs in wo ways: power is delegated to representatives, and a republic can expand and govern far more people and geographical area.

empire: Derived from the Latin word *imperium*, which originally meant "legally granted power." The term came to mean a political area of domination, such as *Imperium Romanum* as the collective description of the Roman Empire. Thence, *imperium* passed into the political language of Europe and, ultimately, the world. In current usage, the term has a connotation of a large number of formerly independent states united under the rule of a single governing power, especially a monarch. Thus, many Americans are unhappy to speak of the "American empire." But the word can be used in quite neutral terms to describe the area under the hegemony or leadership of a superpower.

freedom: The ideal of freedom is in fact composed of three ideals, which do not necessarily include one another. *Individual freedom* is freedom to live as you choose as long as you harm no one else. *National freedom* is freedom from foreign control. *Political freedom* is freedom to vote, to hold public office, to serve on juries, and in general the freedom to be involved in the political process.

Founders: Collective term to describe the leading statesmen of the American Revolution; Founding Fathers and Framers are alternative terms. The Founders include George Washington, John Adams, Thomas Jefferson, James Madison, and James Monroe, as well as Benjamin Franklin and other signers of the Declaration of Independence and Constitution.

Greek (or Eastern) Orthodox Christianity: The doctrine and rituals of the Christian Church dominant in many parts of Eastern Europe and the Balkans, including Russia, Serbia, and Greece. *Orthodox* simply means "right teaching." Formally, the Eastern Orthodox Church and the Roman Catholic Church separated permanently in 1054. However, differences in doctrine, rituals, and philosophical and theological outlook had separated Latin Christianity from Greek Christianity almost since the beginning of Christianity in the 1st century A.D.

historical thought: The use of the lessons of history to make decisions in the present and to plan for the future.

House of Burgesses: Founded at Jamestown, Virginia, in 1619, this is the oldest continually functioning representative legislative body in what is now the United States.

hybris (*hubris*): *Hybris* is the correct transliteration of the Greek term that is best translated as outrageous arrogance that leads to the abuse of power.

information superhighway: A popular and appropriately trendy shorthand for describing the rapid retrieval and transmission and voluminous storage of information made possible by modern technology.

Magna Charta: The Great Charter of English and, hence, American freedom, signed by King John in 1215 and granting to every freeborn subject of his realm certain fundamental rights, such as trial by jury.

Mayflower Compact: A brief agreement signed before the Pilgrims left ship in 1620. By this compact, they agreed to establish just laws for the good government of their new community. It has been called the first written constitution in what is now the United States.

Mesopotamia: "Land between the rivers." A Greek geographical term used to describe an area, now largely in Iraq, between the Tigris and Euphrates Rivers. The area was the site of the early historical civilization of the Sumerians and Babylonians.

Middle East: In this course, we have used the term *Middle East* as a very broad geopolitical designation for the area reaching from Pakistan to the Balkans and the Danube River and to the Atlantic shores of Morocco. The Persian Empire of the 6th and 5th centuries B.C. and Alexander the Great understood this area as a geopolitical whole. It is roughly (excluding Spain) the area in which Islam made its farthest and most permanent advance.

Mongols: One of the most important ethnic groups of the steppes of central Asia. The Mongolian language is part of the broader language family sometimes known as Ural-Altaic, which includes Turkish. The Mongols whom Genghis Khan led to greatness were a mixed confederation of Mongol and Turkic tribes speaking a variety of Turkish and Mongolian languages and sharing a common nomadic lifestyle.

Ottoman Empire: Derives its name from the founder Osman (in earlier European transliteration, Othman); 1288–1326.

republic: See **democracy**.

senate: The term *senate* was a conscious borrowing by the Founders from the Roman *Senatus*. The word literally means "council of old men." The Roman Senate contained roughly 300 members, who were indirectly elected by the Roman people and served for life. The Senate was responsible for finances and foreign policy.

superpower: A political entity that dominates its world or, at least, competes for domination with equal powers. Thus, Rome was the superpower in the Mediterranean world and Western Europe of the first two centuries A.D. Britain, Russia, Italy, France, Germany, and Austria-Hungary were the superpowers (or Great Powers) of Europe on the eve of World War I.

Turks: The Turkic people are one of the most widely spread and historically important nations. Turkic languages are spoken from Siberia to the Balkans. Turks were a major component of the armies of Genghis Khan. Turks are major ethnic components not only of the modern republic of Turkey but also of the central Asian republics of Kazakhstan, Turkmenistan, Uzbekistan, Kyrgyzstan, and Azerbaijan. See also **Mongols**.

tyrant: According to Winston Churchill, an individual who believes that his own ideas and gratification are worth the suffering of millions.

Union of Soviet Socialist Republics (Soviet Union, USSR): The name for the political entity that in 1922 replaced the Russian Empire. In 1992, the Soviet Union was dissolved, splintering into a number of independent nations, one of which is the Russian Federation.

Biographical Notes

Acton, John Emerich Edward Dalberg (1843–1902). British historian. Lord Acton was educated in Germany, where he received historical training far superior to anything available at that time in England. A devout Roman Catholic his entire life, Acton returned to England, where, from 1857–1870, he was involved in a number of journalistic enterprises aimed at bringing the wisdom of history to bear on the liberal reform of the Catholic Church. The proclamation of papal infallibility as Church doctrine at the Vatican Council of 1869–1870 was a profound blow to Acton. He began to plan but never completed a major work on the history of freedom. He became known as the most learned man in England, but he wrote very little for publication. In 1895, Acton was appointed Regius Professor of History at Cambridge, where he performed important service for the academic study of history, including conceiving the idea of the *Cambridge Modern History*. A close friend of Prime Minister Gladstone, Acton was a liberal in the classic sense and believed, as did Winston Churchill, in much of what we associate with modern welfare reforms. Acton called conservatism "the reign of sin." It is ironic and false that contemporary conservatives and libertarians claim him as one of their own.

Augustus (63 B.C.–14 A.D.). Roman emperor and statesman. Born Gaius Octavius, he was the great nephew and adopted son of Julius Caesar. Modern historians generally refer to him as Octavian, from his adopted name of Gaius Julius Caesar Octavianus, in describing his early career and rise to power (44–27 B.C.). With extraordinary political skills, Octavian raised an army at the age of 19 and, by the age of 32, had achieved complete mastery over the Roman world with his decisive victory over the forces of Marc Antony and Cleopatra at the Battle of Actium in 31 B.C. He then carried out a series of political, military, social, religious, and economic reforms that transformed Rome from a republic into the military dictatorship that we call the Roman Empire of the Caesars. In genuine appreciation of his achievement, the Roman people voted that his name be changed to Augustus, which is best rendered in English as "the messiah." The new order of Augustus inaugurated two centuries of unprecedented peace and prosperity for the Roman world, and he is rightly regarded as the greatest Roman statesman of all time.

Bismarck, Otto, Prince von (1815–1898). German statesman. One of the most successful statesmen of the 19th century. Bismarck was born into a Prussian military family. He studied law and entered the Prussian civil and diplomatic service. By 1848, he had become a prominent politician and staunch defender of absolutism and monarchy against the liberal forces then sweeping Germany and Europe. Shrewd, opportunistic, and patriotic, he led the unification of Germany under the leadership of Prussia and its King William I. By careful steps, he defeated Austria, then France. In 1870, after a crushing victory over Napoleon III in 1870, William was proclaimed ruler of the German Empire. Bismarck shaped the new order as chancellor, bringing the benefits of social welfare programs to German workers and making the new Germany into a world power. His personality clashed with the young Emperor William II, and Bismarck was dismissed as chancellor in 1890.

Caesar, Gaius Julius (100–44 B.C.): Roman statesman. Born to an ancient but impoverished family, Caesar was a late bloomer in his political career. However, with military genius and political adroitness, by 48 B.C., Caesar rose to be the leading political figure in the decaying Roman Republic. He was a literary genius, and his *Commentaries* on his war in Gaul and the civil war against Pompey rank as masterpieces of style and narrative. After his military victory over his chief rival, Pompey, in 48 B.C., Caesar set about to transform Rome into a monarchy. By 44 B.C., he had collected all real power in his hands and had been voted dictator for life. The Roman people adored him and viewed him as the only possible salvation for their empire. They did not care about political liberty, and Caesar offered them individual freedom and prosperity. Caesar sought to co-opt his opponents, such as Brutus, by a policy of clemency and conciliation. He understood the need to solve the problem of the Middle East by conquest and annexation of Iran. His plans to carry out that policy and the conquest of the Germans came to naught when he was assassinated by a conspiracy of senators, led by Brutus and Cassius, on March 15, 44 B.C. Such was the impact of Caesar on the idea of empire that his name lived in the title of *kaiser* for the German emperor and *czar* for the Russian emperor.

Churchill, Winston (1874–1965). British statesman and author. Churchill has been called the greatest man of the 20th century. Churchill was half American, the son of an English aristocrat, Lord

Randolph Churchill, younger son of the duke of Marlborough, and Jennie Jerome, a wealthy New York socialite. By the age of 26, Churchill was a war hero, a bestselling author, and a member of Parliament. In World War I, his bold strategy as First Lord of the Admiralty led to the fiasco at Gallipoli and his dismissal from the government. All through the 1930s, Churchill was politically discredited but sought to awaken the British people to the danger of Germany. As prime minister, he led Britain through "its finest hour." He returned as prime minister in 1951–1955, working for close ties with America. His 53 books, including his *History of the Second World War*, won him the Nobel Prize for literature in 1953.

Confucius (551–479). Chinese teacher. One of the most influential figures in history, Confucius never wrote a book. He was a failure in his own attempts at being an administrator. But his teaching shaped centuries of Chinese history and government. He wandered through China during a period of war and oppression. He taught a group of students to take up their responsibility as administrators. His message was one of order and ethical behavior: Let the leaders cultivate the virtues of wisdom, courage, justice, and moderation and the people would follow.

Madison, James (1751–1836). American statesman. Madison studied at Princeton University and served in the Continental Congress during the final stages of the American Revolution. Along with Alexander Hamilton, Madison was a prime mover in bringing about the Constitutional Convention and played a major role in Washington's decision to attend and preside. Madison is known as the "Father of the Constitution." He was one of the most learned of the delegates, drawing on a profound knowledge of Greece and Rome. At the time of the ratification debates, Madison played again a key role with Hamilton and John Jay in authoring the articles now known as *The Federalist* to persuade his fellow citizens of the wisdom of the new constitution. He then served in the first Congress, where he was responsible for drafting the Bill of Rights. He served as secretary of state under President Jefferson. As president himself, Madison led the United States in the War of 1812 with Britain and was the subject of considerable political opposition and hostility.

Muhammad (570–632 A.D.). Prophet and founder of Islam. Muhammad was born in Arabia to a respected family. At age 40, he received his first revelation from God. These revelations are the contents of the Koran. Muhammad began to proclaim his faith to his family and to the citizens of Mecca. He proclaimed the revelation: "There is no God but God and Muhammad is the prophet of God." This was doctrine of uncompromising monotheism to a polytheistic society. For Muhammad, the faith he proclaimed was one of absolute submission to God, who is all-powerful and all-compassionate. Forced to flee from Mecca in 622, Muhammad made his Hegira (his "flight") to the city of Medina. By 630, Muhammad and the new faith were established throughout Arabia. At the time of his death in 632, Muhammad had built a political and military force that would carry Islam into the Middle East, across North Africa, and into Spain and southern France. As a statesman, Muhammad ranks with the great founders of empire. As a religious leader, he ranks with Jesus as the founder of a faith that has transformed history and the lives of countless individuals.

Napoleon III (1803–1873). Emperor of the French. The nephew of the great Napoleon, Louis Napoleon Bonaparte used his name and political adroitness to gain control of French politics in the revolutionary atmosphere of 1848. To a nation that despaired of regaining the glory of the first Napoleon, this counterfeit Napoleon had a fatal attraction. He became a dictator and, in 1852, was proclaimed emperor of the French. Far from being an anachronism, the state of Napoleon III foreshadowed the dictators of the 20th century. France seemed to reclaim its ancient glory. The French began to expand their colonial empire in competition with Britain. But it was a sham. The aim of Napoleon III to recreate a French Empire in Mexico through his puppet, Maximilian von Hapsburg, failed. Outwitted by Bismarck into war, Napoleon led France to a disastrous defeat in the Franco-Prussian War of 1870. Deposed, he died in exile in England. Like his uncle, Napoleon III was fascinated by the legacy of Julius Caesar and wrote an excellent biography of the great Roman.

Bibliography

Note: In the Essential Readings, I have sought to give the firsthand sources in good translations that are conveniently available. In the Supplementary Readings, I have sought to recommend works that I thought best put our discussions into a broader historical context and that I find clearest and most helpful. This means that I have frequently recommended older, more traditional works that are available. I have followed Lord Acton's dictum that it is the mark of an uneducated person to read books he or she agrees with. The educated person reads books he or she disagrees with. Thus, I have frequently recommended books that disagree with me, because these are the ones we find most stimulating.

Essential Reading:

Acton, John Emerich Edward Dalberg. *Selected Writings of Lord Acton*. Ed. J. Rufus Fears. Indianapolis: Liberty Press, 1986–1988. This three-volume edition is the most complete ever published of the writings of the great historian of liberty. It contains much previously unpublished work.

Adler, Mortimer. *The Idea of Freedom: A Dialectical Examination of the Conceptions of Freedom*. Garden City, NJ: Doubleday, 1958. An almost exhaustive collection of meanings that have been attributed to the concept of freedom.

Arberry, A. J. *The Koran Interpreted*. New York: Simon and Schuster, 1996. The best available translation of the Koran.

Arrian. *The Campaigns of Alexander the Great*. Trans. Aubrey de Selincourt. New York: Penguin, 1971. The best source for Alexander, based on excellent eyewitness accounts.

Bakewell, Peter. *A History of Latin America*. Oxford: Blackwell, 2004. A good history of colonial Latin America but very brief on the 20th century.

Brown, Dee. *Bury My Heart at Wounded Knee: An Indian History of the American West*. New York: Holt, Rinehart and Winston, 1970. The book that revised the thinking of many Americans on the history of western expansion.

Bullock, Alan. *Hitler and Stalin*. New York: Knopf, 1991. An outstanding work of historical scholarship, providing parallel portraits in evil.

Carrithers, M., M. Cook, H. Carpenter, and R. Dawson. *Founders of Faith: The Buddha, Confucius, Jesus, Muhammad*. New York: Oxford University Press, 1990. Good survey of the life and teachings of Muhammad and these other seminal figures.

Churchill, Winston. *The Second World War*. Vols. I–VI. Boston: Houghton Mifflin, 1948–1954. Churchill's memoirs, providing his view of why the Second World War was the tragic consequence of the refusal to learn from history.

———. *The World Crisis*. Vols. I–V. New York: Charles Scribner's Sons, 1923–1929. Churchill's memoirs of World War I. Brilliantly written and idiosyncratic in its coverage, it offers unique insight into Churchill's understanding of the wisdom of history.

Collingwood, R. G. *The Idea of History*. New York: Oxford, 1993. This fragmentary work is to me the best single exposition of a philosophy of history, by a scholar who was both a philosopher and historian.

Confucius. *Analects*. Trans. D. C. Lau. New York: Penguin, 1979. The best translation into English, with a valuable introduction.

Dallek, Robert. *Flawed Giant: Lyndon Johnson and His Times*. New York: Oxford University Press, 2005. The best and most balanced biography of Johnson.

DeVoto, Bernard, ed. *The Journals of Lewis and Clark*. Boston: Houghton Mifflin, 1997. The best way to begin a study of Lewis and Clark.

Elliott, John H. *Empires of the Atlantic World: Britain and Spain in America, 1492–1830*. New Haven: Yale University Press, 2006. A superb comparative study.

Ellis, Jeremy. *His Excellency, George Washington*. New York: Knopf, 2004. A most engaging and informative biography.

England, Steven. *Napoleon: A Political Life*. New York: Scribner, 2004. The best recent biography of Napoleon.

Eusebius. *Life of Constantine*. Trans. Averil Cameron. Oxford: Oxford University Press, 1999. A detailed commentary along with translation of the fundamental source for the conversion of Constantine to Christianity.

Fears, J. Rufus. *Books That Have Made History: Books That Can Change Your Life* (2005); *Churchill* (2001); *Famous Greeks* (2001); *Famous Romans* (2001); *A History of Freedom* (2001). Chantilly, VA: The Teaching Company. These lecture courses provide a narrative historical background to themes discussed in our current course.

——. *Cult of Jupiter*. New York/Berlin: De Gruyter, 1981. A study of the transformation of the interpretation of the god Jupiter in Roman history.

——. "The Cult of Virtues in Roman Imperial Ideology." In W. Haase, ed., *Aufstieg und Niedergang der roemischen Reich*. New York/Berlin: De Gruyter, 1981. Division II, vol. XVII, part 1, pp. 7–140. A scholarly examination of the relationship between the power of the emperor and the rise of monotheism.

——. "Freedom: The History of an Idea." *Foreign Policy Research Institute Notes*, May 2007. A short study examining the question of whether freedom is a universal value. Available online at: http://www.fpri.org/footnotes/1219.200706.fears.freedomhistory.html

——. *The Lessons of the Roman Empire for America Today*. Heritage Lectures, 917. Washington, DC: Heritage Foundation, 2005. A broad view of the lessons of Rome for America in the Middle East.

Fehrenbach, T. R. *Lone Star: A History of Texas and the Texans*. Cambridge, MA: Da Capo Press, 2000. A brilliantly written account, useful for understanding the Mexican War and American expansion.

Ferguson, Niall. *Empire: The Rise and Demise of the British World Order and Its Lessons for Global Power*. New York: Basic Books, 2003. A study of the lessons of the British Empire by a prolific and influential contemporary historian.

Ferrell, Robert H. *Presidential Leadership: From Woodrow Wilson to Harry S Truman*. Columbia, MO: University of Missouri Press, 2005. An insightful examination of the leadership qualities of major presidents of this century.

Gibbon, Edward. *Decline and Fall of the Roman Empire*. New York: Random House, 2000. This complete version in three volumes is to be preferred to the various abridged versions. The original was published in 1776–1789, exactly spanning the period from the Declaration of Independence to the ratification of the Constitution.

Hallo, William, and William Simpson. *The Ancient Near East: A History*. New York: Harcourt Brace, 1998. A good brief history of the ancient Near East and Egypt.

Herodotus. *The Histories*. Trans. Aubrey de Selincourt. New York: Penguin, 1954, and subsequent reprints. A good convenient translation.

Homer. *The Iliad*. Trans. Richmond Lattimore. Chicago: University of Chicago Press, 1951. The best English translation of the epic account of the Trojan War.

Josephus. *The Jewish War*. Cambridge, MA: Harvard University Press, Loeb Classical Library, 1927, and subsequent reprints. The best English translation of this contemporary account of the great revolt against Roman rule. Josephus was much read by the Founders of the United States.

Lane, George. *Genghis Khan and Mongol Rule*. Westport, CT: Greenwood, 2004. An excellent recent introduction to Genghis Khan and his legacy.

Lewis, Bernard. *The Emergence of Modern Turkey*. New York: Oxford University Press, 2002. The best discussion of Ataturk and the transformation of his country.

Macmillan, Margaret. *Paris 1919: Six Months That Changed the World*. New York: Random House, 2001. A lively account of the failure and consequences of Wilson and the generation of politicians who blundered in and out of World War I.

Malone, Dumas. *Jefferson and His Time*. Boston: Little, Brown and Co., 1948–1981. The definitive biography, in six volumes.

Morgan, Edmund. *Inventing the People: The Rise of Popular Sovereignty in England and America*. New York: Norton, 1988. An original and stimulating discussion of the English legacy to the American ideal of freedom.

Oates, Stephen B. *With Malice Toward None: The Life of Abraham Lincoln*. New York: New American Library, 1977. Still the best and most readable one-volume life of Lincoln.

Palmer, Robert. *The Age of Democratic Revolutions*. Princeton, NJ: Princeton University Press, 1959–1964. A thoughtful comparative study of the American and French Revolutions.

Plutarch. *Lives of the Noble Grecians and Romans*. Trans. John Dryden. New York: Modern Library, 1992. Plutarch's purpose in writing these biographies was to use the wisdom of history to make his readers better as individuals and as citizens. The edition I recommend contains all the extant *Lives* arranged in the order that fulfills Plutarch's purpose.

Polybius. *The Rise of the Roman Empire*. Trans. Ian Scott-Kilvert. New York: Penguin, 1979. The best selection of Polybius, focusing on the Roman portions of the history. Polybius ranks with Thucydides as an influence on the Founders.

Reinhold, Meyer. *Classica Americana: The Greek and Roman Heritage in the United States*. Detroit: Wayne State University, 1984. A good discussion of the influence of the classics on the political thought of the Founders.

Riasanovsky, Nicholas. *A History of Russia*. New York: Oxford University Press, 2000. The best one-volume history of Russia. Riasanovsky puts less emphasis than I do on the Viking background to Russian history.

Roosevelt, Theodore, *Winning the West*. New York: Charles Scribner's Sons, 1926, and numerous other editions. Professional historians today and many others would sharply disagree with President Roosevelt's interpretation of history, but the book is valuable to us for its vivid portrayal of the conviction that America's expansion was the march of freedom.

Thucydides. *History of the Peloponnesian War*. Trans. Rex Warner. New York: Penguin, 1954. A lively translation of this classic work, in which every generation seems to find new meaning.

Truman, Harry S. *Memoirs*. Garden City, NJ: Doubleday, 1954–1955. One of the best and most honest memoirs ever written by a president of the United States and, perhaps, any politician.

Urofsky, Melvin. *The March of Liberty: A Constitutional History of the United States*. New York: Knopf, 1988. An excellent two-volume history of the Constitution.

Winkler, A. *Franklin D. Roosevelt and the Making of Modern America*. New York: Pearson/Longman, 2006. A good biography for the general reader.

Wright, David. *The History of China*. Westport, CT: Greenwood Press, 2001. A very brief history with a focus on modern times.

Supplementary Reading:

Alvis, Joseph. *Lewis and Clark Through Indian Eyes*. New York: Knopf, 2006. A good way to understand how modern Native Americans view the expedition of Lewis and Clark and its historical impact.

Ambrose, Stephen. *Undaunted Courage*. New York: Simon and Schuster, 1996. A brilliant and moving narrative of the life of Meriwether Lewis and the expedition that made him famous.

Borit, G., ed. *Lincoln: The War President*. New York: Oxford University Press, 1992. A collection of essays by various scholars illuminating Lincoln as commander-in-chief, including one comparing the Civil War with contemporaneous unification movements in Europe.

Brown, J. *Gandhi: Prisoner of Hope*. New Haven: Yale, 1991. A biography that sets the context for the collapse of British rule in India.

Burckhardt, Jacob. *Force and Freedom: Reflections on History*. Indianapolis: Liberty, 1979. Thoughts on the meaning of history by a profound 19th-century historian of culture.

Burns, E. Bradford, and Julie Charlip. *Latin America: An Interpretative History*. Upper Saddle River, NJ: Prentice Hall, 2007. Now in its eighth edition, this is a brief but scholarly history of Latin America.

Butterfield. Herbert. *Man on His Past: The Study of the History of Historical Scholarship*. Cambridge: Cambridge University Press, 1955. A readable and provocative study of historiography by a distinguished historian.

Conquest, Robert. *Stalin: Breaker of Nations*. New York: Viking, 1991. The best short biography of Stalin.

Durant, Will. *The Lessons of History*. New York: Simon and Schuster, 1968. A concise statement of the lessons of history by the man who has introduced several generations of Americans to the study of history with his sweeping history of civilization written for the general reader.

Ellery, Daniel. *Frontiers of History: Historical Inquiry in the Twentieth Century.* New York: Oxford, 2006. A survey and analysis of the main trends in the writing of history as we enter the 21st century.

Ellis, Joseph. *American Sphinx.* New York: Random House, 1996. An engaging and thoughtful one-volume biography of Thomas Jefferson.

Ermatinger, James. *The Decline and Fall of the Roman Empire.* Westport, CT: Greenwood Press, 2004. A short, easy-to-read account.

Esposito, J. *The Oxford History of Islam.* Oxford: Oxford University Press, 2000. A good current source for understanding the history and ideas of Islam.

Fears, J. Rufus. "Natural Law." In Edward McClean, ed., *Uncommon Truths: New Perspectives on Natural Law.* Wilmington, DE: Intercollegiate Studies Institute, 2000. A discussion of the enduring legacy of the Roman Empire.

Ferguson, Niall. *Colossus: The Price of America's Empire.* New York: Penguin, 2004. A widely acclaimed work and one of many books called forth in recent years by the idea of an American empire.

Ferrell, Robert. *Harry S. Truman and the Cold War Revisionists.* Columbia, MO: University of Missouri Press, 2006. An important study by a major Truman scholar of the origins of the Cold War.

Flannagan, James, and Walter Brueggemann, "Samuel, Book 1–2," in *Anchor Bible Dictionary.* Garden City, NJ: Doubleday, 1992. Vol. V, pp. 957–973. The best orientation for the general reader on how modern scholars view the book of Samuel.

Frankfort, Henri. *The Birth of Civilization in the Ancient Near East.* Bloomington, IN: Indiana University Press, 1951. A classic interpretative study, still very valuable, by one of the most original and learned historians of the ancient Near East.

Gandhi, Mahatma. *An Autobiography: The Story of My Experiments with the Truth.* Boston: Beacon, 1993. A recent edition of Gandhi's fascinating and original telling of his search for truth.

Gelvin, James. *The Modern Middle East*. New York: Oxford University Press, 2005. A thoughtful interpretative history.

Glaser, Elizabeth, ed. *Bridging the Atlantic*. New York: Cambridge University Press, 2002. A collection of essays by various scholars comparing the American and German experience, including one comparing Lincoln and Bismarck.

Gooch, G. P. *History and Historians in the Nineteenth Century*. London: Longmans, Green, 1952. A survey of the major themes of historical writing in the era that educated the politicians of World War I.

Green, Peter. *The Greco-Persian Wars*. Berkeley: University of California Press, 1996. A solid, scholarly, and boring account of this heroic struggle.

Hanson, Victor. *A War Like No Other: How the Athenians and Spartans Fought the Peloponnesian War*. New York: Random House, 2005. An attempt to draw lessons for today from the Peloponnesian War.

Heather, P. J. *The Fall of the Roman Empire*. London: Macmillan, 2005. An up-to-date study of contemporary views on the fall of the Roman Empire.

Hegel, G. *Philosophy of History*. New York: Dover, 1956. The most influential philosopher of the 19th century expounds his thesis that freedom is the moving force of history.

Homza, Lu Ann. *The Spanish Inquisition, 1478–1614*. Indianapolis: Hackett, 2001. A collection of fundamental documents on the Inquisition in Spain.

Inalcik, H. *Social and Economic History of the Ottoman Empire*. New York: Cambridge University Press, 1994. The standard work on the Ottoman Empire.

Jones, A. H. M. *Constantine and the Conversion of Europe*. New York: Macmillan, 1948, and subsequent reprints. Remains the best and most original discussion of the historical context of Constantine's conversion.

Kallet-Marx, Robert. *Hegemony to Empire: The Development of the Roman Imperium in the East from 148–62 B.C.* Berkeley: University of California Press, 1996. A detailed, scholarly study of the transformation of Roman aims in the Middle East.

Kelly, Christopher. *The Roman Empire: A Very Short History*. New York: Oxford University Press, 2006. A good introduction for the general reader interested in the basic facts.

Kirk, Russell. *The Roots of American Order*. LaSalle, IL: Open Court, 1977. A detailed intellectual history of several of the currents that have shaped American political ideals.

Lewis, Bernard. *From Babel to Dragomans: Interpreting the Middle East*. New York: Oxford University Press, 2002. An original and thought-provoking study by the most distinguished and influential historian of the Middle East.

Manchester, William. *The Last Lion: Winston Spencer Churchill*. Vols. I–II. Boston: Little, Brown and Co., 1983–1988. The two volumes are all that were completed of what will remain the best account of Churchill and his times.

McClellan, James. *Liberty, Order, and Justice: An Introduction to the Constitutional Principles of American Government*. Richmond, VA: James River Press, 1991. An excellent study of the Constitution and its historical background.

McCullough, David. *1776*. New York: Simon and Schuster, 2005. An engaging and well-written portrayal of this critical year in American history.

Middlekauf, Robert. *The Glorious Cause: A History of the American Revolution, 1763–1789*. New York: Oxford University Press, 1962. The best history of the revolution.

Millar, Fergus. *The Roman Near East, 31 B.C.–A.D. 337*. Cambridge, MA: Harvard University Press, 1993. The most detailed study of the impact of Rome upon the Middle East.

Norwich, J. *Byzantium*. New York: Random House, 1996. A detailed but vivid history of the Byzantine Empire.

Page, D. *History and the Homeric Iliad*. Berkeley: University of California Press, 1959. A provocative study of the archaeological and other evidence for the historicity of the Trojan War.

Richard, Carl. *The Founders and the Classics*. Cambridge: Harvard University Press, 1994. A good, balanced survey of the influence of Greece and Rome on the Founders.

Roberts, J. A. G. *A Concise History of China*. Cambridge: Harvard University Press, 1994. A good introduction to the early history of China.

Rose, J. H. *Life of Napoleon I*. London: Bell, 1924. Old-fashioned but still the most readable biography of Napoleon.

Runciman, Steven. *A History of the Crusades*. Cambridge: Cambridge University Press, 1951–1954. The best and most detailed history of this crucial epoch in the history of Islam and Christianity.

Segue, Count Philippe-Paul de. *Napoleon's Russian Campaign*. New York: Time, 1958. A fascinating contemporary account by an officer who made the march.

Solzhenitsyn, Aleksandr. *The Gulag Archipelago, 1918–1956*. New York: Harper and Row, 1974–1978. A massive indictment of Soviet Communism by the Nobel Prize winner and survivor of the labor camps of Stalin.

Starr, Chester. *The Emergence of Rome as Ruler of the Western World*. Ithaca, NY: Cornell University Press, 1953. An older but very clear and concise discussion of the rise of the Roman Empire by one of the most distinguished historians of his day.

Tarn, W. W. *Alexander the Great*. Cambridge: Cambridge University Press, 1948. Reprinted by Ares, 1981. Still the best modern biography of Alexander.

Turnbull, Stephen. *Genghis Khan and the Mongol Conquests*. New York: Routledge, 2003. A brief introduction to the Mongols, with a focus on military history.

Van Setters, John. *In Search of History: Historiography in the Ancient World and the Origins of Biblical History*. New Haven: Yale University Press, 1983. A scholarly examination of the place of the book of Samuel in the broader context of historical writing in the ancient Near East.

Wills, Garry. *Negro President: Jefferson and the Slave Power*. Boston, New York: Houghton Mifflin, 2003. A controversial study of Jefferson and the slavery question.

Wright and Fuller. *The Book of the Acts of God*. New York: Anchor, 1960. An older but still extremely clear theological and historical appreciation of the Bible.

Wood, Michael. *In Search of the Trojan War*. New York: Facts on File Publications, 1985. A popular account of the use of archaeology to discover the historicity of the Trojan War.

Zacharia, Fareed. *The Future of Freedom*. New York: Norton, 2003. A recent journalistic discussion of freedom and democracy in the contemporary world.

Zimmern, Alfred. *The Greek Commonwealth*. Oxford: Oxford University Press, 1911, numerous subsequent editions and reprints. A highly sympathetic account of Athenian democracy and imperialism, written by a scholar and man of affairs in the heyday of the British Empire.

Internet Resources

http://www.age-of-the-sage.org/history/quotations/index.html
A brief but wide range of famous quotes about the meaning, lessons, and usefulness of history.

http://www.thegreatideas.org/
Mortimer Adler discusses the great ideas and books that have shaped history, including historical studies.

http://historicalthinkingmatters.org
A pedagogical tool to encourage students to use history to understand contemporary politics.

Notes

Notes